Asia-Pacific Economic and Security Co-operation

Also by Christopher M. Dent

THE FOREIGN ECONOMIC POLICIES OF SINGAPORE, SOUTH KOREA AND TAIWAN (2002)

NORTHERN ASIAN REGIONALISM: Learning from the European Experience (co-edited with David Huang) (2002)

THE EUROPEAN UNION AND EAST ASIA: An Economic Relationship (1999)

THE EUROPEAN ECONOMY: The Global Context (1997)

Contents

Asia-Pacific Economic and Security Co-operation

New Regional Agendas

Edited by
Christopher M. Dent
Department of East Asian Studies
University of Leeds

First published 2003 by
PALGRAVE MACMILLAN
Houndmills, Basingstoke, Hampshire RG21 6XS and
175 Fifth Avenue, New York, N.Y. 10010
Companies and representatives throughout the world

PALGRAVE MACMILLAN is the global academic imprint of the Palgrave
Macmillan division of St. Martin's Press, LLC and of Palgrave Macmillan Ltd.
Macmillan® is a registered trademark in the United States, United Kingdom
and other countries. Palgrave is a registered trademark in the European
Union and other countries.

ISBN 1–4039–1803–1

This book is printed on paper suitable for recycling and made from fully
managed and sustained forest sources.

A catalogue record for this book is available from the British Library.

Library of Congress Cataloging-in-Publication Data
    Asia-Pacific economic and security co-operation: new regional agendas /
    edited by Christopher M. Dent.
        p. cm.
    "This book contains the extended and revised versions of presentations given
at the September 2002 research workshop entitled 'Asia-Pacific economic and
security cooperation: new regional agendas" ' – Pref.
    Includes bibliographical references and index.
        ISBN 1–4039–1803–1
        1. Asia – Economic integration. 2. Pacific Area – Economic integration.
    3. National security – Economic aspects – Asia. 4. National security – Economic
    aspects – Pacific Area. 5. Regionalism – Asia. 6. Regionalism – Pacific Area.
    7. Asia Pacific Economic Cooperation (Organization). 8. ASEAN. 9. Asia – Foreign
    economic relations. 10. Pacific Area – Foreign economic relations. I. Dent,
    Christopher M., 1965–

HC412.A724178 2003
337.1'5—dc21   2003046919

10 9 8 7 6 5 4 3 2 1
12 11 10 09 08 07 06 05 04 03

Printed and bound in Great Britain by
Antony Rowe Ltd, Chippenham and Eastbourne

To Angela and Phyllis
For teaching me so many things beyond
what I've learned from reading books

List of Figures and Tables

Figures

Tables

Acknowledgements

I thank Dr. Christopher Hughes for the article 'The Asia-Pacific's New Economic Bilateralism and Regional Political Economy', published earlier in *Security Dialogue* and Sage Publications Ltd. (© PRIO: International Peace Research Institute Oslo, 2001) in granting permission for the re-use of the above article.

Preface

This book contains the extended and revised versions of presentations given at the September 2002 research workshop entitled *Asia-Pacific Economic and Security Cooperation: New Regional Agendas*. It was principally organised by the editor, Christopher Dent, in his capacity as Director of the Institute for Pacific Asia Studies at the University of Hull, UK. The workshop brought together some of Britain and Germany's best young scholars of the Asia-Pacific region, and their fully developed chapters are presented here.

It is an exciting time to be studying the Asia-Pacific's economic and security relations. The region has experienced a period of turbulent change since the mid-1990s. This has mainly centred on two 'shock events', the first being the 1997/98 East Asian financial crisis and the second the al-Qaeda terrorist attacks on the United States on 11 September 2001. These shocks and their subsequent aftermath developments have had significant catalytic effects upon the international relations of the Asia-Pacific, and moreover set the main contextual parameters for the study themes covered by this book. Three 'prime dimensions' to the new economic and security co-operation in the Asia-Pacific are presented in the introductory chapter. The first of these concerns the tension between 'post-shock' forces of *imperative co-operation* and the counter-forces of the region's *complex diversity*. The second 'prime dimension' relates to how *economic and security issues have become increasingly conflated in Asia-Pacific international relations*, particularly since the afore-mentioned 'shock' events. The third examines the relationship between the *Asia-Pacific's new economic and security bilateralism and regional-level forms of co-operation, integration and governance*. As many chapters testify, the relationship between bilateralism and regionalism in the Asia-Pacific has become an increasingly critical one.

I would like to extend profuse thanks to the following people. My former colleague, Tim Huxley, came up with the initial idea for the research workshop and helped me organise the event. Alex Chandra and Ro Soong Chul gave up some of their PhD study time to kindly help out with the logistical organisation of the research workshop. Amanda Watkins at Palgrave Macmillan brilliantly and cheerily guided me through the preliminary stages of producing this book. Thanks also to Kerry Coutts and Mukesh at Palgrave Macmillan. I would finally like to thank my family for their continued love and support in all that I do.

Notes on Contributors

Alan Collins is Lecturer in the Department of Politics and International Relations at the University of Wales, Swansea, UK. Prior to this he held a British Academy Post-Doctoral Fellowship at the University of Wales Aberystwyth. While writing this chapter he was a Visiting Fellow at the Institute of Defence and Strategic Studies, Nanyang Technological University, Singapore. This research was made possible with the award of travel grants from the British Academy and the British Academy's Committee for South-East Asian Studies. He is the author of *The Security Dilemmas of Southeast Asia* (2000), has written articles on Southeast Asian security that have appeared in *Pacifica Review* and *Contemporary Southeast Asia*, and his latest work, *Security & Southeast Asia: Domestic and Regional Issues* is to be published in 2003.

Xiudian Dai is Senior Lecturer in the Department of Politics and International Studies, University of Hull, UK. His main teaching and research interest is the political economy of new media technologies, with particular reference to the European Union and East, South-East Asia, and China. He has published widely on new media technologies, including *The Digital Revolution and Governance* (2000) and *Corporate Strategy, Public Policy and New Technologies* (1996). Dai is currently Programme Director for the MA The Internet and the New Economy.

Christopher M. Dent is Senior Lecturer in the Department of East Asian Studies, University of Leeds, UK. His research interests centre on the international political economy of East Asia. He is more specifically interested in new trade policy developments in the Asia-Pacific; theories of international economic security; the foreign economic policies of Singapore, South Korea and Taiwan; and East Asia's economic relations with the European Union. Recent published books include *The Foreign Economic Policies of Singapore, South Korea and Taiwan* (2002), *Northeast Asian Regionalism: Learning from the European Experience* (co-editor, 2002), *The European Union and East Asia: An Economic Relationship* (1999), and *The European Economy: The Global Context* (1997). He has also published over 40 academic papers, and is currently writing a book on the proliferation of free trade agreement (FTA) projects in the Asia-Pacific.

Jörn Dosch is Senior Lecturer in Asia-Pacific Studies, Department of East Asian Studies, University of Leeds, UK. He was previously Fulbright Scholar at the Asia/Pacific Research Centre, Stanford University (1999–2000), Visiting Professor for International Relations at the International University of the Social Sciences (LUISS Guido Carli) in Rome (March 2000–January

2001), Assistant Professor at the Institute of Political Science, University of Mainz (1993–99). He obtained his PhD from the University of Mainz, Germany in 1996. He has published around 40 academic papers on International Relations in the Asia-Pacific, ASEAN, US-Asia and EU-Asia relations, democratisation in Southeast Asia. He is also a consultant for Deutsche Gesellschaft fuer Technische Zusammenarbeit (German Agency for Development Co-operation) and the Bertelsmann Foundation.

Eric Grove is Senior Lecturer in Security Studies at the University of Hull, UK. He is a graduate of Aberdeen and London Universities, became a civilian lecturer at the Royal Naval College, Dartmouth in 1971 and stayed for thirteen years, leaving as Deputy Head of Strategic Studies. He then worked as a self-employed strategic analyst and defence consultant, among other things starting the Russia–UK–US naval talks, helping design the Sea Power gallery at the National Maritime Museum and teaching at The Royal Naval College, Greenwich and the University of Cambridge. Since 1993 he has been at the University of Hull where he now directs the Centre for Security Studies. His books include *Vanguard to Trident: British Naval Policy since World War II* (1987), and *The Future of Sea Power* (1990). He was also the co-author of the 1995 edition of BR1806 *The Fundamentals of British Maritime Doctrine*. His publications were the basis of a PhD awarded by the University of Hull in 1996. Dr Grove has recently begun to appear frequently on television as a contributor to programmes on modern naval history. He has also worked abroad, with a year of teaching at the US Naval Academy in 1980–81 and six months in 1997 as a visiting research fellow at the University of Wollongong's Centre for Maritime Policy.

Jürgen Haacke is Lecturer in the Department of International Relations at the London School of Economics, UK. He received his PhD from the London School of Economics and Political Science, and is the author of *ASEAN's Diplomatic and Security Culture: Origins, Development and Prospects* (2003). His journal publications have appeared – among other – in *International Relations of Asia-Pacific, Asian Perspective, The Pacific Review*, and *Millennium: Journal of International Studies*.

Christopher Hughes is Senior Research Fellow and Deputy Director at the Centre for the Study of Globalisation and Regionalisation, University of Warwick, and formerly visiting professor at the Faculty of Law, University of Tokyo, and Research Fellow at Hiroshima University. He received his PhD from Sheffield University. Christopher Hughes' research interests include Japanese security policy, Japanese international political economy, regionalism in East Asia, and North Korea's external political and economic relations. He is the author of *Japan's Security Agenda: The Search for Regional Stability* (Lynne Rienner 2003); co-author of *Japan's International Relations: Politics, Economics and Security* (Routledge 2001); and co-editor of *New*

Regionalisms in the Global Political Economy (Routledge 2002). Christopher Hughes has authored a number of articles in journals such as *Survival, Review of International Political Economy, Security Dialogue,* and *The Pacific Review.* He is associate editor of The Pacific Review, and a participant in CSCAP.

Anja Jetschke is Assistant Professor at the Department of Political Science at the Albert-Ludwigs-Universität Freiburg, Germany. Her fields of study are international relations theory, human rights and the international relations of Southeast Asia. Anja Jetschke is a PhD graduate of the European University Institute in Florence, Italy. She has written her dissertation about transnational human rights networks and human rights change in Indonesia and the Philippines and currently works on a project studying the impact of international norms on democratisation.

Simon Lee is Lecturer in Politics at the Department of Politics and International Studies University of Hull, UK. He coordinates the Masters programme in Global Political Economy and co-ordinates the Masters programme in Globalisation and Governance. His principal research interests are in the field of political economy, and in particular the political economy of England. His recent publications include 'The International Monetary Fund', *New Political Economy* 7(2) 2002; (with R.Woodward), 'Implementing the Third Way: The Delivery of Public Services under the Blair Government', *Public Money and Management* October–December 2002; and 'Discovering the Frontiers of Regionalism: Fostering Entrepreneurship, Innovation and Competitiveness in the European Union', in S. Breslin, C. Hughes, N. Philips and B. Rosamond (eds) *New Regionalisms in the Global Political Economy* (2002). His forthcoming publications include *Blair's Third Way.*

Rex Li is a Senior Lecturer in International Relations, Liverpool John Moores University, UK. He is also Associate Editor of *Security Dialogue*, International Peace Research Institutes, Oslo/Sage Publications, London. He has been a Visiting Lecturer at the Joint Services Command and Staff College, UK Defence Academy. He is regularly interviewed by the BBC World Service commenting on East Asian security affairs. His recent publications include, as co-editor, *Fragmented Asia: Regional Integration and National Disintegration in Pacific Asia* (1996) and *Dynamic Asia: Business, Trade and Economic Development in Pacific Asia* (1998). He has also published widely on Chinese foreign and security policy, US–China relations, China–Taiwan relations and other Asia-Pacific security and economic issues, including in *The Journal of Strategic Studies, Pacifica Review, Asia Pacific Business Review, Journal of Contemporary China, The World Today, World Defence Systems* and *Contemporary Politics* journals.

Neil Renwick is Reader in International and East Asian Studies and Co-Director of the Centre for Asia-Pacific Studies at Nottingham Trent University, UK. A graduate of the Australian National University, he has taught at Adelaide and Northern Territory Universities in Australia. Dr Renwick is a former Senior Associate Member at St Antony's College, Oxford and former Reviews Editor for the journal *The Pacific Review*. He is the author of a number of books and numerous articles on international security, identity politics and international political economy related to the Asia-Pacific region. He is currently conducting research on information operations; gender and inequality issues; and on non-tradition security challenges in the Asia-Pacific region. His most recent research is for a book entitled *Northeast Asian Critical Security* (2003).

Jürgen Rüland is Professor of Political Science at the Department of Political Science, University of Freiburg, and Director of the Arnold-Bergstraesser-Institute, Freiburg, Germany. Before joining the University of Freiburg he was a research fellow at the Arnold-Bergstraesser-Institute, Freiburg (1978–91), acting professor at the Department of Political Science, University of Passau (1991–93) and professor of political science at the University of Rostock (1993–98). He is a specialist of governance studies and international relations with an emphasis on Southeast Asia. He has lectured and researched in the Philippines, Thailand, Indonesia, Malaysia, Singapore and Vietnam. Among his over 150 publications are *Asia-Pacific Economic Cooperation (APEC): The First Decade*, London: RoutledgeCurzon, 2002 (co-editor and author), *The Dynamics of Metropolitan Management in Southeast Asia*, Singapore: Institute of Southeast Asian Studies, 1996 (editor and author), *Local Associations and Municipal Government in Thailand*, Freiburg: Arnold-Bergstraesser-Institut (co-author); *Urban Government and Development in Southeast Asia. Regional Cities and Local Government*, Boulder: Westview Press, 1992 (author). His articles appeared in *Asian Survey, Pacific Review, Public Administration and Development, The Philippine Journal of Public Administration, The Asian Journal of Public Administration* and many German scientific journals.

Part I
Introduction

1
New Economic and Security Co-operation in the Asia-Pacific: An Introduction

Christopher M. Dent

1. Asia-Pacific economic and security co-operation: prime dimensions

The Asia-Pacific has experienced a period of turbulent change since the mid-1990s. This has mainly centred on two 'shocks' to the trans-region,[1] the first being the 1997/98 East Asian financial crisis and the second the 11 September 2001 al-Qaeda terrorist attacks on the United States. Both these shock events had significant catalytic effects upon the international relations of the Asia-Pacific. Moreover, they revealed the extent of economic and security interdependence that connect different communities and states in the trans-region, and consequently demonstrate the imperative to enhance different levels and forms of co-operative activity among them. The economic and political shock waves emanating from the near financial meltdown of Southeast Asia in 1997 and the collapse of New York's World Trade Centre in 2001 exposed just how connected people and systems within the Asia-Pacific are, yet at the same time illustrate the 'complex diversity' of the trans-region. This latter aspect has made endeavours to advance co-operative relations somewhat arduous: with 'complex diversity' invariably comes a critical lack of common ground and inherent shared interest required for such relations to develop. Our book contends that it is this tension between the post-shock forces of 'imperative co-operation' and the counter-forces of 'complex diversity' that is shaping new regional agendas in Asia-Pacific economic and security matters at the fundamental level. It is this relationship between *imperative co-operation* and *complex diversity* that forms the first of the book's three 'prime dimensions'.

Let us examine the first of these operative concepts – *imperative co-operation* – in more detail. Shock events such as the 1997/98 financial crisis and the 9/11 terrorist attacks invariably expose critical deficiencies or fault-lines in existing co-operative structures, and furthermore heighten the imperative to better manage the interdependence between shock-affected communities and states. Thus, there is normally sufficient political will generated to establish new forms and structures of co-operation. This in turn can involve a 'creative destruction' process, whereby already existing co-operative structures are either displaced by new structures or substantively reconfigured into something new in itself. The recent 'creative reconfiguration' of the Asia-Pacific Economic Co-operation (APEC) forum, in which its original exclusively economic remit has been more or less recast to embrace new security objectives, is discussed later in this chapter to illustrate such a point. In addition, a variety of new regional co-operative ventures have emerged within the Asia-Pacific in recent years, which may be viewed as the trans-region's latest phase of *new regionalism* development.[2] For example, in 2002 alone, three new multilateral fora of note convened their inaugural meetings. The Boao Forum for Asia first convened in April that year, and is essentially a new non-governmental forum that aims to strengthen economic exchanges and co-operation within the region, and become the Asian version of the Davos World Economic Forum. In May 2002, the first Singapore Shangri-La Dialogue meeting was convened, which is another quasi-official gathering but concerned with security dialogue that brought together defence ministers from Australia, India, Indonesia, Japan and Singapore, as well as US Deputy-Defence Secretary Paul Wolfowitz. A month later in June 2002, Thailand hosted the first Asia Co-operation Dialogue (ACD) meeting, involving ministers from most Southeast Asian states (except Burma), Japan, China, South Korea, Bangladesh, India and Pakistan, as well as, interestingly, Bahrain and Qatar.[3] Discussions under the ACD forum have focused on economic, social and cultural issues rather than security concerns. More generally, with respect to *imperative co-operation*, there may be certain synergies to be had between economic and security co-operation when shock events occur in each sector in close succession to the other, as has been the case for East Asia and the Asia-Pacific. In this sense, new *imperative co-operation* stemming from the 9/11 terrorist attacks have, in particular instances, reinforced or fused with that deriving from responses to the 1997/98 financial crisis shock.

Regarding the second operative concept of our first 'prime dimension', the Asia-Pacific's *complex diversity* is demonstrably salient across a number of domains – economic, business system, political, socio-cultural, socio-religious and so on. The trans-region is home to the world's most advanced industrial states (e.g. the United States, Japan) and also some of its least developed countries (e.g. Cambodia, Papua New Guinea), as well as its broadest strata of newly industrialising economies (e.g. South Korea, Taiwan, Malaysia). Consequently, across the Asia-Pacific a highly asymmetric pattern or distribution of techno-industrial and financial capacities is apparent. It is further demarked by various and significantly contrasting capitalist or business system paradigms, such as East Asia's developmental statism,

Anglo-Saxon market liberalism, and China and Vietnam's socialist market models. In the political domain, well-established liberal democracies, young semi-democracies and (soft) authoritarian systems of governance are situated beside each other. In the Asia-Pacific can also be found ancient countries (e.g. China, Korea), 'new world' countries (e.g. the United States, Australia), and young post-colonial states (e.g. Malaysia, the Philippines). Added to this is a broad mix of Confucian, Buddhist, Muslim and Christian socio-religious or socio-cultural traditions that span the Asia-Pacific. Furthermore, complex interlinking exists between these different domains: the economic, political and business systems of Asia-Pacific states have themselves been significantly determined over time by highly localised socio-cultural and socio-religious factors. Such *complex diversity* cannot be arguably found anywhere else within a defined region or trans-region on the planet, and moreover it is often evident at sub-regional level, for example, Southeast Asia. It is also instructive when making comparisons between specific states. For example, the domestic political determinants behind both Japan and the United States' respective protectionist practices on agricultural trade are extremely different. What is made clear throughout this text is that the Asia-Pacific's *complex diversity* is as deep as it is multifaceted, and consequently presents a ubiquitous set of hurdles in the path of *imperative co-operation*.

The second 'prime dimension' of this book relates to how *economic and security issues have become increasingly conflated in Asia-Pacific international relations*, particularly since the 1997/98 East Asian financial crisis and the 9/11 terrorist attacks on the United States. This trend is evident within various regional fora, and at various levels: for example at the sub-regional level in the Association of Southeast Asian Nations (ASEAN), at the regional level in ASEAN Plus Three (APT), and at the trans-regional level in the Asia-Pacific Economic Co-operation (APEC) forum. The links between economics and security, or the economics–security nexus, have been the subject of scholarly debate for some time.[4] However, these links are becoming increasingly prevalent and significant, as is explored across the various themes discussed in the book. A number of questions are addressed in this respect. For example, how important were the security ramifications of the 1997/98 East Asian financial crisis for the wider Asia-Pacific region? How will the post-9/11 security environment affect the region's international economic relations? To what extent are there security-related motives behind new economic linkages and co-operative endeavours arising within the Asia-Pacific transregion?

The book's third 'prime dimension' concerns the relationship between the *Asia-Pacific's new economic and security bilateralism and regional-level forms of co-operation, integration and governance*. As the authors of many of the chapters note, the relationship between bilateralism and regionalism in the Asia-Pacific has become an increasingly critical one. One may view the recent flourishing networks of bilateral ties as representing a new paradigm of strategic diplomacy in the Asia-Pacific, whereby they offer a viable alternative to economic and security regionalism or trans-regionalism – the limitations of which have, to many, become clearer after the 1997/98 financial crisis and 9/11 shocks. On the one hand, these intensifying bilateral ties may be contributing to regional community-building processes in the Asia-Pacific, being woven from a bilateralised, interlocking 'lattice' base of international relations. In connection to the first 'prime dimension', bilateral co-operative routes could be perceived to have proliferated in the face of constraints impeding the development of wider regionalist arrangements, these constraints deriving principally from *complex diversity* factors. Put alternatively, in a highly diverse regional group of states a large number of bilateral agreements made among them may prove easier to broker than an all-inclusive regional agreement. Yet, this same dense economic and security bilateralism may itself constitute new forms of region-wide – but not necessarily regional – co-operation in the Asia-Pacific, which we may broadly refer to as 'region-convergent' bilateralism. On the other hand, 'region-divergent' bilateralism relates to how the very same dense bilateralism can work against the development of regional-level forms of co-operation, integration and governance. This may arise, for example, through this new trend creating norms of adversarial and competing strategic alliance relationship behaviour amongst Asia-Pacific states that in turn fundamentally undermine regional community-building processes and endeavours. These two opposing perspectives on the bilateralism–regionalism relationship are discussed to some detail in the book's concluding chapter, where it will *inter alia* synthesise the main related arguments on this subject made in preceding chapters.

2. Recent economic and security developments in the Asia-Pacific: a brief overview

2.1. Economic perspectives

As suggested earlier, the most important new changes in the development of Asia-Pacific economic co-operation stem from the catalytic effects of the 1997/98 East Asian financial crisis. For example, we examine later how the crisis exacerbated tensions and conflicts of interest within the APEC group, consequently blowing its regional trade liberalisation project significantly off-course. Another pre-existing regional project – ASEAN's Free Trade Area scheme, or AFTA – also succumbed to crisis-induced pressures and tensions. Since the crisis, many Southeast Asian states have become more preoccupied with protecting domestic economic interests than strictly adhere to their AFTA implementation commitments. Moreover, this 'sub-regional' venture in economic community-building has been in some sense displaced by wider 'pan-regional' ventures as part of the aforementioned 'creative destruction' and 'creative reconfiguration' processes.

This last above point relates to new forms of region-wide economic co-operation and relations in general to have emerged in the 1997/98 crisis aftermath. The most important new regional framework to have emerged in this context is APT, consisting of ASEAN's ten-member states (Brunei, Cambodia, Indonesia, Laos, Malaysia, Myanmar, Philippines, Singapore, Thailand and Vietnam) and the Northeast Asian states of Japan, China and South Korea. The APT group held its first annual summit meeting in December 1997, and its work has mainly focused on improving mechanisms for regional financial governance, as currently developed under the Chiang Mai Initiative. There has also been talk of eventually creating an East Asian free trade zone, and even an Asian monetary union. While these objectives are somewhat utopian, APT is historically significant because it represents the first coalescing of a pan-East Asian economic group.

At the broader Asia-Pacific level of trade diplomacy, there has been a startling proliferation of bilateral free trade agreement (FTA) projects between a growing number of states within the trans-region. This FTA trend has arisen at least partly out of frustrations over the respective trade institutional failures of APEC, AFTA and also the WTO to advance regional and global trade liberalisation. This expanding web of bilateral trade agreements is also strengthening strategic diplomacy linkages within the Asia-Pacific community. For example, Singapore sees its FTA project with the United States as vital to maintaining American interest and engagement in Southeast Asia generally. Japan views its own bilateral FTA policy as an important new vehicle for advancing its (economic) diplomacy influence in the region. Evidence that new sub-regional FTAs could build upon this increasingly dense concentration of bilateral FTA linkages is also emerging, for example in the proposed 'Pacific-3' FTA between Singapore, New Zealand and Chile.

Other significant events and developments in the Asia-Pacific international political economy are noteworthy. Japan's persistent economic problems continue to exert a drag upon the regional economy, yet at the same time Tokyo has become more proactive on the regional economic diplomacy front, as ongoing developments in the APT framework clearly reveal. Meanwhile, China and Taiwan's recent accessions to the WTO have important implications for the region, with both exploring new opportunities for economic diplomacy. The recently initiated ASEAN-China FTA project highlights China's increasingly engaged role in regional economic affairs, and the challenge it poses to Japan as East Asia's regional economic hegemon. At other levels of regional interaction, East Asia continues to develop interregional linkages with the European Union through the Asia-Europe Meeting (ASEM), and with Latin America in the East Asia – Latin America Forum (EALAF). At the same time, various sub-regional 'growth area' development projects – notably in the Greater Mekong Sub-region – have continued to make progress.

2.2. Security perspectives

During the 1990s, Asia-Pacific governments started building pan-regional institutions for security dialogue and confidence-building. The ASEAN group created the ASEAN Regional Forum (ARF) in 1994 in an attempt to extend its own 'good practice', in terms mitigating conflict between members, into the broader East Asian region. The ARF brought together a number of ASEAN's 'dialogue partners' (the United States, Japan, China, Russia, South Korea, Australia, New Zealand, Canada, India and the EU) to discuss security-related issues in general. A more specific aim was to engage China as a co-operative partner in maintaining regional stability and peace. However, the ARF's subsequently unimpressive history prompts the question of why its efforts to build a framework for co-operative security have been so hesitant. At the same time, ASEAN's own security role has faced major challenges, deriving largely from its membership expansion since 1995 to include all ten Southeast Asian states, the impact of economic and political crisis on Indonesia's sub-regional leadership, and an intra-mural debate over the validity of the Association's cardinal principle of non-interference. In early 2001, the first major armed clash between ASEAN members (involving Thailand and Myanmar) seemed to underline the grouping's declining coherence and usefulness in security terms.

One notable phenomenon over the last decade has been the burgeoning non-governmental 'second-track' dialogue on security matters – including 'non-traditional' issues – amongst regional representatives, notably in the context of the various series of CSCAP (Council for Security Cooperation in the Asia-Pacific) meetings and workshops. However, in most East Asian states security policy-making is still a highly secretive matter in which non-governmental actors – or even civilian politicians in some cases – are allowed no significant role. So it is therefore not surprising that the impact of second-track dialogue on regional states' security and defence policies has apparently remained limited.

Meanwhile, as in the economic arena, security bilateralism is thriving in the region. This has involved a growing network of co-operation on defence and broader security matters between regional states, as can be seen within Southeast Asia, within East Asia more broadly, and between the United States or Australia and East Asian partners. The 11 September 2001 attacks on the United States, and more recently the 12 October 2002 terrorist bombing in Bali, Indonesia has provided critical junctures in the development of Asia-Pacific security relations. The new emphasis of the United States and other Asia-Pacific states on combating terrorism appears to have reinforced the new security bilateralism trend, as many chapters in this book discuss in detail. The United States in particular is looking to consolidate an alliance network of (liberal) democratic states in the war on 'terror' through new security and economic diplomacy policies under the George W. Bush administration. The mixed success of this approach, especially in attempts to fortify alliance ties with East Asian states, maybe largely attributed to the Asia-Pacific's *complex diversity*. To some extent, the United States' much criticised actions during the 1997/98 financial crisis may explain why certain East Asian states remain wary of Washington's underlying intentions here. Still, the underlying forces of *imperative co-operation* in the Asia-Pacific's security domain remain reasonably strong.

3. APEC: a case study

In this section, we make a case study on APEC to illustrate some of the main themes covered by this book. APEC is useful in this respect for two main reasons. First, it is the most comprehensively developed regional organisation from either the economic or security domain that spans the Asia-Pacific, and therefore is coincidentally representative of the trans-region as a whole in terms of constituent interests and recent general developments within it. Second, recent developments within APEC itself illustrate well the three 'prime dimensions' of the book and how they interrelate with each other. APEC was established in 1989 with twelve original members that looked to advance regional economic co-operation, broadly conceived (Aggarwal and Morrison 1998, Yamazawa 2000, Ravenhill 2001). By the end of the 1990s, APEC had expanded to twenty-one members, ranging from developing countries such as Papua New Guinea and Peru to advanced industrial states like the United States, Japan and Australia. The wide geographic scope and notably asymmetric development profile of APEC's membership has brought considerable *complex diversity* problematics to the organisation. Moreover, APEC has suffered from a fundamental lack of *imperative co-operation* amongst its diverse membership to drive through its centrepiece project, this being the establishment of a complete 'free trade and investment zone' across the Asia-Pacific by 2020, as laid out at the 1994 summit at Bogor, Indonesia. Several attempts have been made to realise this objective but all have failed or are failing largely owing to different views and approaches to trade policy within APEC. In broad terms, the groups' Anglo-Pacific members (i.e. United States, Canada, Australia, New Zealand) are more interested in pushing trade liberalisation initiatives, whilst APEC's Asian member states are generally more concerned with trade facilitation (Ravenhill 2000). With the growth of trans-pacific commerce naturally intensifying without the help of any formalised regional integration agreement (e.g. an FTA) by the mid-1990s, and with there being much talk of an anticipated 'Pacific Century' around this time, imperative co-operation factors were largely redundant: the trans-region had developed a substantial economic momentum of its own and APEC's co-operative initiatives were essentially riding the crest of this wave.

During the 1997/98 East Asian financial crisis, the fragilities of the APEC economic alliance, as well as its complex diverse membership, were critically exposed. The asymmetric impact of the crisis, in that it only directly affected a sub-group of members within the organisation, was highly relevant. As Chapters 2, 4 and particularly 5 discuss in more detail, the crisis provided imperative co-operation impetus behind the development of the new APT framework (an exclusive East Asian grouping) whilst revealing the divisions in the wider APEC group. This was particularly illustrated in negotiations over APEC's Early Voluntary Sectoral Liberalisation (EVSL) scheme, introduced at the Vancouver summit in 1997 whereby progress towards the organisation's Bogor goal was to be made by liberalising trade in fifteen targeted sectors by the time of the following summit held at Kuala Lumpur in 1998. However, Japan was especially reluctant to make any concessions in liberalising primary sector (mainly fishing and forestry) trade, despite considerable pressure from the United States in particular (Krauss 2003, Rapkin 2001). Like Japan, many other East Asian states advocated for stronger emphasis to be placed on APEC's various trade facilitation and 'ecotech' (economic and technical co-operation) schemes, especially at a time when they wished to insulate domestic markets from the rigours of open engagement with international market forces.

Since this time, APEC has tried to find a new sense of direction and purpose. Various recommendations have been made, either within formal APEC processes or at the informal sidelines. At a pre-summit symposium held in May 2002, long-standing APEC advocate Fred Bergsten proposed that the organisation should adopt a new goal of realising 'shared prosperity in the region' in parallel to the aforementioned Bogor goal of creating a free trade and investment zone by 2020 (Bergsten 2002: 1). This, it was hoped, would counter the resistance to pursue the initial Bogor objective, such resistance essentially stemming from complex diversity factors discussed earlier. Under this new goal, Bergsten envisaged that those adversely affected by liberalisation (e.g. firms, workers, communities) would receive transitional assistance to cope with the dislocations caused by more open and competitive trading conditions. This should, he argued, be combined with improved education and training schemes to exploit the new commercial opportunities presented by more open markets. However, Bergsten was not suggesting that APEC develop its own fiscal redistribution system to operate between group members but rather that each establish its own separate domestic system. Given the complex diversity of the APEC group, the impact of even gradualised trade liberalisation would be significantly asymmetric, with some countries well positioned to exploit the benefits of open regional markets and others not. Moreover, many of APEC's developing country members do not possess the fiscal resources or the technocratic capacity to implement the redistributive schemes proposed by Bergsten. Furthermore, his additional recommendations for creating mechanisms for APEC-wide knowledge sharing of best policy practice on measures such as unemployment insurance, and encouraging external financing from sources like the World Bank would only offer a very minimal level of assistance in this matter.

As it transpired, APEC leaders at the 2002 summit convened in Los Cabos, Mexico, simply pledged 'to continue and accelerate' movement towards the Bogor goals. Once more, no new post-EVSL scheme on trade liberalisation was proposed. Instead, APEC members contented themselves with new, lowest common denominator initiatives on trade facilitation, such as implementing Unilateral Advance Passenger Information systems, the adoption of the revised Kyoto Convention on the Simplification and Harmonisation of Customs Procedures, and the expanded use of electronic certificates of origin.[5] While APEC leaders did endorse a proposal to remove all agricultural export subsidies as part of the WTO's Doha Round of global trade talks, neither the United States nor Japan offered any new commitment to reduce their own agricultural trade protection at the Los Cabos summit.[6] Moreover, New Zealand's Prime Minister, Helen Clark, commented that the 2002 APEC leader's economic declaration resembled those of previous years with no real substantive new project or strategy offered. She more specifically commented that, 'Each year, they make pretty much the same proposals, and each year APEC issues pretty much the same declarations about wanting a strong WTO round promoting trade liberalisation and facilitation.'[7] Meanwhile, in reaction to recent developments in US trade and economic policy (especially in the steel and agricultural sectors), Philippines President Gloria Arroyo commented that, 'they preach trade liberalisation but they practice protectionism'.[8]

In sum, the relative lack of *imperative co-operation* factors spanning the whole Asia-Pacific region in combination with significant *complex diversity* factors has effectively narrowed the scope of APEC economic co-operation to trade facilitation and ecotech fields. Its continued failure to advance its centrepiece project as defined by its Bogor goals, together with the impact of the 9/11 terrorist attacks on the United States has led APEC down a new path where economics and security have become increasingly conflated. As the 2001 and 2002 summits have demonstrated, APEC may require rebranding after security issues coming to the fore. It is also here where APEC may harness whole new forces of imperative co-operation to provide much needed coherence and purpose at a critical juncture of its development. At APEC's 2001 summit at Shanghai, the group's leaders proclaimed in their joint statement that terrorism was 'a direct challenge to APEC's vision of free, open and prosperous economies, and to the fundamental values that APEC members hold'. This was the fundamental linkage point in APEC's new economics–security nexus. From this, APEC governments expressed their commitment to prevent and suppress 'all forms of terrorist acts in the future' in accordance with United Nations resolutions. They more specifically pledged to 'adopt financial measures to prevent the flow of funds to terrorists, to adhere to international requirements on air and maritime security, and to have their transportation chiefs discuss additional measures to enhance airport, aircraft and port security'.[9]

This new approach was followed up at APEC's 2002 summit with new proposed measures under the rubric of 'Counter-Terrorism and Economic Growth' in the context that terrorism was 'a threat to economic stability in APEC, as well as a threat to regional peace and security'.[10] The Bali terrorist bombing incident of 12 October 2002 served to underscore this, as did bombing attacks in the southern Philippines, North Korea's admission of its nuclear weapons development programme, and the hostage crisis in Moscow. The 2002 APEC Leaders Joint Statement went on to reaffirm 'the importance of achieving the twin goals of enhanced security against terrorist threats and continued protection of economic growth', thus formally binding economic and security objectives more closely together. To this end, APEC ministers discussed new co-operative measures in the areas of trade, finance and communications. For example, the Secure Trade in the APEC Region (STAR) Initiative would look to ways to improve transportation security, customs and immigration co-operation while facilitating the movement of goods and people across the Asia-Pacific. Meanwhile, APEC's Action Plan on Combating the Financing of Terrorism aimed to halt the flow of financing to terrorists while ensuring efficient financial markets. In addition, APEC's new Cybersecurity Strategy was intended to debilitate terrorist communication capabilities whilst maintaining the free flow of information that permitted markets to operate effectively.

While, then, APEC's most recent attempts to revitalise its Bogor goal project has been viewed with much scepticism, its gradually veering off its original 'economic-only' remit to embrace security issues in addition has stirred much interest.[11] At the moment, economics remains the primary domain of action in which to realise APEC's security-related objectives: there are no plans to formally discuss or operationalise conventional military security actions within the organisation. Indeed, MacDuff (2002) has argued that the United States is unlikely to have much success in reconfiguring APEC's functional purposes to such ends, and moreover stated that, 'having achieved modest results in the "low politics" of economic co-operation...APEC is unlikely to "graduate" to the "high politics" of traditional security, in which it has little background' (p. 457). MacDuff's somewhat neo-realist interpretation of the 'low-high politics' divide may be viewed by some as creating a false dichotomy in the economics–security nexus in that the two domains have become increasingly intermeshed, as broadening conceptualisations of 'comprehensive security' offered by various academics would suggest (Mathews 1989, Sorenson 1990, Ullman 1993, Katzenstein 1996, Buzan *et al.* 1998). Nevertheless, it is trade that is still viewed as the 'alliance cement' of APEC: securing trade is seen as a means to secure APEC itself as an organisation for promoting regionalised co-operation *per se*. Furthermore, chapters within this book generally concur with the view that the conventional boundaries of the pursuit of 'security' itself have become increasingly blurred. In this sense, APEC's representation of a trade-based alliance between 'civilised' (i.e. non-terrorist sponsoring) nation-states constitutes to many an important forward defence against international terrorism.

Recent developments within APEC are also instructive when studying the third prime dimension of this book, namely the relationship between bilateralism and regionalism. Like many regional fora or organisations, APEC has helped facilitate various forms of bilateral diplomacy. Linking immediately back to the 2002 summit at Los Cabos and security-related issues, Australia used the occasion to announce its US$10 million aid package that was intended to help improve Indonesia's counter-terrorist capabilities by strengthening its airport, immigration and customs-control systems. At the same time, Japan gave US$47 million of emergency aid to assist Bali's recovery. As Chapter 5 elaborates in more detail, though, APEC's relationship with the new trade bilateralism – now a defining feature of the Asia-Pacific's regional political economy – is more relevant and revealing.

It was noted earlier how the proliferation of bilateral FTAs between Asia-Pacific states was at least partly borne from APEC's own failure to advance its regional trade liberalisation project. The organisation is connected to this new bilateralism trend but only in an indirect and somewhat subservient manner. It has become an occasional 'clearing house' for bilateral FTA projects, whereby on *summitry* sidelines new ones are announced, others are further negotiated, and others concluded. Some would say this new trade bilateralism is commensurate with the Bogor goal of eventually creating a free trade zone across the trans-region, and furthermore with APEC's endeavours at regional economic community-building *per se*. In addition, the strategic diplomacy motivations behind the new FTA links being forged in the Asia-Pacific are generally congruent with APEC's recent venturing into the security domain.

However, it is the new bilateral FTA trend's superseding of APEC in the field of region-wide trade diplomacy that is more critically relevant. In this respect, the bilateral FTA phenomenon has made APEC focus on what its relative strengths and real achievements have been to date, namely in trade and investment facilitation as well as ecotech. As noted earlier, it is here where the organisation has been devoting an increasing amount of time and resources, exploiting APEC's revealed comparative advantage. More arguably, and in combination with post-9/11 events and developments, the new trade bilateralism's challenge to APEC's 'Bogor' centrepiece project has helped compel its member states to re-evaluate the organisation's original fundamental purpose, and its subsequent shift towards the economics–security nexus. This further showed the interconnectivity between the three 'prime dimensions' of Asia-Pacific economic and security co-operation.

4. Structure and summary of the text

The book is structured around four main sections. After this introductory chapter (Part I), which has set out the 'prime dimensions' of the text's analysis, Simon Lee and Christopher Hughes offer chapters that cover the global contexts (Part II) to many of the debates presented by subsequent chapters. In Part III, Jürgen Rüland, Christopher Dent and Eric Grove provide regional overviews of new forms and structures of economic and security co-operation arising across Asia and the Asia-Pacific. This is followed by Part IV's more micro-geographic perspectives on events and developments at the sub-regional level. For example, Jürgen Haacke, Alan Collins and Anja Jetschke make respective studies of recent co-operative challenges facing states and communities within Southeast Asia. In his chapter, Jörn Dosch examines developments in sub-regional co-operation in the Mekong Valley 'growth zone', while Rex Li analyses 'Cross-Strait zone' relations between China and Taiwan in an economics and security context. In the last main part (Part V), Neil Renwick and Xiudian Dai present different 'cyber dimensions' to economic and security co-operation in the Asia-Pacific, each considering how new information and communication technologies are posing both new opportunities and threats to the development of international relations in the region.

Thus, the work presented by the authors as a whole offers a rich blend of perspectives on the core theme of Asia-Pacific economic and security co-operation. In the final chapter and part (Part VI), editor Christopher Dent synthesises the main conclusions and findings of preceding chapters within the 'prime dimensions' thematic framework. Further conceptual development and theorising is presented here in an endeavour to better frame our understanding of new forms and structures of economic and security co-operation that have emerged in the Asia-Pacific region over recent years.

Notes

1. The term 'trans-region' with respect to the Asia-Pacific is preferred here as it could be said to straddle or encompass a number of distinct global regions, namely East Asia, North America, Oceania and Pacific Latin America. This term is particularly used in this book when we contrast the Asia-Pacific 'trans-region' to regional (e.g. East Asia) and sub-regional (e.g. Southeast Asia) entities.
2. The 'new regionalism' may be generally contrasted with its more narrow 'old', Euro-centric counterpart by its particular emphasis on: multiple and co-existent levels and forms of regional co-operation and integration (e.g. state-driven, market-driven; sub-regional, trans-regional); a less technocratically determined

and more socially constructed or ideational view to understanding regional community-building; the connections between regionalism and extra-regional processes and structures at the global and multilateral levels. This is not just relevant to the Asia-Pacific but also to most global regions.

3. 'Asian Multilateralism Takes on New Energy', *Japan Times*, 01.08.2002.

4. According to Mastanduno (1998), modern academic studies on the connections between economics and security date back to the 1930s and 1940s when Jacob Viner, E.H. Carr, Albert Hirschman and Edward Mead Earle were amongst the first prominent academics to take an interest in the economics–security nexus. See also Knorr (1977), Leitzel (1993), Neu and Wolf (1994), DeSouza (2000).

5. The APEC Trade Facilitation Action Plan, in which member states aimed to reduce business transaction costs in the region by 5 per cent by 2006, had been introduced a year earlier at the 2001 summit in Shanghai. '*Toward the Shanghai Goal: Implementing the APEC Trade Facilitation Action Plan*', APEC Secretariat, 2002.

6. *The Australian*, 29.10.2002.

7. 'A Little Aid, a Lot of – Political – Trade', *Straits Times*, 29.10.2002.

8. *Stuff.co.uk*, 29.10.2002.

9. From www.apecsec.org.sg.

10. Fourteenth APEC Ministerial Meeting, Joint Statement, 24 October 2002.

11. For example, see 'Japan, APEC Left Out in the Cold on Regional Free Trade', *Asahi Shimbun*, 30.10.2002; 'A Little Aid, a Lot of – Political – Trade', *Straits Times*, 29.10.2002; 'APEC Evolves with Changing Times', *The Star*, 21.10.2002.

References

Aggarwal, V.K. and Morrison, C.E. (eds) (1998) *Asia-Pacific Crossroads: Regime Creation and the Future of APEC*, St Martin's Press, New York.

Bergsten, C.F. (2002) 'Globalisation and Shared Prosperity: The Role of APEC', presentation to the *Dialogue on Globalisation and Shared Prosperity*, Merida, 26 May, Mexico.

Buzan, B., Wæver, O. and de Wilde, J. (1998) *Security: A New Framework of Analysis*, Lynne Rienner, Boulder.

DeSouza, P.J. (2000) 'Introduction and Overview', in P.J. DeSouza (ed.), *Economic Strategy and National Security*, Westview Press, Boulder.

Katzenstein, P.J. (1996) 'Introduction: Alternative Perspectives on National Security', in P.J. Katzenstein (ed.), *The Culture of National Security: Norms and Identity in World Politics*, Columbia University Press, New York.

Knorr, K. (1977) 'Economic Interdependence and National Security', in K. Knorr and F.N. Trager (eds) *Economic Issues and National Security*, Regents Press, Lawrence.

Krauss, E.S. (2003) 'The US and Japan in APEC's EVSL Negotiations: Regional Multilateralism and Trade', in E.S. Krauss and T.J. Pempel (eds), *Beyond Bilateralism: US–Japan Relations in the New Asia-Pacific*, Stanford University Press, Stanford.

Leitzel, J. (1993) (ed.) *Economics and National Security*, Westview Press, Boulder.

MacDuff, D. (2002) 'APEC after Shanghai: Which Path Forward?', *International Journal*, Vol. 57(3), pp. 439–57.

Mastanduno, M. (1998) 'Economics and Security in Statescraft and Scholarship', *International Organisation*, Vol. 52(4), pp. 825–54.

Mathews, J.T. (1989) 'Redefining Security', *Foreign Affairs*, Vol. 68(2), pp. 162–77.

Neu, C.R. and Wolf, C. (1994) *The Economic Dimensions of National Security*, Rand Corporation, Santa Monica.

Rapkin, D. (2001) 'The US, Japan, and the Power to Block: The APEC and AMF Cases', *The Pacific Review*, Vol. 14(3), pp. 373–410.

Ravenhill, J. (2000) 'APEC Adrift: Implications for Economic Regionalism in Asia and the Pacific', *The Pacific Review*, Vol. 13(2), pp. 319–33.

Ravenhill, J. (2001) *APEC and the Construction of Pacific Rim Regionalism*, Cambridge University Press, Cambridge.

Sorenson, T.C. (1990) 'Rethinking National Security', *Foreign Affairs*, Vol. 69(3), pp. 1–18.

Ullman, R. (1993) 'Redefining Security', *International Security*, Vol. 8(1), pp. 129–53.

Yamazawa, I. (ed.) (2000) *Asia-Pacific Economic Co-operation: Challenges and Tasks for the Twenty-First Century*, Routledge, London.

Part II
Global Contexts

2
Asia-Pacific Economic Regionalism: Global Constraints and Opportunities

Simon Lee

1. Introduction

Global economic prosperity and security are vital public goods. They demand co-operation among nation-states for their achievement and maintenance. This fact has been acknowledged in the selection of '*A World of Differences: Partnerships for the Future*' as the central theme for the Asia-Pacific Economic Co-operation (APEC) forum in 2003. The incoming Executive Director of the APEC Secretariat, Piamsak Milintachinda, has affirmed the need for co-operation 'in pursuit of APEC's twin goals of enhancing security against terrorist threats while continuing to promote trade growth and economic development within the APEC region' (APEC 2002: 1). Despite the strength of this rhetorical commitment to regional economic and security co-operation, given the context of a faltering global economy, the October 12 terrorist bombing of Bali and in the light of North Korea's apparent intention to resume its nuclear programme, the reality of Asia-Pacific regionalism has fallen far short of politicians' rhetoric. For example, in the field of economic co-operation through regional trade agreements (RTAs), the World Trade Organization (WTO) has noted that the Asia Pacific is 'the region with the smallest number of RTAs currently in force' (WTO 2000: 22). Furthermore, while a number of states have been actively considering moving from their established policy of Most Favoured Nation-only trade liberalization towards regional co-operation, the WTO has warned that the 'open regionalism' favoured by the APEC may be 'counteracted by a drive towards preferential trade initiatives'. This in turn could threaten trade flows across the Asia-Pacific region because of a damaging lack of uniformity in the rules governing bilateral and 'cross-regional RTAs' (WTO 2002a: 7–8).

Given the disparity between the rhetoric and reality of Asia-Pacific economic and security co-operation, this chapter seeks to explore the relationship between globalization and Asia-Pacific economic regionalism in order to identify the principal constraints and opportunities acting upon the process of regional co-operation. First, the chapter traces how the relationship between global governance and Asia-Pacific regionalism remains as yet unconsummated. Indeed, the potential of regionalism in general, let alone Asia-Pacific regionalism in particular, to contribute to effective global governance of finance, trade and development remains largely unacknowledged and marginalized in recent debates. Second, despite the 'complex diversity' of the Asia-Pacific region (identified by Dent in Chapter 1), it is suggested that there is an opportunity for Asia-Pacific regional economic co-operation to provide an alternative political economy to the neo-liberal orthodoxy of the 'Washington Consensus' which has delivered turbulence, instability and financial crises as much as sustained prosperity and growth for major economies in the Asia-Pacific region during the past decade (Lee 2003a). Third, the chapter explores the prospects for Asia-Pacific regionalism by evaluating recent proposals for enhancing regional financial co-operation, concluding that such co-operation affords the Asia-Pacific in general and East Asia in particular the opportunity to develop a degree of ideological and policy autonomy from the global constraints of the 'Washington Consensus'.

2. The relationship between global governance and Asia-Pacific regionalism

One of the most important trends in the world economy in the past seven years has been the acceleration in the pace and coverage of regional economic co-operation in the field of trade policy. According to the WTO, 'the number of regional trade agreements (RTAs) being negotiated has increased exponentially and their scope as well as their geographical reach have both broadened and expanded' (WTO 2002a: 3). As a consequence, by March 2002, 250 RTAs had been notified to the GATT/WTO, of which 168 remain in force. Indeed, since 1 January 1995, a further 125 new RTAs have been notified, with an average of 15 notifications every year to the WTO, compared with an annual average of less than three during the four and half decades of the GATT. However, the WTO has also noted that, despite the size of its market, the Asia-Pacific is the region with the smallest number of RTAs in force. Furthermore, there has been a recent trend in the region away from 'open regionalism', since 'most of the major players at the regional level are increasingly looking beyond their regional borders for partners in selective (often bilateral) preferential trade agreements'[1] (WTO 2002a: 8).

The danger inherent in a move away from regionalism towards bilateralism in trade agreements is that 'the states which benefit most from such arrangements are those with the largest market access to offer, the largest security umbrella to share, and the greatest capacity to threaten negative consequences from non-compliance or exclusion' (Woods 2002: 39).

The penalty for states in the Asia-Pacific region of their failure to make more rapid progress in the development of region-wide RTAs is that they will be exposed to a huge asymmetry in political and economic power when negotiating with the United States. Because the United States, as the most powerfully armed nation with the largest domestic market, possesses 'disproportionate power in every international organization to which it belongs' (Woods 2002: 38), the pursuit of bilateralism has risked exposing weaker states to the aggressive unilateralism frequently characteristic of US trade policy, notably during the presidency of George W. Bush. President Bush's trade strategy has sought to promote trade liberalization 'on multiple fronts: globally, regionally, and with individual nations' in order to create 'a competition in liberalization with the United States as the central driving force' (USTR 2002a: 1). Thus, on 26 November 2002, the United States called upon the member states of the WTO 'to eliminate all tariffs on consumer and industrial goods by 2015', a move which it was claimed would yield 'a world income gain of US$832 billion from free trade in all goods including agriculture, of which US$539 billion (65 per cent) would flow to developing countries' (USTR 2002b: 1–2).

While superficially attractive, given its apparent synergy with the principles and purpose of APEC's 'open regionalism', the attendant danger is that this strategy – against the backdrop of rising US trade deficits since 1995, which reached US$376 billion in 2000 (3.8 per cent of GDP) before falling back to US$351 billion in 2001 (3.4 per cent of GDP) – will be used by Bush in the run-up to the November 2004 Presidential election to justify more aggressive, unilateralist and potentially punitive and damaging trade measures against Asia-Pacific economies. Indeed, the lack of American commitment to regional co-operation in trade has been noted by the President's own annual report on United States' trade which has conceded that while 'there are 130 regional free trade and customs agreements in the world; the United States is a party to only three'[2] (USTR 2002a: 10). The dangers of a more aggressive trade policy under Bush, designed to reinforce the United States' competitive advantage over its commercial rivals, are becoming increasingly manifest.

This highly dynamic context for Asia-Pacific economic co-operation has placed a premium on a clear understanding of the relationship between regionalism and global governance. Held and McGrew (2002) have portrayed the institutional architecture of global governance as having five principal facets, namely, that it is multilayered; polyarchic or pluralistic; of variable geometry; structurally complex; and has made national governments increasingly important as 'strategic sites … [for] suturing together these various infrastructures of governance and legitimizing regulation beyond the state' (p. 9). Not only is global governance increasingly complex. The uncomfortable fact remains, as demonstrated by the causes and consequences of the 1997/98 East Asian financial crisis, that neither the architecture of global or regional governance of finance, trade and development has been able to keep pace with the dynamism of private sector networking at the regional and global levels (Lee 2003b). Furthermore, as Woods (2002) has noted, while the desire to democratize global governance remains a laudable and morally desirable objective, there remain major practical problems in the implementation of democratization beyond the nation-state. As a strategy for global governance, multilateralism does at least afford the benefits of being both representative and accountable to a significant degree. However, as Woods (2002) further acknowledges, multilateralism in the contemporary world has to surmount two major obstacles. First, the fact that many states have decided that their interests are not necessarily best pursued through multilateral agencies such as the International Monetary Fund (IMF) and World Bank, but are better pursued through alternative routes, notably bilateralism on the part of the United States. Second, many people have not accepted that their interests are represented in multilateral institutions and resent the intrusion of structural adjustment programmes and the General Agreement on Trade in Services (GATS)[3] upon their domestic political sovereignty.

As an alternative to bilateralism, one of the principal constraints upon the further development of Asia-Pacific regional and security architectures has been the marginalization of regionalism, and the virtual invisibility of Asia-Pacific regionalism, in recent debates about global governance. For example, in a major recent analysis of the role of the G8 group of leading industrialized economies,[4] the potential for Asia-Pacific regional institutions to work more closely with the G8 in the field of economic and security co-operation has been confined to the acknowledgement – based upon the G8's experience of working with the EU – of the opportunities which might arise from the G8's association with 'leader-led regional organisations with global visions' (Kirton 2002: 201), such as APEC. Moreover, in an analysis of the prospects for renewal of the United Nations (UN), Falk (2002) has pointed to the potential for regionalism to either displace or complement the United Nations, but identified the parallel deficits in both accountability and transparency in even the most long established regional actor (i.e. the EU) as a constraint for regionalism to play a more salient role in global governance. In a similar vein and in identifying a series of 'missing institutions' in global governance – especially in relation to the governance of financial markets – Nayyar (2002) has joined the ranks of those who have proposed global solutions to governance questions, notably a Financial Stability Forum or World Financial Authority,[5] rather than new regional institutional frameworks.

A rare exception to this trend of largely ignoring the potential contribution of Asia-Pacific regionalism to global governance, has been provided by the report of the International Forum on Globalization (IFG), a three-year project to define an alternative paradigm for global governance, which has recommended the decommissioning of the Bretton Woods institutions and their replacement by a new set of institutions. Among these new institutions, the IFG has revisited the idea of an Asian Monetary Fund (AMF)[6] by proposing the creation of regional monetary funds, accountable to the region's governments, which would provide 'quick-response, short-term emergency loans in the event of an unanticipated foreign exchange shortfall' (IFG 2002: 234). Crucially, the IFG has proposed that, while states would be free to send observers to any of the regional monetary funds established in different parts of the world, 'no country should be allowed to be a voting member of more than one regional fund' (ibid). In this way, the United States would be forced to limit its direct participation to either a regional monetary fund of the Americas or the Asia-Pacific, but not to both, thereby alleviating potentially some of the principal tensions that have constrained the development of APEC as an effective regional institution.

3. An alternative political economy to the Washington Consensus

To depict the relationship between global governance and regional institutions in the wake of the East Asian financial crisis, Acharya (2001) has proposed the notion of 'post-hegemonic regional orders', based in turn upon two key assertions. First, by implication, 'continued acknowledgement by regional elites and institutions of the salience or even the "inevitability" of economic globalization and the structural power of the US that underpins it'. Second, the argument that 'for a variety of reasons and in a variety of ways, regional actors may be prompted to redefine and broaden their regional space so as to move it beyond and outside of the framework of hegemonic regionalism' (p. 297). The motives for such action could include disillusionment with the benefits of the neo-liberal global order (especially in the light of the huge economic, political and social costs to the Asia-Pacific region of the East Asian financial crisis), the impact of domestic politics upon regional agenda and the need to respond to particular transnational challenges. However, any or all of these motives could and should be used to legitimize the development of a degree of ideological and institutional autonomy from the neo-liberal orthodoxy of the 'Washington Consensus'.

In the aftermath of the 1997/98 East Asian financial crisis, which as Harris (2002) has suggested 'enhanced understanding of the region's vulnerability to forces external to the region' (Harris 2002: 119), much of the blame for the crisis was attributed to the deficiencies of Asian models of political economy. For example, the World Bank (1998) maintained that 'corruption and poor institutional performance shoulder much for the blame for the crisis' (p. 92), while Krugman (1998) claimed that 'the region's downfall was a punishment for its sins ... a dark underside to "Asian values" ' (pp. 28–9), namely crony capitalism. Subsequent events in the United States, notably at Enron

(Cruver 2002, Fox 2003), have demonstrated that cronyism and corruption are endemic to many capitalist economies. At the same time, an extensive critique has emerged of both the 'poor institutional performance' of the IMF and the neo-liberal political economy underpinning its actions. From his close scrutiny of the IMF, Joseph Stiglitz (former Chief Economist at the World Bank) has asserted that the actions of the IMF in the East Asian financial crisis were anti-democratic, hypocritical, lacking transparency and based upon 'what seemed a curious blend of ideology and bad economics, dogma that sometimes seemed to be thinly veiled special interests' (Stiglitz 2002: xiii). Furthermore, in the most authoritative statement of an alternative regional political economy to the neo-liberal orthodoxy shaping global governance, Will Hutton has emphasized the importance of recognizing that 'the so-called "Washington consensus", enshrining balanced budgets and the urgency of implementing pro-market solutions, is not just an economic doctrine to be applied universally; it has profound social and political repercussions'. Those repercussions have been particularly damaging for large parts of the Asia-Pacific region during the past decade. Therefore, Hutton's contention is that public goods such as security and prosperity in the twenty-first century will not be achievable if they are provided 'as any one country dictates, or as a by-product of what it considers its interests'. The implication for regional economic and security co-operation is that 'their provision needs to be international and predicated upon an acknowledgement of interdependence'. Furthermore, 'there must be scope within globalisation for different cultures and approaches to capitalism to flourish; we cannot all be homogenised around the principles of American conservatism' (Hutton 2002: 11–12).

The primary importance of regional economic and security co-operation is that it affords the opportunity to develop an alternative political economy and structure of governance of the market in the Asia-Pacific region. However, for such regional co-operation to evolve beyond its existing and limited foundations, regionalism cannot be conceived as a functionalist, technocratic project. The first step in the future evolution of Asia-Pacific regionalism, albeit an extremely contentious but nonetheless unavoidable step, must be a fundamental re-examination of the institutional and ideological framework of growth and the assumptions about that growth process in the Asia-Pacific. As Woo-Cumings (1999) rightly asserts, this process should particularly take into account 'a sense of East Asia in *time* and *place*', and understand 'the historical interplay of forces-historical, political, market, security that have determined the structure of opportunity in East Asia' (and the Pacific), so as to be able 'to delineate the limits of feasible reform in East Asia today' (p. xi). As an alternative political economy to the neo-liberal orthodoxy of global governance, and as a potential ideological basis for Asia-Pacific regionalism, the East Asian developmental state tradition should not be dismissed as nothing more than 'crony capitalism'.

While that tradition could structure market incentives that enrich the state 'and its friends at the expense of consumers, good jobs, and development' (Johnson 1999: 48), it could and did govern the market for several decades to achieve both spectacular national developmental goals and enterprise viability. The World Bank's (1993) erroneous dismissal of the developmental role of the state in East Asia as 'largely ineffective' (p. 312), and its claim that the East Asian financial crisis has 'undermined faith in the East Asian model' (Yusuf and Evenett 2002: 2) should not be allowed to pass uncontested. Asia-Pacific regionalism – based on East Asian developmental modalities – could yet provide the focal point for an ideological and institutional bulwark against the damage wrought by such 'market fundamentalism' (Soros 1998) whose natural counterpart was 'a volatile politics of economic insecurity' (Gray 1998: 213) for so much of the global economy during the 1990s.

This form of economic and security co-operation would require the creation of an alternative Asia-Pacific region paradigm based upon principles similar to those envisaged by Gore (2000) in his notion of a 'Southern Consensus' on development. Gore has outlined five tenets of an alternative paradigm to the Washington Consensus that appear applicable to the definition of a regional foreign economic policy for the developmental state in the Asia-Pacific. First, the principle that economic growth and structural change is best accomplished through a phased 'strategic integration' of national economies into the global economy rather than a sudden liberalization. The crisis-hit economies of the region would need little convincing of this truth, which has been grudgingly acknowledged by the IMF. Second, the principle that growth and structural change is best achieved through the co-ordination of a growth-oriented macroeconomic policy with a 'productive development policy' incorporating technology policy, financial policy, human resource development, physical infrastructure development, and industrial organization and competition policy. It is only through regional co-operation and co-ordination of monetary, fiscal and competitiveness policies that the Asia-Pacific will be able to develop relative autonomy from its dependence on the US economy. Third, the prerequisite for implementation of these principles is 'government business co-operation within the framework of a pragmatic developmental state'. While greater transparency is needed to avoid the damage caused by 'crony capitalism', a viable regionalism could not detach itself from a close working relationship with transnational corporations. Fourth, in order to maintain the legitimacy of the growth process, its distributional consequences must be managed to ensure an equitable and inclusive distribution of income and wealth. This principle would appear entirely consonant with the political economy of most Asia-Pacific economies, save for the United States itself. Fifth, national development strategies must incorporate a major element of regional integration and co-operation in order to furnish a viable 'post-Washington

Consensus' developmental paradigm, capable of seizing the opportunities presented by globalization but also recognizing and dealing with the vulnerabilities and constraints arising from globalization (Gore 2000: 796–9). In this latter regard, Dent (2002, 2003) has argued in his work on the foreign economic policies of East Asian states that recent changes in their developmental political economies have predisposed them to new regionalist, and regional co-operative possibilities. For Japan, Singapore, South Korea and Taiwan especially, this concerns the evolving nature of their respective developmental statist paradigms and an associated shift from national to regional economic management. In their adaptation to new global, multilateral and post-crisis circumstances, East Asia's developmental states have become increasingly interested in inter-state co-operation designed to better manage their common regional developmental space. In this sense, the new regional financial co-operation that has developed within the ASEAN Plus Three (APT) framework, as later discussed in this chapter, not only represents an attempt to avert another financial crisis but also ultimately safeguards the structural integrity and politico-ideological basis of the East Asian regional economic system. Additional co-operative exercises in regional community-building by East Asia's developmental states concern their pursuit of 'broadband' bilateral free trade agreements (FTA) with each other, whereby their FTA element is embedded in a wider economic co-operation agreement (e.g. Japan–Singapore Economic Partnership Agreement, Japan–Korea Economic Agenda 21) that possess 'developmentalist' co-operation mechanisms, covering areas such as science and technology, education and training, and e-commerce (see Chapter 5).

While regional economic and security co-operation affords the opportunity to fashion an alternative political economy for the Asia-Pacific, a more immediate imperative for accelerating the pace of regional co-operation is the imminent threat of slower global growth, driven by the prospect of a severe recession in the United States' domestic economy. Whichever institution's statistics are used, the outlook for the global economy in general and the Asia-Pacific region in particular was not rosy in 2002/03. For example, in its December 2002 *Economic Outlook*, the Organization for Economic Co-operation and Development (OECD) has forecast a hesitant and less widespread than expected global economic recovery, with world trade predicted to grow by only 2.6 per cent in 2002 (OECD 2002). In its September 2002 *World Economic Outlook*, the IMF (2002) has forecast weaker than expected global growth of 2.8 per cent in 2002, rising to 3.7 per cent in 2003. Furthermore, it has acknowledged that even this degree of economic recovery is heavily dependent on the outlook for the United States, and that there might yet be 'significant risk of a more subdued recovery' (p. 11), given the problems besetting other G8 economies.

Despite a 15 per cent rise in flows of foreign direct investment (FDI) to China in 2001, overall FDI flows to the developing economies of the

Asia-Pacific region have fallen by 24 per cent in 2001, reflecting a 53 per cent fall in global FDI to US$735 billion (UNCTAD 2002). For its part, the World Bank's November 2002 overview of the East Asia and Asia-Pacific region forecasted that while East Asian GDP growth was expected to rise in 2002 to 5.4 per cent, from 3.5 per cent in 2001, it will not reach the 7.6 per cent achieved in 2000. Furthermore, within the region, while China forecasted to grow by 7.7 per cent in 2002, Japan's economy was forecasted to further deflate by 1.0 per cent, following a 0.3 per cent contraction in 2001. At the level of the international competitiveness of individual national economies, the faltering global and regional economies have worrying implications given the trend towards declining competitiveness. While 2002 saw the United States being ranked as the most competitive economy for the fifth consecutive year, Singapore saw its ranking decline to fifth from second (in 1998–2001), and Hong Kong saw its ranking fall to ninth (compared to sixth in 2001, and fifth in 1997). No other Asia-Pacific economy was ranked in the top ten, with South Korea ranked only 27th, Japan 30th and China 31st (IMD 2002). With intra-regional trade in ASEAN falling by more than 10 per cent in 2001, compared to a less than 2 per cent fall in the European Union and 7 per cent decline for the North American Free Trade Agreement (NAFTA) economies (WTO 2002b), the opportunity for regional economic co-operation to provide a robust platform for development in the Asia-Pacific economies is apparent. More importantly, because the region can no longer rely upon consumer demand in the United States to act as the motive force for the post-East Asian financial crisis recovery, regional economic co-operation has become a critical imperative method for prosperity-generation in the Asia-Pacific.

4. The potential for regional financial co-operation

In the face of such sharply rising external and domestic threats to both economic performance and security, the World Bank (2002) has advocated the advancement of reforms 'to strengthen public security, reduce vulnerability to shocks and foster domestic productivity growth' (p. 2). However, to resolve the ideological and policy dilemmas confronting the governance of the markets in the Asia-Pacific region in the immediate future, the Bank has not endorsed but merely noted recent developments in regional co-operation. It has instead recommended that the route to greater competitiveness, at least for East Asia, lies with a further embracing of a market-driven and entrepreneur-driven model of innovation, competition and clustering (Yusuf and Evenett 2002), previously recommended as a solution to Japan's economic woes (Porter et al. 2000). This agenda would see the Asia-Pacific region converging towards an Anglo-Saxon model of competitiveness long established in the United States (Porter and van Opstal 2001). By contrast, in an important study of the potential for regional financial co-operation, Henning (2002) has identified the opportunity for a genuinely divergent regional political economy. Indeed, Henning has contended that regional financial co-operation would be beneficial because it would reflect a commonality of interest in economic prosperity and crisis prevention; facilitate the reduction of reserve holdings of foreign exchange; redress asymmetries in size between national economies and international financial firms; render economic decision-making less cumbersome and more expeditious, leading to faster financial assistance; supplement the resources of the IMF and multilateral institutions; and enhance regional surveillance.

Henning's (2002) advocacy for regional financial co-operation is, however, heavily qualified by his desire to firmly locate regional co-operation within the existing institutional and ideological framework of global governance. His contention is that multilateral approaches to financial stabilization focused on the IMF remain 'first best for the time being and the foreseeable future', but that 'regional financial arrangements can nevertheless serve as useful adjuncts to the multilateral framework and as second best' (p. 76). Among his recommendations, Henning proposes that the relationship between regional and multilateral structures of governance should be clarified and strengthened by the member states of the IMF creating 'the financial equivalent of GATT Article XXIV as a formal set of principles'[7] (p. 78). Furthermore, the APT framework should further enhance what Henning portrays as the complementarity between the Chiang Mai Initiative and the IMF through greater reliance on the IMF's Contingency Credit Line, or CCL (see Chapters 4 and 5). Indeed, he suggests that such a move 'could well raise interest in, attract applicants to, breathe life into the CCL' (p. 91). In overall terms, Henning wishes 'to continue to base regional co-operation upon multilateral institutions, and the IMF in particular, where possible' (p. 94).

While providing a welcome recognition of the potential contribution of regionalism towards global governance, Henning's recommendations would further entrench East Asia within the multilateral institutional framework of the Washington Consensus, the very framework that ushered in the East Asian financial crisis. In his conclusion, Henning (2002) has acknowledged that, 'the formation of an Asian Monetary Fund could well be desirable as a contribution to international economic stability', and furthermore 'the case for the AMF would be particularly strong if, owing perhaps to inadequate reform of the international financial architecture, the multilateral system failed to prevent crises and stabilize economies in the region' (pp. 93–4). Henning sees the case for an AMF being strengthened by possible future failures of institutional architecture of the multilateral system. However, given the successive failures of bilateral and multilateral surveillance in the recent past to detect financial crises and contagion from Mexico in December 1994 via East Asia in 1997, Brazil and Russia in 1998 and Argentina in 2002 – and the huge cost of the resulting multi-billion dollar bailouts for both the IMF member states and the crisis-hit economies

(Lee 2002) – one wonders what scale of future financial catastrophe would persuade Henning to contemplate abandoning the notion that the IMF is 'first best' in the delivery of financial stability.

Henning's (2002) thesis for maintaining the subordination of regional financial co-operation in East Asia to multilateral arrangements, where the IMF is held to enjoy 'a comparative advantage over other regional and multilateral organizations in the specification of conditionality', is based upon the questionable assertion of the 'analytical resources, experience and expertise of IMF staff ... [and] its global perspective' (p. 80). Given its highly chequered recent track record of non-intervention and subsequent belated interventions in financial crises, as well as the critique of the efficacy of the conditionality attached to its loans (Stiglitz 2002), Henning's thesis appears to have been based upon some highly suspect foundations. The 'market fundamentalism' of the Washington Consensus may have been global in its reach and impact in the past decade but many in crisis-hit Asian economies would question whether its rationale was truly to promote global welfare rather than to further entrench American hegemony and structural power. Henning's study concedes that, 'if a regional group wishes to fully displace the IMF with a more ambitious regional arrangement and is willing to commit the resources to do so effectively, as Europe has done, then the IMF and other member governments have few legitimate objectives' (p. 83). While Henning rejects the 1997 AMF proposal, on the grounds that it could have undercut 'IMF conditionality and weakened the impetus for economic adjustment in the region' (p. 84), it could be asserted, on the contrary, that the undermining of IMF conditionality would have been a very welcome development because it could have paved the way for an AMF-led alternative political economy on which to base economic adjustment. Henning's very choice of the CCL as a potential instrument of financial stabilization in East Asia is itself a testament to the constraints that the 'Washington Consensus' could yet place upon the political economy of Asia-Pacific regional co-operation. As Henning himself has conceded, the CCL, which was 'introduced in April 1999, in the wake of the Asian and Russian financial crises, as precautionary lending facility to increase investor confidence in those emerging market economies in possession of macroeconomic policies and financial systems complying with IMF best practice' (Lee 2002: 293–4), has failed to attract a single signatory. States have simply refused to sign up on the grounds that this very act might be sufficient to trigger further financial panic, instability and contagion among private investors. To inflict the CCL upon Asia-Pacific economies would appear to be a dubious recruitment technique for a discredited symbol of the failure of the international architecture of the Washington Consensus to deliver financial stability.

5. Conclusion

As Mittelman (2000) has asserted, regionalism may both legitimize and resist the neo-liberal orthodoxy on globalization and governance. While others (Henning 2002, Katzenstein 2000) have contended that regionalism can and should complement the multilateral institutions of global governance, this chapter has argued that the greatest potential of Asia-Pacific regionalism resides in its potential to diverge from those institutions. This is because the greatest global constraint acting upon Asia-Pacific economic and security co-operation remains the institutional and policy straightjacket provided by the 'Washington Consensus', a constraint now being reinforced by the consequences of the domestic recession in the United States. As the ease with which the US Treasury Department saw off the Japanese proposal for an AMF in 1997 demonstrated, the greatest regional constraint upon Asia-Pacific regionalism – particularly that based on East Asian developmentalism – remains ideological, in the reluctance of its major constituent Asian economies to challenge Washington's institutions and policies. As the chequered history of the APEC has shown, this constraint may appear insurmountable given that, as the largest single regional economic and military power, the United States itself has defined its foreign economic policies on principles that have departed substantially from those particularly of its Asian regional partners.

The greatest opportunities for Asia-Pacific regionalism arise from the potential to use regional co-operation as a platform for the development of an alternative political economy more attuned to the region's values and goals. As the US$1 trillion of foreign exchange reserves possessed in 2003 by the APT economies demonstrates, the region possesses the financial resources to develop its own escape route from global economic turbulence should it develop a viable political economy to mobilize co-operation. The greatest regional imperative for co-operation resides with the need to develop a regional institutional capacity to redress the future consequences of a global economic recession. As Hutton (2002) has suggested, 'In an era of globalization all nation-states need to co-operate and collaborate if they want to represent their citizens' interests. Such co-operation works best among those who share values and goals; and it works most efficiently if it is entrenched in permanent institutions' (p. 47). For the Asia-Pacific region, the future governance of the market does not have to be confined to the 'permanent institutions' of the IMF, World Bank and WTO, any more than it was before the policy prescriptions of the Washington Consensus immersed the global economy in instability, uncertainty and turbulence. It is primarily to East Asian capitalism, rather than its US-led Anglo-Saxon counterpart, that the Asia-Pacific should look as the platform upon which to build regional co-operative endeavours and regional economic coherence in the trans-region generally.

Notes

1. See Chapter 5 for more discussion on the recent proliferation of bilateral free trade agreements (FTAs) in the Asia-Pacific.
2. These were the North American Free Trade Agreement (NAFTA) and bilateral agreements with Israel and Jordan.
3. Deriving from the Uruguay Round of GATT, signed in 1994.
4. Namely the US, Japan, Canada, Britain, Germany, France, Italy and Russia.
5. See Eatwell (2000) for more on this.
6. See Chapter 5 for discussion on Japan's AMF proposal.
7. Article XXIV covers the WTO's prime rules on regional trade agreements.

References

Acharya, A. (2001) 'Regionalism: The Meso Public Domain in Latin America and South-East Asia' in D. Drache (ed.), *The Market or the Public Domain: Global Governance and the Asymmetry of Power*, Routledge, London.

APEC (2002) '2003 APEC Themes: Security and Economic Development Regardless of Differences', *APEC Media Release*, 13 December, Singapore, Asia Pacific Economic Co-operation Secretariat.

Cruver, B. (2002) *Anatomy of Greed: The Unshredded Truth from an Enron Insider*, Hutchinson, London.

Dent, C.M. (2002) *The Foreign Economic Policies of Singapore, South Korea and Taiwan*, Edward Elgar, Cheltenham.

Dent, C.M. (2003) 'Northeast Asia: Developmental Political Economy and the Prospects for Regional Economic Integration', in F.K. Liu and P. Regnier (eds), *Regionalism in East Asia: Paradigm Shifting?*, RoutledgeCurzon, London.

Eatwell, J. (2000) *Global Finance at Risk: The Case for International Regulation*, New Press, New York.

Falk, R. (2002) 'The United Nations System: Prospects for Renewal', in D. Nayyar (ed.), *Governing Globalization: Issues and Institutions*, Oxford University Press, Oxford.

Fox, L. (2003) *Enron: The Rise and Fall*, John Wiley, New Jersey.

Gore, C. (2000) 'The Rise and Fall of the Washington Consensus as a Paradigm for Developing Countries', *World Development*, Vol. 28(5), pp. 789–94.

Gray, J. (1998) *False Dawn: The Delusions of Global Capitalism*, Granta, London.

Harris, S. (2002) 'Asian Multilateral Institutions and Their Response to the Asian Economic Crisis', in S. Breslin, C. Hughes, N. Phillips and B. Rosamond (eds), *New Regionalisms in the Global Political Economy*, London, Routledge.

Held, D. and McGrew, A. (2002) 'Introduction', in D. Held and A. McGrew (eds), *Governing Globalization: Power, Authority and Global Governance*, Polity, London.

Henning, R. (2002) *East Asian Financial Co-operation*, Institute for International Economics, Washington DC.

Hutton, W. (2002) *The World We're In*, Little Brown, London.

IFG (2002) *Alternatives to Economic Globalization: A Better World is Possible. A Report of the International Forum on Globalisation*, Berrett-Koehler, San Francisco.

IMD (2002) *World Competitiveness Yearbook 2002–3*, Institute for Management Development, Geneva.

IMF (2002) *World Economic Outlook: Trade and Finance, September*, International Monetary Fund, Washington DC.

Johnson, C. (1998) 'Economic Crisis in East Asia: The Clash of Capitalisms', *Cambridge Journal of Economics*, Vol. 22, pp. 653–61.

Katzenstein, P.J. (2002) 'Regionalism and Asia', in S. Breslin, C. Hughes, N. Phillips and B. Rosamond (eds), *New Regionalisms in the Global Political Economy*, Routledge, London.

Kirton, J. (2002) 'The G8, the United Nations, and Global Security Governance', in J. Kirton and J. Takase (eds), *New Directions in Global Political Governance: The G8 and International Order in the Twenty-First Century*, Aldershot, Ashgate.

Krugman, P. (1998) 'Saving Asia: It's Time to Get Radical', *Fortune*, 7 September, 27–32.

Lee, S. (2002) 'The International Monetary Fund', *New Political Economy*, Vol. 7(2), pp. 283–98.

Lee, S. (2003a) 'The Political Economy of the Third Way: The Relationship between Globalization and National Economic Policy', in J. Michie (ed.), *The Handbook of Globalisation*, Edward Elgar, Cheltenham.

Lee, S. (ed.) (2003b) *The Asian Financial Crisis: Causes and Consequences*, Lynne Rienner, Boulder.

Mittelman, J. (2000) *The Globalisation Syndrome: Transformation and Resistance*, Princeton University Press, Princeton.

Nayyar, D. (2002) 'The Existing System and the Missing Institutions', in D. Nayyar (ed.), *Governing Globalization: Issues and Institutions*, Oxford University Press, Oxford.

OECD (2002) *OECD Economic Outlook No.72*, December, Organization for Economic Co-operation and Development, Paris.

Porter, M., Takeuchi, H. and Sakakibara, M. (2000) *Can Japan Compete?*, Macmillan, London.

Porter, M. and van Opstal, D. (2001) *US Competitiveness 2001: Strengths, Vulnerabilities and Long-Term Priorities*, Council on Competitiveness, Washington DC.

Soros, G. (1998) *The Crisis of Global Capitalism: Open Society Endangered*, Little Brown, London.

Stiglitz, J. (2002) *Globalisation and its Discontents*, Allen Lane, London.

UNCTAD (2002) *The World Investment Report 2002: Transnational Corporations and Export Competitiveness*, United Nations Conference on Trade and Development, New York.

USTR (2002a) *2002 Trade Policy Agenda and 2001 Annual Report of the President of the United States on the Trade Agreements Program*, Office of the United States Trade Representative, Washington DC.

USTR (2002b) 'US Proposes Tariff-Free World, WTO Proposal Would Eliminate Tariffs on Industrial and Consumer Goods by 2015', *USTR Press Release*, 26 November, Office of the United States Trade Representative, Washington DC.

Woo-Cumings, M. (1999) 'Preface', in M. Woo-Cumings (ed.), *The Developmental State*, Cornell University Press, Ithaca.

Woods, N. (2002) 'Global Governance and the Role of Institutions', in D. Held and A. McGrew (eds), *Governing Globalization: Power, Authority and Global Governance*, Polity, London.

World Bank (1993) *The East Asian Miracle: Economic Growth and Public Policy*, Oxford University Press, Oxford.

World Bank (1998) *East Asia: The Road to Recovery*, Oxford University Press, Oxford.

World Bank (2002) *Making Progress in Uncertain Times: Regional Overview, East Asia and Pacific Region*, World Bank, Washington DC.

WTO (2000) *Mapping of Regional Trade Agreements*, World Trade Organization, Geneva.

WTO (2002a) *Regional Trade Integration under Transformation*, World Trade Organization, Geneva.

WTO (2002b) *International Trade Statistics-2002*, World Trade Organization, Geneva.

Yusuf, S. and Evenett, S. (2002) *Can East Asia Compete? Innovation for Global Markets*, World Bank, Washington DC.

3
Globalisation and Security in East Asia*

Christopher Hughes

1. Introduction: connecting globalisation and security

Globalisation and security are two of the most poorly understood concepts in the academic and policy worlds. Security has been described as an under-developed concept (Buzan 1991), and globalisation, for a variety of reasons and as briefly described below, has been subject to any number of defini-tions. The inability of academics and policy-makers alike to agree on the individual definitions and implications of these two issues, despite the fact that they are seen to be of great contemporary importance, is worrying. Even more worrying is the lack of attempt to study in depth the intersection between the two concepts and consequences for international stability. We are thus faced with a pressing need to define and interconnect the twin issues of globalisation and security. Pioneering attempts have already been made to investigate the relationship between globalisation and security, in terms of its creation of new security actors, problems and responses (Cha 2000). However, although very valuable in providing a starting point and emergent framework for consideration of the globalisation–security nexus, these attempts have tended to lack a strong empirical basis and geographi-cal focus. This type of focus is important because globalisation is likely to differ in its security impact between regional contexts.

All of this argues for the need to combine the study of globalisation and security, but that this should also be carried out through the balanced application of analytical frameworks to particular regional cases. The objec-tive of this chapter is to make an initial contribution to the examination of globalisation and security by following this very approach. Hence, the chapter attempts, in a number of stages, to both build upon the existing globalisation–security nexus literature and to extend it to the case of the East Asia region in the post-Cold War (or following the clear impact of the

* Reprinted by permission of Sage Publications Ltd. from Hughes, C., 'Conceptualizing the Globalization ...' in *Security Dialogue*, Vol. 32(4), 2001.

financial crisis on East Asia after 1997 and arrival of globalisation forces, what we might want to call the 'post-globalisation') period. The first of these stages defines more fully the essence of the term 'globalisation', and the inherent problems that it presents more generically for the existing international order. The second stage then examines the general impact of globalisation upon security, in especial regard to its generation of new and re-emergent security actors, threats and policy responses. In the third stage we apply this model to East Asia to assist our understanding of the differential impact of globalisation in the region, and the particular problems posed for East Asia's states and citizens.

2. Conceptions of globalisation

2.1. Definitions

As noted before, globalisation is a supremely slippery concept and has produced a bewildering number of definitions (Scholte 2000). Globalisation has been defined variously as universalisation (the expansion of cultures across the globe); internationalisation (increased interaction and interdependence between people in different states); Westernisation or Americanisation (the homogenisation of the world along Western or US standards); and liberalisation (the spread of deregulated forces of technology, production, trade and finance across borders). Many of these definitions are indeed facets of globalisation, both in terms of its causation and eventual outcomes (Clark 1998). But these definitions still fail to capture the qualitatively different nature of globalisation from other processes and phenomena associated with the interaction of social forces on a global scale.

Globalisation represents a qualitatively different process due to its essential de-territorialisation, or put conversely, supra-territorialisation of social interaction (Scholte 1997). That is to say, globalisation is a process that increasingly reconfigures social space away from and beyond notions of delineated territory, and *transcends* existing physical and human borders imposed upon social interaction. For instance, global financial transactions, facilitated by information technology, can now often operate without reference to physical territorial distance or human-imposed territorial barriers. It is important to avoid the type of 'hyper-globalisation' thesis that views the world as moving towards a condition of being totally 'borderless'. For it is apparent that there is considerable territorial 'drag' upon the free-flow of globalisation forces, wide disparities in the degree of globalisation across different regions of the world, and both resistance to and reversibility in the process itself. Nevertheless, globalisation as a process of supra-territorialisation is increasingly affecting large sections of the world, and must be acknowledged as a markedly different (although certainly not unrelated) process to those other definitions of social interaction noted above.

Hence, even though universalism, internationalisation, westernisation and liberalisation may eventually result in globalisation, the fact that they may not necessarily be entirely detached from territorialisation means that they remain on a qualitatively different level to the inherently supra-territorial phenomena of globalisation. After all, if we could exactly equate globalisation with any of these other phenomena, then there would be little need to consider it is as anything new or to search for new vocabulary to describe it, and policy prescriptions would already be in our hands.

2.2. Globalisation and challenges to the state

The phenomena of globalisation as supra-territorialisation and the reconfiguration of social space carries significant implications for existing forms of social organisation, and, most importantly in the case of security issues, the dominant position of the nation state (or far more accurately for many states, sovereign state) within the existing globality. Needless to say, the state, with its monopoly of exclusive jurisdiction and sovereignty over a particular social and territorial space, delineated by a combination of physical geography and most especially human construction, has been the basic unit for the division of global space in the modern era. States have in the past attempted both in theory and practice to exercise sovereign control over all forms of social interaction in the political, economic and security dimensions, both within and between their territorial borders. Quite clearly, and as elucidated below with reference to the East Asia region, not all states throughout history have been able to exercise the same degree of sovereign control over all forms of social interaction. But nevertheless, sovereign states rooted in territorial notions of social space have been the prime unit for facilitating, impeding and mediating interaction between the social groups, organisations and citizens and other categories of collective and individual social units contained within their borders. Hence, to date, global social space has been primarily international, or inter-sovereign state, social space.

However, the inherent nature of globalisation as a process that transcends and overrides territoriality as the dominant principle for the organisation of social space now poses a fundamental challenge to the sovereign state as the basic social unit, which exemplifies and undergirds this very territorial principle. Sovereign states must now contend with the freer flow of social forces on a global scale that move with declining reference to the previous limitations and channels imposed by state borders. This increasing porosity or irrelevance of state borders, relative decline in the *de facto* sovereign authority of states over forms of social interaction, and corresponding increased exposure of 'internal' social groupings to 'external forces' (or even indeed the removal of the traditional international–domestic divide to create an 'intermestic' arena for social interchange) has a number of outcomes for security. For if global social space has been primarily international or inter-sovereign state space for much of the modern era, then the security order as one aspect of social interaction has been primarily built around the inter-state order. But it is clear that the security order is now pitted against the phenomenon of globalisation, which generates security issues diametrically opposed to and often beyond the limits of sovereign state authority.

2.3. Globalisation: causation and policy response

Before examining the general consequences of globalisation for security and thereafter applying these conceptions to the East Asian context, it is first necessary to take note briefly of the causes that lie behind the phenomena. Only if we are equipped with a clearer understanding of the causes of globalisation and its relation to insecurity can we then also attempt to tackle conceptually the possibilities of framing an effective security policy response. This need to consider the causes of globalisation is made all the more important by the fact that all too often it is viewed in a deterministic fashion – especially in neo-liberal economic analysis – as a phenomena which somehow occurs naturally through spontaneous and unconscious social interaction amongst rational economic actors, and which is largely inevitable and irreversible in its trajectory. To be sure, and as will be argued below in the case of East Asia, globalisation is caused to a large degree by the release of liberal economic forces (hence the point that globalisation may bring about but is not necessarily coeval with liberalisation), is in part the outcome of unconnected actors seeking to exploit economic complementarities that subvert the economic spaces centred on sovereign states, and is on a powerful forward trajectory in its diffusion across the core economic regions of the globe.

Nonetheless, it is important to understand that the role of liberal economic forces in propelling globalisation forward is in turn the outcome of conscious decisions (or more usually non-decisions, and the acquiescence in policies of inaction so as to avoid perceived costly policy choices) on the part of political actors. Hence, whether these actors are states, social groups, individuals, or organisations such as transnational corporations (TNC), they have to be seen as the prime movers in constructing the socio-political structures, which underpin the dominance of liberal economics and the consequent spread of globalisation (Higgott 1999). If we then view globalisation as a *process* which is driven by human choice and the deliberate pursuit of liberal economic gains, rather than as some form of leviathan which is no longer subjugated to the dictate of humans but has acquired a life of its own, then it is possible to understand the causation and the reversibility, or at least manageability, of the process. Based on this understanding, the fate of security still lies in human hands, and it should also be possible to conceptualise policy responses to the security impact of globalisation.

3. Globalisation's impact on security: levels, dimensions, responses

If we are to view globalisation as a process that is driven forward by political choice in favour of liberal economics, and results in forms of social interaction, which transcend territorial borders and state sovereignty, then it is possible to conceive of its impact on security in a number of areas. These involve both the *vertical* extension of security in terms of levels of actors, and the *horizontal* extension in terms of dimensions of security issues.

3.1. Levels of actors

The first of these areas concerns the identification and expanding number of security actors under conditions of globalisation. Arguably, three broad categorisations of security actors can be identified: those actors subject to security threats (often termed the referent object of security); those actors that impose security threats upon others; and those that supply security to others. Clearly, none of these identities is mutually exclusive, and a certain actor may assume different identities according to the context and perception of onlookers, that is, the rather tired but still valid adage that one man's terrorist is another man's freedom fighter. Indeed, the appeal for public legitimacy of certain states and groups as victims rather than imposers of insecurity, and the consequent blurring of security actor identities is one by-product of the diffusion of the mass media and globalisation. Moreover, security actors themselves can move between and assume different identities, as in the case of narcotics cartels, which, although often categorised as forms of social organisations, can also virtually usurp the functions and identities of states. But just as significant as the ability of the globalisation process to obscure the identities of security actors has been its ability to expand the range and level of actors that can assume the three identities.

One noticeable impact of globalisation has been to accentuate the concept, which has pre-existed in certain contexts, that the state's position as the prime referent object of security is now rivalled by other social groupings. The study of security has traditionally rested upon the assumption that the security of the institution of the sovereign state can be necessarily conflated with the security of the 'nation' or general population and citizenry contained within that state's borders. Hence, in the past and still in the contemporary period, the tendency of security studies has been to argue that the survival of states, as institutions which are created as the embodiment of collective national will, and which serve as the point of interface or 'gatekeeper' to shield their citizenry and populations from external threats, is indivisible from the survival of peoples and nations. The result has been to produce a view of security which concentrates not just upon states as the key referent objects of security (Wæver 1995), but also mainly upon the external aspects of state security. For the traditional paradigm, then, security is concerned with external threats to states, and especially those threats imposed upon states by inter-sovereign state conflict: the natural outcome of friction in an international system dominated by states as the major actors, all seeking to ensure the security of their own populations from external challenges.

The identity and role of sovereign states as the referent object of security, undoubtedly remains central to our understanding of security in the contemporary era, and this may be especially so for those states which can assert with conviction the character of being nation states, marked by a cohesive association between the security interests of state as an institution and its 'national' population as a whole. In other instances, though, the assumption that the security of states as referent objects approximates with that of the population or nation at large, and consequently that all states focus upon external threat perceptions, is inaccurate. The tendency of the traditional security paradigm to 'black box' internal state dynamics means that inevitably it neglects also those internal threats which arise from a fundamental divergence between the perceived security interests of states themselves and segments of their population. Newly established and late-starter sovereign states with borders cutting across and encompassing a variety of national and ethnic groups are particularly sensitive to internal security threats. It is often the case that such states face small or large numbers of ethnic groups that reject the definition of nation and state emanating from the government and view themselves as subject to oppression. The result being that these groups seek instead to secure autonomy or to secede, and may often launch insurgency movements, so challenging the integrity and internal stability of the state.

Another internal security problem, often independent of but also at times interlinked with and capable of reinforcing ethnic separatism, is that of a crisis of the state's political legitimacy and leadership amongst the general population. In certain states, the majority of the population may support the cause of national and state integrity, but come to reject the political legitimacy of the government system or governing regime and elite. The antagonism of the general population towards the political regime may be aroused by a variety of factors centring on perceptions of misgovernment, including the management of the economy, issues of crime and corruption, and the commitment to stable or democratic government. The outcome can be political turmoil, violent demonstrations, revolt and even revolution. If prolonged, political unrest can bring the prospect of factionalism and civil war. Most explosive of all is a combination of political crisis and ethnic separatism, which can threaten the internal disintegration of a state. As will be mentioned below, many states in East Asia, as developing sovereign states, but often only partially 'nation' states, are subject to these twin problems of ethnic separatism and political legitimacy. Consequently, these states have focussed much of their security policy-making energy on dealing with internal rather than external security threats.

Therefore, the argument that the state cannot be considered as the exclusive, or even main, referent object of security, and that there is a need to give our attention to problems of the internal security of social groupings contained within the state's sovereign territory, is not new. Globalisation's impact, though, has been to heighten this consciousness of the potential divisibility of the security of the sovereign state from that of its internal social elements. As explained above, globalisation as a process which transcends territorial and sovereign boundaries, and thus which penetrates with relative ease the internal social space of the state, inevitably also brings with it security effects that diminish the role of the state as the barrier to external threats and that impact directly and differentially upon internal social groups. For instance, globalisation has such an impact in the dimension of economic security, whereby the free flow of market forces across borders, and the accompanying wealth creation but also economic dislocation that it can create, undercuts the ability of the sovereign state to act as the principal arbiter of the economic welfare of its internal society. The result, as is well known from the 1997/98 East Asian financial crisis, is that social groups (ethnic and economic) and individual citizens may endure economic costs which the state is unable to mitigate and redistribute. In these circumstances, even though the apparatus of the state may remain intact, social groups and individual citizens may view the state as a redundant framework for the preservation of their economic security interests and can detach themselves from it, resulting in the type of crisis of political legitimacy for the state described above. Globalisation's capacity to strip the protection of the state away from social groups and citizens then helps to explain why there has been a significant shift in security perspectives away from those fixated on the state, and towards the irreducible, yet ultimate, level of individual and 'human security' (Commission on Global Governance 1995, Tow *et al.* 2000).

Likewise, if the state's position as the principal referent object of security is challenged by globalisation, so also must we begin to review its position as always the principal actor responsible for the imposition and defence of threats. States clearly continue to dispose of the greatest economic and military power capabilities, and to deny or provide internal and external security to others on the largest scale. However, again whilst it is not an entirely new trend, globalisation has accentuated the perception that other social actors are capable of not just consuming security, but also denying and supplying security to others. For example, ethnic and minority groups can infringe the security of states and other sets of groups and individuals if they are perceived to threaten stability by embarking on a political or military struggle, especially if they become involved in criminal or terrorist activities. But the opposite is also true, that these groups can be regarded as freedom fighters and the providers of security to minorities subject to repression by states. Moreover, in much the same way as individuals can be regarded as the irreducible referent object of security, so they must also be regarded as the irreducible deniers and providers of security functions. Individuals even within the legal framework of a state do still retain the capacity to inflict violence and damage upon each other and other security actors. Acts of individual murder and assault remain commonplace, and individuals can even pose threats to a society as a whole if they adopt terrorist techniques and gain access to the means of violence, as shown by the emergence of one-man bombing campaigns in the United States (Unibomber) and the United Kingdom (racist bombings) in the 1990s. Individuals in many societies may also feel the responsibility to provide for their own security, especially where the internal policing functions of the state have broken down or where they are perceived to be too severe, for example, US militias suspicious of government attempts to limit the right to possess firearms.

Furthermore, TNCs now have to be considered within the scope of deniers and providers of economic, environmental, and even military security. Corporations can clearly impose conditions of economic insecurity on states, societal groups and individuals, through their business activities and competition which can lead to differential patterns of poor working conditions, unemployment and underemployment, poverty and general economic dislocation. The activities of corporations can also lead to environmental degradation, and have detrimental effects on military security, not only by the creation of a prosperous or poor economic climate which can be conducive to increased tensions amongst security actors and the build-up or reduction of military capacities, but also in terms of the business of the global arms trade which facilitates these processes. Yet, TNCs too can be a source of security. They can foster ties of interdependence that may promote external security amongst states or alternatively provide the economic strength to promote independent security. Furthermore, they may also provide wealth and employment to segments of a state's population that delivers general stability and internal security. In addition, TNCs and private firms generally can provide an income and various welfare benefits, and thus improve economic security for individual workers and their families. Transnational corporations may also provide 'privatised' military security in a direct fashion through the employment of private armies and mercenaries to protect their business interests and even assist the stabilisation of sovereign states (Shearer 1998).

Finally, globalisation and the trans-sovereign problems that it creates have thrust to the fore another potential category of societal organisation which can provide security, namely non-governmental organisations (NGOs). The legitimacy of NGOs as security actors in some case can certainly be questioned on grounds of accountability. Nevertheless, the ability of NGOs to exploit open economies and new developments in technology in order to organise across borders means that they can contribute both directly (aid activities; anti-land mine movement) and indirectly (campaigns for debt relief; environmental protection) to the military, economic and environmental security of individuals.

The argument of this chapter is certainly not that globalisation has directly created these groups anew as security actors. As will be noted with reference to East Asia, the problems that motivate these actors originate in the constituent nature of states and the process of state-building. Nonetheless, globalisation has impacted in such as way as to sap the economic and military ability of states to threaten or provide for the security of others, and thereby create greater freedom for these alternative level security actors to operate. If states are viewed as incapable of providing security due to their own military or economic weakness, often generated by the destabilising effects of globalisation, then other actors have to step into the breach.

3.2. Dimensions of threat: economic, environmental, societal, military

The second impact of globalisation on security has not necessarily been to create new dimensions of threats, but to revive and exacerbate both latent and existing security problems, so leading to the horizontal extension of security concepts mentioned earlier. Globalisation's most obvious impact has been its integrative and disintegrative economic characteristics, and the consequent knock-on effects upon the economic and then military security of states and their social constituents. The spread of liberal market forces is capable of bringing economic inclusion and interdependence, which may contribute to social stability and peaceful relations internally and externally (a form of 'democratic peace' argument). Nevertheless, the disintegrative effects of globalisation can simultaneously contribute to insecurity in a number of ways:

- *Economic exclusion*: Globalisation can produce economic exclusion for states and individuals marked by disparities of welfare, which may feed through into military tension amongst states in an attempt to wrest economic benefits from others, or result in internal unrest within states.
- *Economic disparity*: Globalisation is capable of re-mapping economic and social space, with the frequent result that economic interdependency can pull actors and sub-state regions away from the defined territorial space of the sovereign state and towards sub-state regions incorporated within other states. China may be such a case, whereby under conditions of globalisation and market liberalisation the density of its provinces' economic linkages gradually shifts towards regions in other states, so generating problems for the control of the centre over the provinces. In these kinds of instances, the rise of regionalisation can lead to the disintegration of state structures, with unforseen consequences for internal and external security.

- *Economic competition*: Globalisation can generate economic competition amongst states, TNCs, social organisations and individuals for scarce natural resources, again often threatening to spill over into military conflict. Moreover, the wealth it produces can fuel arms races.
- *Economic dislocation*: As already mentioned, globalisation often leads to economic poverty, crises and insecurity for states, social groups and individuals, all leading to social instability within and amongst state and possible armed conflict.

Moreover, sitting in between these integrative and disintegrative economic effects of globalisation are those security problems connected with transnational or trans-sovereign crime. Globalisation promotes trans-sovereign crime because economic integration and disintegration in tandem create both supply and demand, or push and pull factors, for those actors engaged in criminal activities. By this it is meant that economic dislocation and disparities within a certain state or social grouping create incentives to engage in wealth-generating activities by engaging in the supply of illicit products such as narcotics or arms. In turn, globalisation's creation of economic wealth in certain areas of the world creates a market and demand for the supply of these economic commodities. Crime as an economic activity and the trade in 'illicit' commodities is clearly not a new phenomenon. Indeed, in the past, the chief suppliers of narcotics have been sovereign states themselves, the opium trade being one notable example. But economic globalisation, facilitated by transport and telecommunications technology, has enabled crime organisations to mimic the behaviour of TNCs (Flynn 2000), to move with still greater ease across deregulated economic space, and thus to impinge even more directly upon the welfare of other social groups and individuals.

The other most notable security effects of economic globalisation are environmental. Although in the past socialist systems have been responsible for some of the worst examples of environment degradation, the spread of liberal economic globalisation has arguably taken these problems to new heights. Liberal capitalism's vast and largely unimpeded appetite for natural resources, and the pollution that usually results, not only threatens directly the health of groups of individuals in various regions (e.g. water and river pollution in Europe; air pollution and forest fires in Southeast Asia; nuclear accidents in Japan), but also threatens indirectly the existence of humankind through the total destruction (e.g. global warming; sea level changes) of the biosphere.

Globalisation can also be said to encompass and exacerbate other dimensions of security such as the societal and military dimensions. Globalisation impacts upon the societal dimension of security, defined as the perceived erosion of the collective identity of certain social groups (Buzan *et al.* 1998), due to its promotion of trans and intra-national migration which can bring different ethnic or religious groups into contact and occasionally conflict. Globalisation's principal impact in the dimension of military security is indirect. The onset of globalisation and its related integrative and disintegrative economic effects can both lay the grounds for and exacerbate military conflicts. Finally, as well as globalisation's influence upon the interlinking of the different dimensions of security, it also clearly intermeshes or supersedes the domestic and international security agendas: the conflict generating effects of globalisation on the domestic level often threatening to spill over into international tensions and conflicts.

3.3. Responses

The objective of this chapter is simply to stress that the inherent nature of globalisation and its supra-territoriality means that its associated security problems cannot be responded to within the traditional confines of the territorial sovereign state or by utilising the traditional tools of security policy. Globalisation's ability to circumvent territorial boundaries gives all of its security-related dimensions a transnational and trans-sovereign character; thus, economic dislocation, crime and environmental pollution increasingly transcend sovereign frontiers in a globalising world system. States are then faced with security problems that demand policy responses that are also trans-sovereign. This makes clear the need for multinational co-operation and, most controversially, the (hopefully voluntary) abrogation at times of the principle of exclusive sovereignty in order to construct policies, which can also pursue global security problems across state frontiers. However, whilst the sovereign state, due to its continued overwhelming disposition of power, certainly remains the principal supplier of security in an era of globalisation, the analysis above has also indicated that it needs to share this role with other actors, including international organisations, social groups, TNCs and NGOs. Moreover, the nature of globalisation as often an economic phenomenon also means that military power alone is not sufficient to meets its security demands. Thus, there is a need for comprehensive approaches to security that employ military power in balanced combination with economic power.

4. Globalisation and security in East Asia

4.1. Differential impact of globalisation in East Asia

This chapter has already described a number of security problems that have occurred in the East Asia region, and moreover those that are associated with globalisation. The 1997/98 East Asian financial crisis has been the most prominent of these and has impacted on all levels of security from that of the state to the individual, and across all dimensions from the economic to the environmental, and even to the military, at least in terms of scaling back of arms procurements. But the financial crisis was only one indication of the ongoing impact of globalisation upon the security of the region. The continuing integration of the region into the global political economy is likely to only accentuate problems of economic security. For instance, economic exclusion can be said to have underlain many of North Korea's internal and external security problems in the post-Cold War period; economic disparity and uneven growth presents problems for the territorial and political unity of China and the Russian Far East, and the internal political stability of a number of Southeast Asian states; economic competition has given rise to concerns about conflict over energy resources in the region; and economic dislocation is a continuing problem for states in both Northeast and Southeast Asia. Meanwhile, trans-sovereign crime is growing in the region (Dupont 1999), with renewed problems of narcotics cartels and piracy in Southeast Asia; and environmental degradation is also continuing largely unchecked in the region, as demonstrated by the reoccurrence of the 'haze' in Indonesia and Malaysia since 1997. All these problems also draw attention to the fact that security situation in the region is affected by TNCs, NGOs, social groupings and individuals as well as by sovereign states.

It is possible, then, to identify a host of problems in East Asia that illustrate the crucial interconnection between globalisation and security. Moreover, from the evidence of the East Asian financial crisis, it might be possible to argue that the security impact of globalisation has been differentially heavy in East Asia compared to many other regions. The limited space of this chapter does not allow for a more detailed attempt to catalogue all of the problems of the globalisation–security interconnection in the region. Instead, the remaining part of this analysis is devoted to an investigation of the possible reasons as to why the region may be particularly prone to the effects of post-globalisation security problems.

As stated in the chapter's introduction, it is important to understand the relationship between globalisation and security through reference to both generic analytical frameworks and specific regional contexts. It was also argued earlier on that the essence of globalisation as a security problem is to be found in its transcendence of barriers to interaction across social space, and hence its challenge to the sovereign state as the existing basis for the global security order. The forces of globalisation quickly search out any inconsistencies and flaws in the structure of the sovereign state, and can prise open its external security barriers. Consequently, this suggests that in order to comprehend the reasons for the differential impact of globalisation across regions then it is necessary to examine the differential nature of sovereign states in each region, and their ability to absorb and withstand the security shocks associated with globalisation processes. Much of what follows is painted in very broad-brush strokes and its generalisations cannot capture the entire complexity of the region. But it is hoped that at the very least it will provide a framework for making intelligible the nature of states and the political economy in East Asia.

4.2. Vulnerable sovereign states: decolonisation, bipolarisation and globalisation

If attention is then turned to examining the condition of sovereign states in East Asia, it can be seen that they are particularly vulnerable to the inherent qualities of globalisation due to the dual influence of decolonisation and bipolarisation upon the state-building process in the post-war period. The effect of decolonisation upon the East Asia region was to create states modelled, in theory, along the lines of the sovereign and nation states of their former colonial masters, but which, in practice, have not always conformed to these ideals. In many instances, the idea of the sovereign state came before or diverged from that of the nation state: shown by the fact that the territorial and sovereign space of states in the region was often delineated along former colonial borders which had been drawn in arbitrary fashion and in contradistinction to trans-border ties of ethnicity and religion. These contradictions between sovereign space and societal composition clearly weakened from the start the internal political cohesion of states in the region, and laid the ground for the potential divisibility between the security interests of the state and its social constituents. Moreover, the common legacy of distorted development from the colonial period also placed these states in a disadvantageous economic position to maintain their internal stability. Therefore, the preoccupation of many East Asian states since the postcolonial period has been to preserve their internal integrity by advancing the process of state-building, and particularly in the economic sphere, as a means to reconcile these structural contradictions (Ayoob 1995). The most notable example of this state-building project has been that of Indonesia and the attempt to forge a centralised and integrated state from the colonial territory inherited from the Dutch as the former imperial power (Huxley 2002). However, other states such as the Philippines, Malaysia and Burma have been engaged in similar exercises.

The problematic position of newly established sovereign states in the region was further compounded either during or immediately after the decolonisation phase by the impact of the onset of the Cold War. The translation to East Asia of the contest between the ideologies and political economies of the United States and USSR led to the division of certain states and the bipolarisation of the region to varying degrees. As is well known, the bifurcation of the region in the early Cold War period was to create a legacy of military confrontation, which has endured in many cases to this day. Nevertheless, perhaps more important when considering the post-Cold War and post-globalisation security agendas is the affect of the Cold War upon the state-building agenda and related political economies of many of the new states in the region. The Cold War in effect divided the East Asia region into three zones of political economy (Spero 1997): a zone of independence centred for the early part of the Cold War upon a socialist bloc under the auspices of the USSR; a zone of interdependence centred upon the United States, and increasingly Japan as well, throughout most of the Cold War; and a zone of dependence, consisting mainly of the newer sovereign states in Southeast Asia, which although seeking economic independence was increasingly drawn into the zone of interdependence, with Japan playing a major role in this process. The zone of independence created an alternative economic system to that of liberal capitalism and ensured the security of many of its members, although it showed increasing signs of breaking down throughout the latter period of the Cold War and as the USSR and China split the zone internally. However, this zone of independence was also eventually to be rendered asunder by the economic pressure from the zone of interdependence at the end of the Cold War, so leaving the already internally weak states of the zone exposed to the forces of liberal capitalism.

Meanwhile, the zone of interdependence can be conceived of in the Cold War period as a form of proto-globalisation and liberal economic system under the leadership of the United States. This system was also to affect the state-building efforts of those states within its ambit. On the one hand, the system provided markets and aid that accelerated the economic growth of certain states on the semi-periphery and later at the core, such as Japan, as well as pulling along the growth of other states on the periphery and located in the zone of dependence in Southeast Asia. In this way, states were able to develop distinctive variations of developmental capitalism and to use economic growth to mitigate problems of internal stability. On the other hand, though, the system – revolving as it did around a form of proto-globalisation that was designed to support the security interests of the United States, and thus insulate these states to some degree from full competition – also had particular effects on the evolution of these states' political economies. Hence, extreme case states in the region, such as Marcos' Philippines, were propped up by external aid. More usually, though, the states of the region took advantage of US largess to evolve political economies that were developmental in orientation but still systemically vulnerable to the fully unleashed global capitalism. Thus, these states may have been able to overcome to some extent the economic shocks of the early 1970s and to move towards a new path of development in the new international division of labour. Yet, at the same time, these states were still given special dispensations within the zone of interdependency, consisting of access to technology and the developed markets of the United States and the West, whilst simultaneously being able to restrict access to their own markets (Strange 1996).

Therefore, the twin processes of decolonisation and bipolarisation have had a distinct impact upon the development of the sovereign states of East Asia. First, these processes have created states marked by internal

contradictions between the delineation of territorial space and societal composition, and a consequent preoccupation with attempts to reconcile the
two by the defence of the principle of sovereignty. Despite all these efforts,
there still remains a near ineradicable and potential divisibility between the
proclaimed security interests of East Asian states and large sections of their
citizenry, the very conditions which globalisation is capable of highlighting
to the detriment of security. Second, they have created states either fundamentally unprepared to cope with global economic forces as in the case of
certain former members of the zone of independence, such as North Korea,
or states driven by the need to exploit the benefits of liberal capitalism to
preserve their own internal stability, but which have been insulated in the
past from the full effects of capitalism's tendency towards periodic crises. In
sum, East Asia has been characterised by states vulnerable to those forces
that attack territorial sovereignty and generate external economic shocks, so
frustrating state-building agendas.

Based on this understanding of the nature of sovereign states in East Asia,
the reasons for the differentially heavy impact of globalisation in the region
become clearer. Quite simply, globalisation, especially when it generates
seismic economic shocks on the scale of the 1997/98 East Asian financial
crisis, represents the very antithesis of state-building agendas in the region.
Globalisation is mercilessly capable of laying bare the internal weaknesses
of states. This is not to say that states cannot adapt to and successfully ride
the globalisation wave, and then utilise the benefits of economic growth to
push forward their state-building efforts. But globalisation is also a double-
edged sword, due to its ability to undermine sovereignty and produce economic dislocation. Moreover, with the end of the Cold War and merging of
the zones of independence, dependence and interdependence, there is no
longer a great incentive for the United States to provide special economic
dispensations to the states of East Asia, so increasing the pressure for them
to adopt neo-liberal modes of capitalism. The final outcome is then to
deepen and widen the process of globalisation in East Asia and to expose its
political economies to greater security risks in the process of adjustment to
liberal capitalism.

5. Conclusion: the future security agenda of East Asia

This chapter has attempted to sketch the connection between globalisation
and security through the use of generic frameworks for analysis and the
regional context in East Asia. It has demonstrated how globalisation as a
qualitatively new phenomenon is capable of transcending territorial and
sovereign space, and has challenged us to extend our conceptions of security both vertically and horizontally. Globalisation requires us to consider
security from the level of the state down to that of the individual, and across
the dimensions of economic, environmental, societal and military security.

Moreover, it has been shown how globalisation has a differential impact across regions in accordance with the ability of sovereign states – the existing unit for ordering social space – to resist the impact of trans-sovereign problems. In the case of East Asia, the twin processes of decolonisation and bipolarisation have placed relative limits upon this ability for states, and enabled globalisation to exacerbate existing security problems in the region.

In turn, the continuing spread of globalisation in the region indicates that it is increasingly necessary to place alongside the traditional post-Cold War military security agenda of policy-makers an alternative – and certainly not an entirely new in the case of many states in the region long preoccupied with problems of internal and comprehensive security – one which focusses upon problems in the economic, environmental and societal dimensions. The creation of optimum policy response of states to these problems – as for the time being at least these are the only social units with sufficient resources and legitimacy to spearhead the defence of other social groupings from globalisation's worst excesses – is still an ongoing process. However, it is perhaps clear that the sovereign state, mismatched as it is in its capabilities against a phenomenon which challenges its very *raison d'être* of sovereignty, can only hope to respond effectively to the challenges of globalisation by also assuming more flexible and adaptive forms. All too often in East Asia there is an underlying assumption (eminently understandable, though it may be) that globalisation is simply another historical phase, like that of the Cold War, which disadvantages the states of the region but which can be adapted to if the 'rules of the game' are simply relearned. There is a sense that the states of the region can come away relatively unscathed from the hazardous game of globalisation if they exercise sufficient guile and use a 'pick and mix' approach to the phenomena: taking the positive benefits but screening themselves off from the perceived negative aspects of globalisation.

Larger states in the region such as China may well be better positioned to follow this approach. China is blessed with a geographical size that to some degree provides it with scope to dampen over the short term, although certainly not halt over the longer term, the onset of centrifugal globalisation pressures; whilst the perceived size of its market and position as a production base equips it with a certain degree of structural power in the international political economy to influence the pace and terms of globalisation. Other states such as Japan have had the good fortune of the 'window of opportunity' of the Cold War and alignment with the United States. These have enabled Japan to climb to a level of economic development in the international political economy, and continue with state-building attempts, to the point whereby it is sufficiently strong as a state to weather the impact of globalisation.

But the fact that even states such as China and Japan, with their mixed advantages of size, wealth and strategic position, are shaken by globalisation is suggestive of the fact that it is likely to have a far graver impact upon the smaller and weaker states of the region. For these states there is less oppor-tunity to pick and choose from the globalisation menu and they have to increasingly take the phenomena wholesale. In this situation, they are unable to just learn or influence the rules of an existing game, but have to learn a new game entirely; a game that increasingly negates or reinvents the function of sovereignty and which further redistributes power to the large states and to non-state actors. It is only by taking on board this painful les-son that states can adapt to globalisation and tackle their security-related issues. However, that this realisation may not yet have dawned on many of the political elites in the region only gives cause for concern.

References

Ayoob, M. (1995) *The Third World Security Predicament: State Making, Regional Conflict, and the International System*, Lynne Rienner, Boulder.

Buzan, B. (1991) *People, States and Fear: An Agenda for Security Studies in the Post-Cold War Era*, Harvester Wheatsheaf, London.

Buzan, B., Wæver, O. and de Wilde, J. (1998) *Security: A New Framework for Analysis*, Lynne Rienner, Boulder.

Cha, V.D. (2000) 'Globalization and the Study of International Security', *Journal of Peace Research*, Vol. 37(3), pp. 391–403.

Clark, I. (1998) 'Beyond the Great Divide: Globalization and the Theory of International Relations', *Review of International Studies*, Vol. 24, pp. 479–98.

Commission on Global Governance (1995) *Our Global Neighbourhood*, Oxford University Press, Oxford.

Dupont, A. (1999) 'Transnational Crime, Drugs and Security in East Asia', *Asian Survey*, Vol. 39(3), pp. 433–55.

Flynn, S.E. (2000) 'The Global Drug Trade Versus the Nation State', in M.K. Cusimano (ed.) *Beyond Sovereignty: Issues for a Global Agenda*, St Martin's Press, New York.

Higgott, R. (1999) 'Economics, Politics, and (International) Political Economy: The Need for a Balanced Diet in an Era of Globalisation', *New Political Economy*, Vol. 1, pp. 23–36.

Huxley, T. (2002) *Disintegrating Indonesia? Implications for Regional Security*, Adelphi Paper 349, Oxford University Press/Institute for Strategic and International Studies, Oxford.

Scholte, J.A. (1997) 'Global Capitalism and the State', *International Affairs*, Vol. 73(3), pp. 427–52.

Scholte, J.A. (2000) *Globalisation: A Critical Introduction*, Macmillan, London.

Shearer, D. (1998) *Private Armies and Military Intervention*, Oxford University Press, Oxford.

Spero, J.E. (1997) *The Politics of International Economic Relations*, Routledge, London.

Strange, S. (1996) *The Retreat of the State: The Diffusion of Power in the World Economy*, Cambridge University Press, Cambridge.

Tow, W.T., Thakur, R. and Hyun, I. (2000) *Asia's Emerging Regional Order: Reconciling Traditional and Human Security*, United Nations University Press, New York.

Wæver, O. (1995) 'Securitization and Desecuritization', in R.D. Lipschutz (ed.) *On Security*, Columbia University Press, New York.

Part III
Regional Overviews

4
Asian Regionalism Five Years after the 1997/98 Financial Crisis: A Case of 'Co-operative Realism'?

Jürgen Rüland

1. Introduction: the basis of 'co-operative realism' in Asia

Until the late 1980s, theorists of international relations paid little attention to the Asian region. The overwhelming majority of studies tacitly rested on mainstream realist assumptions and beyond that were more or less descriptive, chronological and narrative (Huxley 1996). Theory-building at the time was mainly inspired by superpower relations, transatlantic relations and European integration. This state of affairs changed markedly in the late 1980s. Two developments caught the interest of international relations scholars: the impact of the end of the Cold War and the Sino-Soviet conflict on international relations in Asia, on the one hand, and the enormous changes caused by economic globalization on the other. While the end of the Cold War seemingly lessened security risks and shifted attention from military affairs to economic development, the region's unprecedented economic boom, intensifying trade relations, foreign investment and capital flows spurred economic integration in the region, creating hitherto unknown economic and political interdependencies.

Like many other world regions, Asia responded to the opportunities and pressures of globalization with the formation of new or the revitalization of existing regional organizations. Through the participation in inter-regional and trans-regional fora such as the Asia-Europe Meeting (ASEM) and the Asia-Pacific Economic Co-operation (APEC) forum, Asia also became firmly linked to Europe and North America, the other two constituent regions of the 'triad'. While these inter-regional and trans-regional fora served as intermediaries between the regional and the envisaged global level of international relations, subregional transborder institutions such as the so-called growth triangles and quadrangles linked the regional level with the nation states (see Chapter 9). This differentiation of international relations characterizing the so-called *new regionalism* thus nested Asia into the emerging multilayered structures of global governance (Rüland 2002a,b). These changes prompted many scholars to propose new paradigms for the study of international politics in Asia. Realist orthodoxies were increasingly challenged by institutionalist and social constructivist approaches. Although acknowledging that Asian regionalism differs from European integration, there was nevertheless a tendency to view co-operation as a more or less auto-dynamic process, that is driven by functional spillovers, networks of transnational actors, learning effects, and collective identities based on shared norms (Higgott 1994, Acharya 1997, Dosch 1997, Busse 1999). Optimistic authors – downplaying or ignoring the warnings of early integration theorists and, more recently, regime theorists about integration reversals (Müller 1993) – even went so far as to declare these changes irreversible (Dosch 1996).

The 1997/98 East Asian financial crisis shattered these new paradigms and the beliefs associated with them. Nowhere else was the stagnation and even reversal of regional co-operation more visible than in the paralysis and subsequent decline of the Association of Southeast Asian Nations (ASEAN), established in 1967 and Asia's oldest and at the same time most sophisticated and prestigious regional organization (Funston 1999, Wesley 1999, Rüland 2000, Möller 2002). It is thus no accident that the financial crisis and its repercussions on regional co-operation have once more stimulated theorizing. Consequently, institutionalist and social constructivist approaches have been criticized for placing too much emphasis on institutional learning, spill-overs and the intrinsic capacities of institutions for maturing and deepening. Like in other areas of political science, there is increasing reservation towards thinking in linear developments and deterministic patterns. One area where this has led to fruitful conceptual innovation is democratization research. Discarding teleological concepts of democratization, recent studies have been able to overcome the rigid dichotomy between authoritarianism and democracy and developed new analytical tools to better capture hybrid types of government. 'Competitive authoritarianism' is one such category which acknowledges that a regime applies electoral procedures and allows for a certain level of limited pluralism, while at the same time seeking to contain dissent by manipulating political institutions and, if needed, even resort to outright repression. The concept also conveys the message that such hybrid political systems are regime types in their own right. They are permanent and while at one point may develop more democratic, at another more authoritarian features, they are essentially authoritarian in nature and fail to graduate into a full-fledged democracy (Diamond 2002, Levitsky and Way 2002).

Such category-building tempts drawing analogies to the field of international relations in Asia. Here, too, operating with dichotomies such as the realism–institutionalism paradigms – even if acknowledging a growing congruence of the two schools of thought (Baldwin 1993) – may not capture the realities of Asian international relations that well. While international relations in the developed world basically function along institutionalist lines – a certainty which in itself is increasingly called into question by American unilateralism and the renewed priorities attached to plain military power in the present war against international terrorism – it is misleading to depict Asian international relations exclusively in realist terms, and even more misleading to portray them primarily by institutionalist parameters. As Simon (1995) has already rightfully argued years ago, Asian international relations are more complex, operating on the basis of realist premises and very often simultaneously on institutional logic. This seeming paradox may be well captured by the concept of 'co-operative realism' – a concept derived from earlier work of Link (1998) who spoke of 'co-operative balancing' and 'competitive co-operation' in order to categorize such hybrid scenarios in international relations.

As a concept, 'co-operative realism' modifies the low priority classical realists' (and most structural realists, too) accord to co-operation. It reflects the changes that have taken place in the post-Cold War era in much of Asia and recognizes that, as elsewhere in the world, co-operative institutions have mushroomed in Asia under the auspices of what is known since the 1990s as *new regionalism*. Asian foreign policy-makers responded to the (Western-inspired) new dominant discourse in international relations, which as a rational answer to the challenges of globalization emphasizes international institution-building and global governance. As a result, but also in line with traditional requirements of legitimacy, Asian states have begun to accord greater priority to economic objectives, although it is open to contestation if and to what extent they place them over military issues. What, however, may be said with greater confidence is that much less than, say, three decades ago, they are now less prepared to use military force in the pursuit of national interests or as a means to solve disputes. Yet, some actors such as China, India, Pakistan and North Korea are still prepared to resort to brinkmanship, and possibly force when it suits their interests. Therefore it may be more adequate to speak of 'co-operative realism' than 'co-operative balancing', as the latter term basically refers to processes of institutional balancing.

Despite these undisputable changes in international policy behaviour of Asian governments, a closer look quickly exposes the newly established fora and institutionalist policies as a thin veneer cast over otherwise deeply entrenched realist traditions. As highlighted by McCloud (1995) there is an almost complete lack of co-operative experiences in the region. In fact, more than peaceful co-operation, most Asian peoples have strong collective memories of the chaos produced by the anarchical power descending on them for centuries. The perception of the outside world as an essentially hostile environment has been impressed on the people time and again by the incessant invasions of warring pre-colonial kingdoms, colonialism, Japanese imperialism, the Second World War and finally the Cold War which, unlike in Europe, escalated into wars in Asia. Much more than in post-Second World War Europe, arch enmities and pre-colonial struggles for regional hegemony still determine the attitudes and perceptions of politicians and peoples towards their neighbours, maintaining high levels of distrust and creating formidable barriers for co-operation. Such insecurities persevere even in the post-Cold War era as numerous irredenta, unsolved territorial disputes and arms build-up create the perception that the regional power balance is unstable and in flux. Co-operation is thus suspected of creating relative gains for potential adversaries, thereby negatively affecting one's own position.

That plain force and military potentials shape external relations is thus a deeply internalized and widely shared perception in Asian societies. Hinduistic concepts of statecraft originating in South Asia and adopted by the Indianized states of Southeast Asia share with Chinese strategic thinking and writings on the art of war a highly negative and sceptical perception of the outer world. They translate into cynical policy recommendations of proportions even dwarfing a Machiavelli (von Glasenapp 1958, Fitzgerald 1973, Zimmer 1976, Johnston 1996). These pessimistic perceptions of the outer world have a lasting effect on politicians, diplomats and, in particular, military officers throughout much of Asia, which through discourse analysis can be verified without much effort in everyday politics. It is exactly this collective memory to which Wendt (1999) refers when he distinguishes collective knowledge from individual beliefs and attitudes. Collective knowledge is much deeper entrenched in the memories of the people than beliefs and attitudes influenced by the *zeitgeist*. Such collective worldviews tend to have a particularly powerful impact on the mental disposition of people in times of crises when they find that more recent interpretations of reality are at variance with the existing situation. They respond to this seeming contradiction by seeking orientation in age-honoured myths and narratives.

With these concepts usually goes an essentially strongly ethnocentric worldview. I have argued elsewhere that the concept of geometric politics is inherent in the *mandala* concept of the Indian *Arthashastra*, which involves a decidedly expansionistic logic. The essence of the *mandala* concept, that only amoral power assures political survival, is driven home by epics such as the *Ramayana* or the *Mahabharata* and other arts genres related to them. These epics form part of the school curricula in much of Southeast Asia up to the present day. The *Ramayana*, for instance, socializes readers in the belief that only the rigorous and uncompromising use of power promises protection against the deadly threats emanating from chaos-creating demons. Ethnocentric worldviews can also be found in Chinese notions of the Middle Kingdom, the Japanese 'kokutai' (van Wolferen 1990) and the Korean *Tan'gun* myths (Allen 1990) or at a religious level in the Buddhist *Chakravartin* concept.

Ethnocentric traditions are a breeding ground for nationalist sentiments which are still strong in most Asian societies. The colonial domination has nurtured deep sensitivities towards national sovereignty and economic nationalism which find their expression in the desire to pursue an autonomous foreign policy and to achieve economic autarky. The Indonesian doctrines of *'bebas dan aktif'* (free and active) and *'ketahanan nasiona'* (national resilience) are adequate expressions of these notions. Both are not at all amenable to supranational concepts of integration and deep institutionalization and rather facilitate unilateral policy patterns. Also the spates of ethnic nationalism – indicating that the nation-building process is uncompleted – has a bearing on state-led nationalism.

Further exacerbating the propensities for *realpolitik* is the salient role played by the military in foreign policy-making. Military officers tend to dislike the growing interdependencies of a globalized world as it erodes their cherished goal of autarky and, albeit in the post-Cold War era to a lesser extent, seem to assess foreign policy options from an exclusively military-guided national security perspective. With these legacies still alive, the co-operative element in 'co-operative realism' strongly tilts towards *realpolitik*. Co-operation in regional organizations is basically viewed as a vehicle to increase national power, to balance shifts in the international power equation and to enhance bargaining power in international organizations with the objective of getting more influence on international rule-making.

That balancing is perhaps the most important rationale for co-operation agreements have far-reaching repercussions on the institutional arrangements, even as the power game is shifting from the military into the institutional arena. As balancing basically responds to short-term shifts of political and economic power, and alliances are abandoned when they lose their rationale, building strong institutions is regarded as an unreasonably costly investment. Asian governments are thus averse to sovereignty pooling and in many cases even give second thoughts to resource pooling. 'Soft institutionalization' and the reliance on 'soft law' are thus the preferred modes of co-operation and a trademark of 'co-operative realism'. The extreme pragmatism – some would even say opportunistic behaviour – enabled by shallow institutionalization and exacerbated by cultural aversions towards 'deep institutionalization' and 'hard law' is thus a major factor for the erosion of co-operative arrangements in times of crisis and the subsequent return to *realpolitik* and unilateralism. Moreover, such policy preferences are, contrary to what some social constructivists tend to believe, also difficult to transcend by collective identity-building, especially if identity-building is based, as in most Asian co-operation agreements, on very general norms. The remainder of this chapter examines new developments, forms and structures of economic and security co-operation that have emerged since the 1997/98 financial crisis.

2. The Association of Southeast Asian Nations (ASEAN)

From the outset, regional co-operation in Southeast Asia has been strongly influenced by realist perceptions. Military potentials dominated and still dominate the way policy-makers look at the international environment. Accordingly, even member states of ASEAN, by all standards the most advanced regional organization in Pacific Asia, tend to pursue foreign policies based on realist concepts such as balancing and bandwagoning which they also extend to the institutional arena. It was thus no accident that ASEAN was formed at the height of the Vietnam War in 1967. The grouping was in the first place a creature of the Cold War and initially served an anti-communist cause. ASEAN was formed as a second-line defence against a seemingly aggressive communist expansion which many believed would spill over from Indochina to other parts of Southeast Asia as predicted by the then prevailing 'domino theory'.

Institutionalists and social constructivists challenged such views by arguing that ASEAN was not conceived as a military pact and never developed into one (Busse 1999). This is certainly true, but does not refute the realist argument. For one, relying on the American security umbrella, no matter whether directly or indirectly, must be regarded from the perspective of ASEAN members as an act of bandwagoning. Moreover, in the light of the founding father's staunch anti-communism, even the emphasis on economic co-operation as laid down in the 1967 Bangkok Declaration may be perceived in realist terms as an act of balancing. As a regional organization fostering economic co-operation ASEAN was expected to spur socio-economic development in member states, and thus serve as an internal safeguard against communist penetration.

Liberal institutionalists also tend to reject realist interpretations of ASEAN by the claim that original members initiated the grouping as a means to resolve intra-regional conflicts peacefully. As examples for the conflictual relationship between member states, they cite the Indonesian *konfrontasi*, the Philippine claim to Sabah and maritime disputes in the South China Sea. Heavily drawing from early functionalism and Deutsch's transactionist theory, they argue that with advancements in co-operation and the evolving interdependencies, solving disputes by force would create unacceptably high costs.[1] David (2002), however, rightly contends in my view that even though interdependencies may indeed deter protagonists to use force there is no guarantee that relations between partners are free of tensions. He illustrates this point with the persistently strained and unfriendly relations between Singapore and Malaysia, the by far most interdependent ASEAN members. Both approach each other much more in realist terms as their arms modernization programmes and Singaporean steps towards resource-autarky show.[2] Moreover, a functionalist interpretation ignores the order of priorities. While the formation of ASEAN was in the first place a response to an external threat, peaceful dispute settlement among the members became a prerequisite for successful co-operation. Restraining intra-regional conflicts may thus be seen as a secondary priority derived from the higher priorities of bandwagoning and balancing.

After a short-lived thaw in ASEAN–Indochinese relations in the mid-1970s, beginning with the Vietnamese invasion of Cambodia, ASEAN co-operation was again predominantly driven by security concerns. For most of the 1980s, ASEAN pursued a basically confrontational policy towards Vietnam even though Malaysia and Indonesia recognized genuine Vietnamese security interests and pleaded for a more accommodating policy. Not surprisingly, therefore, the relationship between the two sub-regional blocs in this phase was primarily assessed in terms of military capacities.

Although economics assumed a considerably greater role in post-Cold War international politics, military potentials still greatly determined the way ASEAN foreign policy-makers looked at the evolving new regional order. Such thinking was inspired by the lingering suspicions towards hegemonic designs of rising regional powers such as China, India and a potentially resurging Japan, which were seen as filling the vacuum left by the retreating super powers. Arms build-ups, euphemistically called defence modernization in the region but in reality being a near perfect example for an evolving security dilemma, were one obvious response, and the continued use of realist foreign policy doctrines another one. As already mentioned earlier, doctrines such as *ketahanan nasional* and *bebas dan aktif* stress national strength in an anarchic environment, foreign policy autonomy and economic autarky (Anwar 1995, Suryadinata 1996). Ethnocentric world-views such as the Thai *Suwannaphume* concept also continued to flourish. Although *Suwannaphume* essentially pursued an economic rationale by designating Thailand as an economic hub in mainland Southeast Asia, the way Thailand conducted economic co-operation with her Indochinese neighbours was perceived by the latter as aggressive and exploitative. The co-operative element in the relationship thus became discredited as a thinly veiled form of resource imperialism (Rüland 2000).

Like elsewhere, the intensifying process of globalization has gradually shifted the attention of ASEAN policy-makers more towards to the economic realm. However, attitudes towards globalization are quite ambiguous in Southeast Asia, being perceived as a chance by some but as a threat by many others. Even in the boom years preceding the 1997/98 East Asian financial crisis, which seemingly corroborated the reservations of those who felt threatened by it, globalization was generally viewed more in terms of competition and challenges than co-operation and networking. The decision of the Fourth ASEAN Summit in 1992 at Singapore to seriously venture into economic co-operation and to strengthen ASEAN institutions was thus in the first place a defensive move, primarily guided by intentions to ward off economic challenges from outside the region such as NAFTA and what was seen as an emerging 'Fortress Europe'. Hence, the balancing argument prevails irrespective of the fact that it is now extended to the institutional arena. Regional co-operation was thus seen as a response to the changing relations inside the triad.

The widening of ASEAN was also depicted by analysts and policy-makers in these terms. An enlarged ASEAN would develop greater economic weight and improve its stature in international institutions. Moreover, widening was also determined by internal dynamics, especially the rivalries between Indonesia and Thailand over leadership, and externally the forays of China into the South China Sea and its growing presence in mainland Southeast Asia (Rüland 2000). While institutionalists were confident that co-operation would stimulate institutional learning, soften apprehensions about the anarchical nature of international relations, thereby gradually changing interests of the members, and, by coincidence, facilitate processes of institutional deepening, admission of new members was in fact tantamount to a perpetuation of soft institutionalization and soft law. Reinforcing the cardinal principles of the so-called 'ASEAN way' (see Chapters 7, 8 and 10) – for example that of non-interference in each other's domestic affairs – in fact put a brake on institutional deepening.

The dilemma of reconciling the inevitable contradictions between widening and deepening were compounded by the 1997/98 financial crisis, which jeopardized much of the co-operative capital accumulated over the last thirty years. After a short-lived period of solidarity that, however, was more inspired by populism and conspiration theories than carefully designed collective action, ASEAN slid back into unilateralism, newly erupting bilateral conflicts and, even more serious, divisive debates over the grouping's co-operation principles.[3] The inability of ASEAN to take a common stance *vis-à-vis* the International Monetary Fund (IMF) and the failure to display leadership in the East Timor crisis, were testimony of a regional organization in disarray. Moves towards damage control at subsequent formal and informal summits and the annual ministerial meetings achieved little, and were time and again overshadowed by acrimonious debates over the future of the grouping. Neither the formation of a troubleshooting 'Troika' and the activation of the ASEAN High Council nor initiatives such as the establishment of a monetary surveillance mechanism, ASEAN Vision 2020, the ASEAN Investment Area, the ASEAN Industrial Co-operation and the 'Hanoi Bold Measures' were able to pull ASEAN out of the doldrums. On the contrary, Malaysia's unilateral decision to impose capital controls in September 1998, the three-year delay in engaging its automotive industry from trade liberalization under the ASEAN Free Trade Area (AFTA) exacerbated sentiments of doom pervading ASEAN. Yet, and perhaps the most telling sign for the loss of confidence in ASEAN – and, by coincidence, Asian regionalism as a whole – is the continued talk about new regional bodies such as Pacific-5, the Big Asia Five, a South-West Pacific Dialogue Forum, ASEAN Plus Three (APT), and, most recently, the conclusion of bilateral free trade agreements spearheaded by Singapore. These new fora and co-operative arrangements have been proposed and promoted by different ASEAN members, and if not being an expression to great power ambitions, as in the case of Indonesia's proposal of a Big Asia Five, they are at least an expression of their aspirations to pursue an independent foreign policy based on short-term national interests.

The recent conclusion of an anti-terrorism agreement with the United States hardly changes this state of affairs. First of all, it glosses over intra-ASEAN policy disagreements as how to fight terrorist movements, and, second, it touches upon very sensitive national security issues which most ASEAN members are not prepared to discuss in depth with their neighbours. While it may be true that Washington has reassessed the strategic priority of Southeast Asia, which it considers a second front in the war against terrorism, and is now dealing with ASEAN as an entity, the agreement is couched in the language of 'soft law' and does not create binding obligations for ASEAN members to co-operate closer among themselves (see Chapter 7). To assign to the United States the role of an external federator, as recently the *Far Eastern Economic Review* implicitly did, exaggerates the co-operative effects of the agreement.[4] On the contrary, there is a greater likelihood that anti-terrorism co-operation will tilt foreign policies of ASEAN members even more towards the realist paradigm.

3. Other regional organizations

The Asian forum presently getting most attention is APT. While it certainly has a noteworthy co-operative component (Bowles 2002, Stubbs 2002), analyses viewing it as the thriving force of a more intensive and much deeper institutionalized East Asian regionalism must be treated with caution. Foremost among such interpretations is Dieter's (2000) concept of an emerging East Asian 'monetary regionalism'. As monetary co-operation is placed very high on the integration hierarchy, they project a considerable institutional deepening of co-operative arrangements in the region. Yet, the failed Latin American experiences of the 1960s and 1970s have shown that the level of integration does not necessarily correlate with successful deepening. To talk about projects such as an East Asian monetary union or an East Asian economic community is academically challenging, but in my view premature. Unchanged habits and recent developments seem to confirm my scepticism. For one, most East Asian governments are still hesitant to provide full insight into their state finances which is a precondition for the monitoring mechanism installed under the Manila Framework to be efficient. Second, the Chiang Mai Initiative has not lived up to the high expectations it generated. The fourteen bilateral currency swaps either signed or to be concluded by May 2003 – the date set for completing the whole CMI swap network – will together only amount to US$36 billion, a total far below what is needed to weather a serious currency crisis (see Figure 5.6). Moreover, an Asian Monetary Fund (AMF) has not yet emerged and currency swaps of a certain magnitude are still subject to IMF approval. Christopher Dent discusses these matters in more detail in the following chapter.

While there was a flurry of new activities during the 8th ASEAN Summit and the subsequent 6th APT Summit in November 2002, such as Japan's Initiative for Development in East Asia (IDEA), the Joint Declaration of ASEAN and China on Co-operation in the Field of Non-Traditional Security Issues, the Joint Declaration of the Leaders of ASEAN and Japan on the Comprehensive Economic Partnership (or JACEP), and the Framework on ASEAN-China Economic Co-operation (including a free trade agreement between both sides), they are still declarations of intent and it remains to be seen as to what extent they differ from earlier initiatives. Similarly uncertain is the impact of the report submitted by the APT Vision Group to the 5th APT Summit at Brunei in 2001[5] which among many other initiatives also proposed the establishment of an East Asian Free Trade Area or Zone, with the objective of liberalizing trade ahead of APEC's own target date of 2020. It may be remembered in this respect that only a few years ago, Asian APEC members had rejected the term 'community' for the forum and persistently diluted bolder moves of the Anglo-Pacific members towards trade liberalization when prior to the 1997/98 East Asian financial crisis their economies were in much better shape than now (see Chapter 1). Initially launched with great fanfare, most 'vision groups' have so far failed to meet expectations: cases in point are the Eminent Persons Groups of APEC, the ASEAN-EU Eminent Persons Groups and the ASEM Vision Group over the mid-to-late 1990s. Many of the above-mentioned new initiatives are related to the threat of international terrorism and moves of balancing the increasingly assertive role of the United States in the Southeast and East Asian region. In the economic realm, they are expressions of an intensifying competition between China and Japan for influence in Southeast Asia. For ASEAN, East Asian regionalism and the ensuing co-operative structures are recognition that the grouping is too weak to weather deepening globalization, and that it urgently needs to strengthen its bargaining power in international fora. Yet, taking into account the diversity of interests of leading members, there is a great likelihood that even as a bargaining coalition, APT may be confined to the lowest common denominator.

Compared to ASEAN and APT, co-operation in other regional organizations in Asia is even less advanced. To a considerable extent this must be attributed to the fact that realist attitudes of foreign policy-makers by far outweigh institutionalist policies. Among all Asian regional organizations, the South Asian Association for Regional Co-operation (SAARC) is probably the grouping most entangled in realist thinking. This is hardly surprising as the region is the theatre of one of the most dangerous conflicts on the globe.

Since independence in 1947, India and Pakistan have fought three wars over Kashmir. For much of the 1990s, both amassed tens of thousands of troops in the Himalayas. Apart from almost daily skirmishes along the demarcation line, on two occasions (in 1990 and 2002) both sides went dangerously close to a nuclear show-down. No wonder that the power equation in the region is exclusively evaluated in military terms. Security agreements with extra-regional powers, arms races and the refusal of India and Pakistan to sign the Nonproliferation and the Comprehensive Test Ban Treaties set the parameters for realist interpretations of South Asian politics. Another obstacle standing in the way of more co-operation is the Tamil conflict in Sri Lanka, as well as a number of nonviolent bilateral conflicts between India and her neighbours (Wagner 2002).

Yet, the regional organization is unable to provide a forum for resolving these conflicts as Article X of the SAARC Charter explicitly rules out the discussion of bilateral and contentious issues. However, to be fair, bilateral meetings at the sidelines of the grouping's (irregular) summits have occasionally at least temporarily defused the conflicts. Moreover, where the power equation is as precarious as in South Asia, relative gains by other players must be avoided by all means. Hence, even intra-regional trade hovers at a level that is appallingly low even by the low standards of most Third World regional organizations. Taking into account all these adverse circumstances, one cannot but side with those analysts who argue that already the existence of the grouping and its low profile co-operation in a number of low politics areas is to be commended and is a sign of hope.

Formed in 1997, the Bangladesh, India, Myanmar, Sri Lanka, Thailand Economic Co-operation (BIMSTEC) forum is a subregional grouping bridging South and Southeast Asia. Although hard empirical evidence is difficult to get, its formation must most likely be attributed to the geopolitical balancing objectives of some members. Thailand and India, for instance, had a strong interest to create such a regional grouping in order to engage Burma. India, and to some extent Thailand too, were increasingly worried about the close co-operation between Burma and China, which covers military affairs as well. Her presence in Burma would give China access to the Indian Ocean which India considers as a threat to her declared sphere of influence. On the institutionalist side, India may have been interested in creating an additional avenue for bringing the country in closer contact with the fora and organizations of Pacific Asia of which it was hitherto excluded. The Thai government, for her part, may have believed that by engaging Burma in another grouping, this would facilitate the process of socializing it into ASEAN to which Rangoon was admitted in the same year. Five years later, it seems that BIMSTEC is more or less dormant. Member states did not bother to create viable institutions and the East Asian financial crisis has dried out the resources available for joint projects and private sector investment.

The Shanghai Organization for Co-operation, formalizing earlier bilateral ties in 1998 brings together China, Russia and the former Soviet Republic of Kazakhstan, Krygistan, Tadjikistan and Uzbekistan. The organization shares many of the obstacles for deeper co-operation outlined in the previous cases. It is thus far-fetched to expect that the organization would spur moves towards an Asian security forum that rests on CSCE (Conference on Security and Co-operation in Europe) principles (Wacker 2001).

4. Asian participation in trans-regional fora

Studying inter- and trans-regional fora constitutes a new area of research in international relations. Asia participates in several such fora. The most important of them are APEC, ASEM and – to a much lesser extent – the Indian Ocean Rim Association for Regional Co-operation (IOR-ARC). The literature attaches several functions to them which may be linked to the main strands of international relations theory: balancing and bandwagoning to realism, institution-building, rationalizing (decision-making processes of global-multilateral fora) and agenda-setting to liberal institutionalism and collective identity-building to social constructivism (Maull and Tanaka 1997, Roloff 1998, Dent 1999, Rüland 1999, Hänggi 2000, Gilson 2002).

Although empirical evidence is so far limited, it seems that balancing prevails among these functions. For instance, APEC is widely perceived as a response to plans arising in the 1980s for the European Single Market and the Canada–United States Free Trade Area. Viewed through the Asian lens, ASEM was essentially a response to APEC and the increasing economic dominance of Japan and the United States over the East Asian growth region, as well as European overtures to Mercosur and bilateral free trade agreements with Mexico and South Africa. Finally, the IOR-ARC is a recognition of the fact that most of its members have been marginalized by globalization and the institutions created by the *new regionalism*. In other words, it represents a coalition of the periphery.

Institution-building is limited as all trans-regional fora with Asian participation have adopted ASEAN principles of co-operation. Under these auspices, co-operation is non-binding, consultative, negating interferences into the internal affairs of members and characterized by 'soft law' and 'soft institutionalization' (Kahler 2000). Agenda-setting and rationalizing have taken place occasionally, but neither APEC nor ASEM have thus far assumed a major role here. APEC has virtually ceased as an agenda setter and rationalizer since the 1997/98 East Asian financial crisis. Its trade liberalization programme came to a virtual standstill, with the unresolved issues (primarily between Japan and the United States) arising from APEC's ill-fated Early Voluntary Sectoral Liberalisation scheme being transferred to the World Trade Organization (WTO). The United States has increasingly lost interest in it as a forum for trade liberalization, and now uses APEC as a multi-purpose vehicle (see Chapter 1). While the United Nations (UN) intervention in East Timor prepared at the 1999 APEC summit in Auckland may be read in institutionalist terms, the post-9/11 anti-terror coalition is evolving within APEC under a genuinely realist scenario based on the understanding of an anarchical international environment. Moreover, leaders increasingly use the summits of regional and trans-regional fora for bilateral talks at the sidelines of the official programme. Reducing regional and trans-regional fora to such functions sets the wrong signal: they are rationalizing bilateralism instead of multilateralism.

Identity-building has undoubtedly taken place even more through ASEM than through APEC. Yet, ASEM did not go as far as to transcend balancing and Asian propensities towards shallow institutions. To a much greater extent did it foster coalition-building in East Asia for the sake of enhancing Asian bargaining power in trans-regional fora and in global-multilateral organizations such as the UN and the WTO. Moreover, the 1997/98 East Asian financial crisis has softened the voices of East Asian exceptionalism on which much of the pre-crisis identity-building rested. Very telling in this respect is an article entitled 'East Asia is diverse and unstoppable', which authored by Singaporean diplomat and intellectual Tommy Koh appeared in December 1997 in the *International Herald Tribune*.[6] Emphasizing the diversity of East Asia is a thinly veiled attempt to distance Singapore, which spearheaded the Asian value *mantra* from her crisis-ridden neighbours. This shows that the ideational cement of East Asian regionalism is weak, and is unable to create sufficient commitment to long-term regional co-operation. Moreover, regional solidarity seems to give way to egoistic pragmatism, especially in times of crisis. Therefore, the new regional organizations mentioned above that have been formed or proposed since 1999 are as much a vote of no-confidence for APEC as for ASEAN.

5. The Asian Regional Forum (ARF)

Like the trans-regional fora with Asian involvement, the Asian Regional Forum (ARF) has also adopted the ASEAN formula of co-operation (Johnston 1999). This has led to a situation in which 'governments are less concerned with solving international problems through co-operative security than protecting sovereignty from ARF intervention' (Simon 2002: 19). Hence, progress towards institutionalist security policies remains limited. The gains in terms of transparency and actor predictability are thus likewise modest at best (Garofano 2002, Möller 2002). Among the achievements in this direction are a number of confidence-building measures (CBMs) such as the Defence White Papers published by some Asian governments including China, and the exchange of information on defence doctrines, arms acquisition plans and military manoeuvres. However, much of the information provided did not go beyond what was already common knowledge in the defence community (Leifer 1996).

As a result, ARF has so far been unable to venture beyond the first stage of the three-stage agenda adopted in its 1995 Brunei meeting. Progress towards preventive diplomacy and the development of mechanisms for conflict resolution have so far been hampered by fears that they would open the flood gates for intervention into members' internal affairs. Hence, the inability of the ARF to solve even one of the more serious issues in the region. In fact, the ARF has neither been able to slow down the competitive regional arms-build up, which is gaining new momentum after many governments temporarily shelved their arms purchases due to the 1997/98 East Asian financial crisis, nor to address effectively the border and territorial disputes in the region, and even less the region's numerous communal conflicts and insurgencies. Progress is also limited to tackle non-conventional security issues such as transborder migration, transnational crime, narcotics trafficking and environmental hazards.

While the ARF has facilitated the rise of an impressive array of track two processes (e.g. the Council for Security Co-operation in the Asia-Pacific, CSCAP), their influence on government decision-makers remains ambiguous. There is no doubt that the track two dialogues enhanced the consciousness of decision-makers and the wider public for a broad range of security risks in the region which, if left unattended, have the capacity to evolve into serious crises. Yet, they have not effected paradigmatic changes in the region's strategic thinking, and the role attached to them by some observers as 'propellers of policy learning' must be placed in proper perspective (Nesadurai and Stone 2000: 183). In fact, track two dialogues are no panacea where track one failed (Kraft 2000).

While there are certainly cases, where governments accepted recommendations from think tanks and track two meetings, recent studies show that these informal dialogues suffer from a number of flaws. Most Asian participants continue to stick to a conservative, state-centric security concept centring on eminent realist concepts such as 'balancing' and 'power' (Kraft 2000, Nesadurai and Stone 2000, Simon 2002). Moreover, in many Asian countries, track two participants are very close to the government and subject themselves to varying degrees of 'self-censorship'. Finally, track two meetings have been rightfully criticized as an 'exclusivist club' (Kraft 2000) involving the same core personnel that, despite the establishment of working groups, addresses a broad range of issues. Innovation is therefore piecemeal at best and a *deja vu* effect associated with many arguments is hardly deniable.

6. Transborder co-operation and bilateral free trade agreements

Transborder co-operation assuming the form of growth triangles and quadrangles have to a lesser extent been balancing devices. As Chapter 9 later shows, ASEAN member states have been especially active in setting up such transborder, sub-regional economic 'growth areas'. Spearheaded by the Indonesia–Malaysia–Singapore Growth Triangle (IMSGT, linking Singapore to Indonesia's Riau province and Malaysia's Johor province), which was later considerably extended, they include the so-called Northern triangle covering Penang and Northern Malaysia, Southern Thailand and Northern Sumatra (or Indonesia–Malaysia–Thailand Growth Triangle), the Greater Mekong Sub-Region (GMS) scheme and the East ASEAN Growth Area consisting of Eastern Malaysia, Brunei, Sulawesi, Kalimantan, the Moluccas, West Papua and Mindanao (BIMP-EAGA).

In some cases, such as the IMSGT, they were a response to stagnation of ASEAN co-operation, in other cases an approach of national governments to develop their hinterlands which they have so far neglected. Yet, cross-regional institution-building is weak and, if at all, rarely goes beyond loose inter-governmental officials' meetings. Even worse, most of these 'growth triangles' were badly affected by the 1997/98 financial crisis and the political turbulences in its aftermath. This holds particularly true for the BIMP-EAGA, which due to the resurgent Moro rebellion in the Southern Philippines and the communal violence in Sulawesi, the Moluccas and West Papua is more or less moribund and only hesitantly revived. The Mekong Basin projects, too, have been affected as private investment capital from ASEAN countries was drying out (Freeman 1999). It remains also to be seen what impact the chaotic decentralization process in Indonesia will have on transborder co-operation. Provinces are increasingly emancipating themselves from the central government in Jakarta and may try to develop their own border-crossing relations. This may however cause a backlash from the central government, which may see in enhanced provincial activities an undesirable strengthening of centrifugal forces and a threat to national cohesion.

As Chapter 5 discusses far more extensively, several Asian governments (particularly Singapore) have become increasingly active in developing bilateral free trade agreement (FTA) projects with partners from both inside the region and across the wider Asia-Pacific. In contrast to some authors, who attach a generally positive meaning to them as far as their influence on the perspectives for co-operation in the region is concerned, I would argue that this is a one-sided view which overlooks the risks inherent in them. Co-operative bilateralism as practised in these agreements creates a lot of incentives for balancing. The competition between China and Japan to conclude FTAs with ASEAN is a point in case. Whether an increasingly dense network of bilateral agreements facilitates the return to multilateral regionalism is questionable in the light of the distrust sowed by the inevitable rivalries of successive balancing moves. 'Multiple bilateralism' is thus even less conducive to deep institutionalization than 'multiple regionalism' (Bowles 1997).

7. Conclusion

Departing from a critique of linear concepts of regionalism as explicitly or implicitly pursued by the majority of institutionalist and social constructivist analyses of Asian regionalism, this chapter has argued that foreign policy-making in the Asia-Pacific region is still very much driven by realist premises. Yet, analyses of Asian international relations exclusively relying on the tenets of classical or structural realism, with their explicit pessimism towards international co-operation and institutions, do not capture realities on the ground very well. They are unable to adequately take into account the grey areas where power-driven, state-centric and unilateralist policies combine with limited co-operative efforts and 'soft institutionalization' on the basis of 'soft law'. The growth of new regional and sub-regional institutions under what has been called the *new regionalism* are testimony of this latter trend. In order to highlight the simultaneity of *realpolitik* and institutionalist policies, with the institutionalist logic however often subordinated to power politics, this chapter has introduced the concept of 'co-operative realism'. It connotes that foreign policy in Asia is still predominantly adhering to age-honoured perceptions of the outer world, which are highly power-conscious and rest on the firm belief in self-help, yet that (when environmental factors are conducive) go hand in hand with policies of cautious institution-building and co-operation that, though, are void of a long-term perspective. The concept also suggests that Asian-style co-operation deviates from a teleological, linear and autodynamic concept of co-operation driven by the proverbial spill-over effects and the belief in institutional learning. It consequently reasons that international relations in the Asia-Pacific are coloured to a considerable extent by a distinct regional security culture. The mix between realist and institutionalist policies is more prone to realist reversals than to progress towards institutionalist patterns. In other words co-operation does not transcend a certain point.

Unsurprisingly, the 1997/98 East Asian financial crisis has thrown most of the regional organizations into disarray. As a consequence, intra-regional relations have been tilting back towards unilateralism and pragmatic egoism. The retreat of Asian regionalism – which is not counterbalanced but rather underlined by the rise of new regional institutions such as ASEAN Plus Three (APT) and others – is corroborated by a similarly conspicuous return to bilateralism and, to a lesser extent, to global institutions. Bilateralism eventually works in favour of *realpolitik* as it allows the stronger and more resourceful partner the better deal which is not cushioned by the checks and balances otherwise provided by regional-multilateral institutions. Global-multilateral institutions provide better perspectives for institutionalist policies, yet due to the existing power equation in the world, with the United States relying without reservations on its superpower status by openly despising international institutions, it is questionable whether global fora constitute an alternative to *realpolitik* for the medium-sized and smaller states in the Asia-Pacific.

Notes

1. See Chapter 9 for more on this view.
2. Long-standing negotiations between Singapore and Malaysia over the former's freshwater supply dependency on the latter is a high profile case of this, whereby Singapore has sought to develop new desalination plants and technologies to ease this 'supply security' predicament (Dent 2001).
3. See Chapters 7, 8 and 10 for more discussion on this.
4. *Far Eastern Economic Review*, 15.08.2002, p. 24.
5. The report is entilted '*Towards an East Asian Community*'.
6. *International Herald Tribune*, 17.12.1997, p. 6.

References

Acharya, A. (1997) 'Ideas, Identity, and Institution-Building: From the 'ASEAN Way' to the 'Asia-Pacific Way', *The Pacific Review*, Vol. 10(3), pp. 319–46.

Allen, C.T. (1990) 'Northeast Asia Centered Around Korea: Ch'oe Nam-son's View of History', *Journal of Asian Studies*, Vol. 49(4), pp. 787–806.

Anwar, D.F. (1995) *Indonesia in ASEAN. Foreign Policy and Regionalism*, Institute of Southeast Asian Studies, Singapore.

Baldwin, D.A. (ed.) (1993) '*Neorealism and Neoliberalism: The Contemporary Debate*', Columbia University Press, New York.

Bowles, P. (1997) 'ASEAN, AFTA and the New Regionalism', *Pacific Affairs*, Vol. 70(2), pp. 219–34.

Bowles, P. (2002) 'Asia's Post-Crisis Regionalism: Bringing the State Back In, Keeping the (United) States Out', *Review of International Political Economy*, Vol. 9(2), pp. 230–56.

Busse, N. (1999) 'Social Constructivism and Southeast Asian Security', *The Pacific Review*, Vol. 12(1), pp. 39–60.

David, H. (2002) *Die ASEAN zwischen Konflikt, Kooperation und Integration*, PhD Thesis. University of Rostock.

Dent, C.M. (1999) 'The EU-East Asia Economic Relationship. The Persisting Weak Triadic Link?', *European Foreign Affairs Review*, Vol. 4(3), pp. 371–94.

Dent, C.M. (2001) 'Singapore's Foreign Economic Policy: The Pursuit of Economic Security', *Contemporary Southeast Asia*, Vol. 23(1), pp. 1–23.

Diamond, L. (2002) 'Elections Without Democracy. Thinking About Hybrid Regimes', *Journal of Democracy*, Vol. 13(2), pp. 20–35.

Dieter, H. (2000) 'Ostasien nach der Krise: Interne Reformen, neue Finanzarchitektur und monetärer Regionalismus', *Aus Politik und Zeitgeschichte*, B 37/38/2000, 8. September 2000.

Dosch, J. (1996) 'Die ASEAN-Kooperations- und Integrationsleistungen, Perspektiven', in G. Eilenberger and M. Mols and J. Rüland (eds), *Kooperation, Regionalismus und Integration im asiatisch-pazifischen Raum*, Mitteilungen des Instituts für Asienkunde, Hamburg.

Dosch, J. (1997) *Die ASEAN. Bilanz eines Erfolges. Akteure, Interessenlagen, Kooperationsbeziehungen*, Abera Networks, Hamburg.

Fitzgerald, C.P. (1973) 'Zum chinesischen Ethnozentrismus', in D. Frei (ed.), *Theorien der Internationalen Beziehungen*, R. Piper&Co. Verlag, München.

Freeman, Nick J. (1999) 'Greater Mekong Sub-Region and the "Asian Crisis": Caught Between Scylla and Charybdis', *Southeast Asian Affairs*, Institute of Southeast Asian Studies, pp. 32–51.

Funston, J. (1999) 'Challenges Facing ASEAN in a Modern Complex Age', *Contemporary Southeast Asia*, Vol. 21(2), pp. 205–19.

Garofano, J. (2002) 'Power, Institutions, and the ASEAN Regional Forum: A Security Community for Asia?', *Asian Survey*, Vol. 42(2), pp. 502–21.

Gilson, J. (2002) *Asia Meets Europe: Interregionalism and the Asia-Europe Meeting*, Edwin Elgar, Cheltenham.

Glasenapp, H. von (1958) *Indische Geisteswelt. Glaube, Dichtung und Wissenschaft Indiens*, Band II, Harrassowitz, Wiesbaden.

Hänggi, H. (2000) *Regionalism Through Interregionalism: East Asia in ASEM*, unpublished paper.

Higgott, R. (1994) 'Ideas, Policy Networks and Policy Co-ordination in the Asia Pacific', *The Pacific Review*, Vol. 7(4), pp. 397–409.

Huxley, T. (1996) 'Southeast Asia in the Study of International Relations: The Rise and Decline of a Region', *The Pacific Review*, Vol. 9(2), pp. 199–228.

Johnston, A.I. (1996) 'Cultural Realism and Strategy in Maoist China', in P.J. Katzenstein (ed.), *The Culture of National Security. Norms and Identity in World Politics*, Columbia University Press, New York.

Johnston, A.I. (1999) 'The Myth of the ASEAN Way? Explaining the Evolution of the ASEAN Regional Forum', in H. Haftendorn, R.O. Keohane and C.A. Wallander (eds), *Imperfect Unions. Security Institutions over Time and Space*, Oxford University Press, Oxford.

Kahler, M. (2000) 'Legalization as a Strategy: The Asia-Pacific Case', *International Organization*, Vol. 54(3), pp. 549–71.

Kraft, H.J.S. (2000) 'The Autonomy Dilemma of Track Two Diplomacy in Southeast Asia', *Security Dialogue*, Vol. 31(3), pp. 343–56.

Leifer, M. (1996) *The ASEAN Regional Forum*, Adelphi Paper 302, Oxford University Press/Institute for Strategic and International Studies, Oxford.

Levitsky, S. and Way, L.A. (2002) The Rise of Competitive Authoritarianism, *Journal of Democracy*, Vol. 13(2), pp. 51–65.

Link, W. (1998) *Die Neuordnung der Weltpolitik. Grundprobleme globaler Politik an der Schwelle zum 21. Jahrhundert*, Beck'sche Reihe, München.

Maull, H.W. and Tanaka, A. (1997) 'The Geopolitical Dimension', in Council for Asia-Europe Co-operation (ed.), *The Rationale and Common Agenda for Asia-Europe Co-operation*, CAEC Task Force Reports, London.

McCloud, D.G. (1995) *Southeast Asia. Tradition and Modernity in the Contemporary World*, Westview, Boulder.

Möller, K. (2002) *Pacific Sunset. Vom vorzeitigen Ende des ostasiatischen Jahrhunderts*, Stiftung Wissenschaft und Politik, Berlin.

Müller, H. (1993) *Die Chance der Kooperation. Regime in den internationalen Beziehungen*, Wissenschaftliche Buchgesellschaft, Darmstadt.

Nesadurai, H. and Stone, D. (2000) 'Southeast Asian Think Tanks in Regional and Global Networking', *Panorama*, Vol. 1, pp. 19–36.

Roloff, R. (1998) 'Globalisierung, Regionalisierung und Gleichgewicht', in C. Masala and R. Roloff (eds), *Herausforderungen der Realpolitik. Beiträge zur Theoriedebatte in der internationalen Politik*, SB-Verlag, Köln.

Rüland, J. (1999) 'The Future of the ASEM Process: Who, How, Why and What', in W. Stokhof and P. van der Velde (eds), *ASEM. The Asia-Europe Meeting. A Window of Opportunity*, Kegan Paul, London.

Rüland, J. (2000) 'ASEAN and the Asian Crisis: Theoretical and Practical Consequences for Southeast Asian Regionalism', *The Pacific Review*, Vol. 13(3), pp. 421–51.

Rüland, J. (2002a) 'APEC, ASEAN and EAEC – A Tale of Two Cultures of Co-operation', in J. Rüland and E. Manske and W. Draguhn (eds) *Asia-Pacific Economic Co-operation (APEC): The First Decade*, RoutledgeCurzon, London.

Rüland, J. (2002b) 'The Contribution of Track Two Dialogue towards Crisis Prevention', *ASIEN*, Vol. 85, pp. 84–96.

Simon, S. (1995) 'Realism and Neoliberalism: International Relations Theory and Southeast Asian Security', *The Pacific Review*, Vol. 8(1), pp. 5–24.

Simon, S.W. (2002) 'The ASEAN Regional Forum Views the Councils for Security Co-operation in the Asia Pacific: How Track II Assists Track I', *NBR Analysis*, Vol. 13(4), pp. 5–23.

Stubbs, R. (2002) 'ASEAN Plus Three: Emerging East Asian Regionalism?' *Asian Survey*, Vol. XLII(3), pp. 440–55.

Suryadinata, L. (1996) *Indonesia's Foreign Policy under Suharto. Aspiring to International Leadership*, Times Academic Press, Singapore.

Wacker, G. (2001) *Die Shanghaier Organisation für Zusammenarbeit: Eurasische Gemeinschaft oder Papiertiger?* Stiftung Wissenschaft und Politik, Berlin.

Wagner, C. (2002) *Die 'verhinderte' Grossmacht? Die Aussenpolitik der Indischen Union, 1947–1998*, Habil.Schrift, Universität Rostock.

Wendt, A. (1999) *Social Theory of International Politics*, Cambridge University Press, Cambridge.

Wesley, M. (1999) 'The Asian Crisis and the Adequacy of Regional Institutions', *Contemporary Southeast Asia*, Vol. 21(1), pp. 54–73.

Wolferen, K. van (1990) *The Enigma of Japanese Power: People and Politics in a Stateless Nation*, Knopf, New York.

Zimmer, H. (1976) *Philosophien und Religionen Indiens*, Suhrkamp Verlag, Frankfurt.

5

The Asia-Pacific's New Economic Bilateralism and Regional Political Economy

Christopher M. Dent

1. Introduction

It is generally accepted that the two most significant recent developments in the Asia-Pacific regional political economy[1] concern the proliferation of bilateral free trade agreement (FTA) projects between an increasing number of the region's states, and the emergence of the ASEAN Plus Three (APT) framework that has coalesced a region-wide set of East Asian states into an operationalised economic grouping for the first time. In both cases, the 1997/98 East Asian financial crisis proved to be a major catalyst behind these developments. From its conception, the APT framework has sought to establish regional financial governance mechanisms that were devised to avert another crisis from occurring. A key factor in the expansion of bilateral FTA projects amongst Asia-Pacific states derives from new post-crisis formulas to improve international economic relations generally. The 11 September 2001 terrorist attacks on the United States has further intensified both processes, and moreover has introduced a stronger security dimension to the strategic diplomacy motives that are driving them forward.

The bilateral FTA trend and the APT framework demonstrate well the three key dimensions of this book. First, the 'imperative co-operation' forces behind their development are strong, and yet this is occurring under the duress of various 'complex diversity' counter-forces that impede the progress of both. Second, as noted above, each demonstrates how economic and security matters are conflating within international co-operative ventures in the Asia-Pacific. Third, even the seemingly regionalist arrangement such as APT is essentially founded on bilateralism at the framework's sub-structural level, as shown by the series of bilateral currency swap agreements brokered under the Chiang Mai Initiative – APT's centrepiece project. As is argued in this chapter, however, the trade bilateralism embodied by the new FTA trend and the finance bilateralism within the APT framework provide themselves a sub-structural basis on which new forms of regional economic community-building in East Asia and the Asia-Pacific may be developed. Different aspects of this bilateralism–regionalism relationship are explored here, and how they are shaping the contemporary Asia-Pacific regional political economy. Furthermore, we shall examine the growing connections between the bilateral FTA trend and the APT framework.

2. New FTA projects in the Asia-Pacific

As Figures 5.1–5.5 indicate, the proliferation of new FTA projects in the Asia-Pacific has been startling. At the time of the 1997/98 East Asian financial crisis, there were only a small handful of FTA projects in the Asia-Pacific trans-region. The United States, Canada and Mexico had formed the North American Free Trade Agreement (NAFTA) in 1993; the Closer Economic Relationship (CER) agreement between Australia and New Zealand was established in 1983; Chile and Mexico signed a FTA deal in September 1991, while a Chile–Canada FTA was signed in 1997; Costa Rica had signed an FTA with Mexico in 1995 and was negotiating another with Chile by 1993 ASEAN member states began implementing its Free Trade Area (AFTA) project from 1993 onwards; and finally, the United States and Chile had been considering a bilateral FTA deal since 1995 (Figure 5.1). At eight projects in

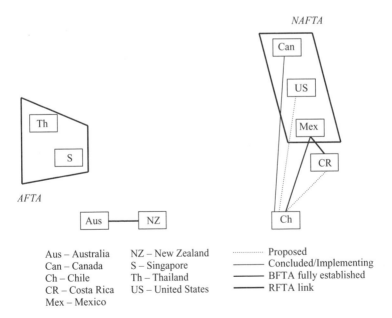

Figure 5.1   Asia-Pacific free trade agreements (before 1998).

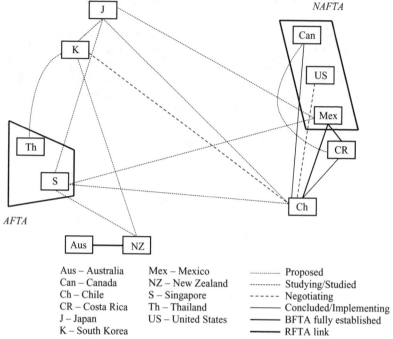

Figure 5.2   Asia-Pacific free trade agreements (by end of 1999).

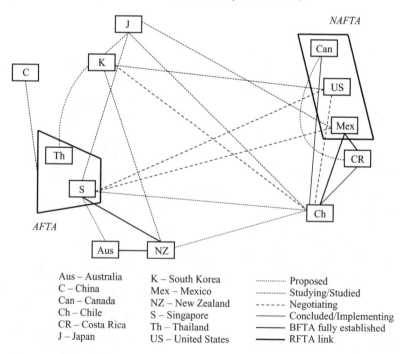

Figure 5.3   Asia-Pacific free trade agreements (by end of 2000).

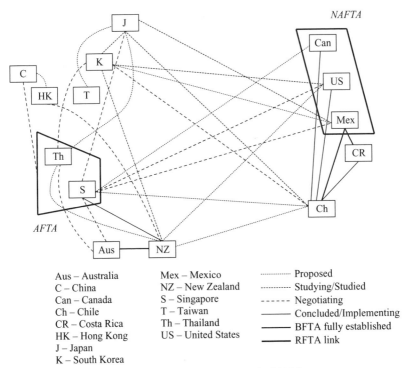

Figure 5.4 Asia-Pacific free trade agreements (by end of 2001).

total, this represented a very small number by global region comparison. Yet within a few years the Asia-Pacific had become host to the world's fastest growing concentration of new FTA projects. By the end of 2002, the trans-region was host to a total of 45 FTA projects in various stages of development (Figure 5.5), with 13 new projects initiated in the latter half of that year alone.

This bilateral FTA project phenomenon has thus become a new defining feature of the Asia-Pacific regional political economy (Dobson 2001, Webber 2001, Lloyd 2002, Dent 2003, Ravenhill 2003). Bilateral FTAs are now seen as the most viable way to advance freer trade in the region, especially in the wake of failed attempts by the Asia-Pacific Economic Co-operation (APEC) forum to achieve the same (see Chapter 1). More importantly, though, these bilateral FTA projects constitute new mechanisms for cultivating closer economic and political ties between Asia-Pacific states. For example, Japan and South Korea's bilateral FTA project plays an integral part of their longer-term reconciliation process. Singapore's securing of an FTA with the United States is not just driven by market access interests but by the objective of tying American interests more generally to the city-state's regional locale. China's FTA deal with the ASEAN group is intended to further demonstrate to the outside world the country's willingness to engage in substantive international partnerships, and thus an attempt to dispel the anxieties of those

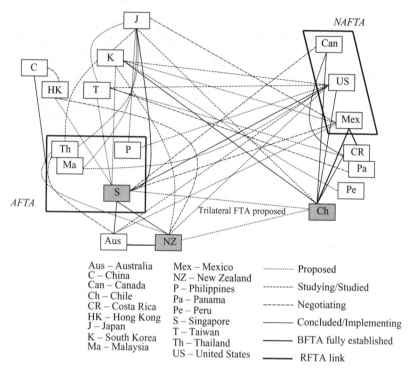

Figure 5.5   Asia-Pacific free trade agreements (by end of 2002).

Note: Chile FTAs with other Pacific Latin American countries include Colombia and Ecuador, both in force from 1995. These two countries have been omitted because they have no FTA project links with other sub-regions in the Asia-Pacific. Chile also had an FTA link with the Central American Common Market (CACM) group by this date, in which Costa Rica was the first to start implementing (noted). Costa Rica is the only CACM member with FTA project links with other sub-regions in the Asia-Pacific. Mexico has negotiated FTA links with other CACM members by 2000, a CACM-Panama FTA was signed in 2002, a CACM-Canada FTA talks started in November 2001, and CACM-US FTA talks since 2003.

fixated with the perceived economic and political threats China poses. Both Australia and New Zealand's FTA policies are the latest trade diplomacy tactics employed within their respective longer-term strategies of forging closer economic community links within the trans-region. Chile and Mexico's new FTA projects across the Asia-Pacific represent just an extension of their already well-established FTA diplomacy.

For the United States – which came quite late to this new FTA trend – bilateral FTA projects have provided an opportunity for the George W. Bush administration to prove its free trade credentials. Although the previous Clinton Government had initiated some kind of bilateral FTA policy in the

Asia-Pacific, it achieved little in progressing beyond the United States' relatively limited FTA portfolio, this comprising its participation in NAFTA and bilateral FTAs with Israel and Jordan. Fresh impetus was, though, provided by the 11 September 2001 terrorist atrocities. The US's bilateral FTA projects now form part of Washington's broader strategy of international coalition-building against the spectre of terrorism, with these trade agreements now viewed as cementing alliance ties amongst 'democratic' or at least like-minded partner states (US Department of State 2002). However, this would not be possible without the Bush administration's securing of 'Trade Promotion Authority' (TPA) in 2002, which now enables the US Trade Representative (USTR) Office to more effectively expedite trade deals in general.[2]

From field research thus far conducted, interviewed policy-makers and other stakeholders generally cite 'strategic diplomacy' factors as the most important current determinant behind the new bilateral FTA trend, especially after this trend has reached a critical level of self-momentum. To use a computer software analogy, it is viewed as increasingly disadvantageous not to be participating in this emerging 'network standard' of trade diplo-. macy, and the growing number of bilateral FTA players in the Asia-Pacific reflects this. The new FTA trend started with around nine states back in 1999 but this had gradually risen to 18 by the end of 2002 (Figures 5.2 and 5.5). While there is a strong underlying political aspect to these strategic diplomacy motivations (i.e. consolidating inter-state alliance ties, improving bilateral relations in general), the economic or more specifically 'market access' dimension is invariably just as strong. An important factor behind the gradual intensification of this new FTA is the fear of trade diversion. For instance, New Zealand Prime Minister Helen Clark quickly reinvigorated her country's attempts to secure a FTA with the United States after Washington and Canberra had agreed in November 2002 to commence bilateral FTA negotiations in March 2003. Clark recognised an FTA between Australia and the United States – the first and third most important trade partners for New Zealand respectively – would place New Zealand's firms at a significant disadvantage given their Australian-based and US-based rivals' free trade access to these important markets.[3]

The market access issue is also highly relevant to earlier critical determining factors behind the new FTA trend at its outset. As noted earlier and indicated by Figure 5.1, the Asia-Pacific was a region comparatively devoid of FTAs by the mid-to-late 1990s. However, this ran against the prevailing global trend. By the time of the 1997/98 financial crisis, there were over 140 preferential trade agreements (PTAs)[4] in force around the world, around 100 of which had been notified to the WTO since 1990. There was thus a growing feeling amongst Asia-Pacific states that they were falling behind in the global FTA trend, and that the game of 'FTA catch-up' with other regions (especially Europe and Latin America) should be quickly initiated in accordance to their broad market access security interests. It was this realisation together with the catalysing effects of the 1997/98 East Asian financial crisis that helped spark the new FTA trend in the Asia-Pacific.

The catalysing role of the 1997/98 crisis can be viewed from two main perspectives. First, it created the general conditions for 'imperative co-operation' in that bilateral FTAs were perceived as integral to better managing economic interdependence in the region, and this of course particularly applied to East Asia states. The second and more specific perspective relates to how the crisis brought fatal pressures to bear upon existing regional trade institutions or projects, these being APEC and AFTA. Efforts made within APEC to advance towards its 1994 Bogor summit goals of creating a free trade and investment zone by 2010 and 2020 deadlines[5] had made slow progress by 1997, but the crisis effectively derailed it. At the 1998 summit in Kuala Lumpur, the growing resentment of many East Asian states over the United States' opportunistic behaviour during the crisis helped fuel a heated dispute concerning APEC's Early Voluntary Sectoral Liberalisation (EVSL) scheme, its latest strategy to advance towards the Bogor goals. Japan was especially reluctant to make any concessions in liberalising primary sector (mainly fishing and forestry) trade, despite intense pressure from the United States (Rapkin 2001, Scollay and Gilbert 2001). Unable to broker a resolution, the dispute was referred to the WTO for possible inclusion in the then named 'Millennium Round' agenda for global trade talks, due to be launched at the WTO's Seattle Ministerial in December 1999. This episode further undermined APEC's credibility on trade liberalisation (see Chapter 1).

Meanwhile in Southeast Asia, the crisis had significantly tested ASEAN member states' resolve to keep the AFTA project on track (Mahani 2002). They not only became increasingly preoccupied with domestic economic problems (including recourse to protectionist measures to help crisis-compensate domestic firms) but also saw the crisis considerably undermine the regional market appeal of AFTA itself. Thus, both APEC and AFTA in their own ways could not offer Asia-Pacific states the market access security they sought. This was further exacerbated by the trade institution failure at the global-multilateral level. Although the new bilateral FTA trend in the Asia-Pacific had been initiated before the WTO's abject failure to launch the aforementioned 'Millennium Round' at Seattle in December 1999, this incident and subsequent problems experienced by the organisation did undoubtedly help accelerate the trend over 2000 and 2001.[6] On the one hand, the 'Seattle debacle' did not pose an immediate threat to the market access security interests of Asia-Pacific states, but it did cause them to re-examine their long-term 'insurance policy' options in case the Seattle debacle was the first chain event in a further, more serious undermining of the multilateral trade order. In sum, the combined effects of trade institution failures on various fronts compelled Asia-Pacific states to look to alternative market access routes, and bilateral FTAs were deemed the most practical alternative in this respect during the early phase of this regional trend.

The relationship between the bilateral FTA project trend and APEC is a particularly interesting and one worth exploring further given that trade bilateralism seems to have now totally marginalised a regional trade organisation's (i.e. APEC's) endeavours at advancing trade liberalisation in the Asia-Pacific. On the one hand, these bilateral trade deals are hoped by many to realise APEC's aforementioned 'Bogor objectives' (see Chapter 1 for more analysis on APEC). Bergsten (2000, 2001) has even made the claim that the bilateral approach was APEC's latest trade liberalisation strategy.[7] On the other hand, the new FTA bilateralism has seriously challenged the guiding principles and *modus operandi* of APEC. For example, it denotes a switch in 'reciprocity choice' in trade liberalisation, from the *diffuse* reciprocity principle – on which APEC 'open regionalism' is based[8] – to the *specific* reciprocity basis on which bilateral FTAs are negotiated and have developed. In other words, APEC member states have clearly shown their predilection for simultaneous and direct *quid pro quos* in trade deals (the bilateral way) rather than voluntarily contributing to a common pool of trade liberalisation benefits that all contributors also draw from, that is, diffuse reciprocity, or the APEC way. In this sense, the 'concerted unilateral liberalisation' underlying APEC's Individual Action Plans (1995–96) scheme and the earlier noted EVSL programme have been displaced by the 'concerted bilateral liberalisation' approach.

More importantly, while these proposed bilaterals may be consistent with WTO rules on FTAs (as primarily encoded in Article XXIV), their preferential character runs counter to the fundamental multilateral principles of the WTO. Hence, this discriminatory bilateralism could be viewed as an inversion of APEC's 'open regionalism' and advocacy of multilateralist approaches on trade liberalisation. Bilateral FTA projects may well have made technical breakthroughs on services trade liberalisation, e-commerce, investment and other new complex trade issues from which WTO processes could learn – an argument particularly made by the Singapore Government – but their reconciliation with APEC's core principles remains nevertheless problematic. Furthermore, Bergsten's notion that APEC has primarily facilitated the bilateral FTA phenomenon is highly questionable, at least in a fundamental sense. It has not developed through any formalised APEC framework; it has essentially arisen within the vacuum created by APEC itself on regional trade liberalisation. Indeed, APEC has been from the very beginning subservient to the bilateral FTA process and not vice versa. This is perhaps best demonstrated by how its meetings provide opportunities for member states to talk further about new or existing projects. For example, many of the bilateral FTA projects concluded by the end of 2002 (Singapore–New Zealand, Japan–Singapore, South Korea–Chile, and Australia–Singapore) were initially proposed at previous APEC summit meetings (see Figures 5.2 and 5.5). At the 2002 APEC summit, the United States used the opportunity to launch its 'Enterprise for ASEAN Initiative (EAI)', which offered the future prospect of bilateral free trade agreements to ASEAN countries. After having almost secured its FTA with Singapore by this time, the United States expressed a specific interest in exploring similar bilateral FTA projects with Malaysia, the Philippines and Thailand.[9] Meanwhile, Japan and Mexico used the 2002 APEC summit platform to announce their intention to conclude a bilateral FTA by next year's summit, and Indonesia's Trade and Industry Minister, Rini Soewandi, suggested to Japan's Senior Vice Minister of Economy, Trade and Industry, Sanae Takaichi, that the two countries consider a bilateral FTA project between them.[10]

We should not, however, assume that these new bilateral FTA projects avoid similar difficulties experienced by APEC on advancing trade liberalisation in the region. Many of the obstacles encountered by APEC initiatives in the 1990s remain in place. Addressing entrenched protectionist interests is the key problem area for bilateral FTA negotiators, and this especially relates to agriculture. Even during the negotiations of the Japan–Singapore Economic Partnership Agreement (JSEPA), the Japanese agricultural lobby became notably anxious, though not because of competition from Singapore's agriculture sector (surely, only the Vatican's is less significant by international comparison) but because of the precedent it would set for other future FTAs Tokyo intended to sign. Elsewhere, highly competitive American farmers continue to lobby Washington over allowing free market access to their even more competitive Australian rivals. Having said this, South Korea and Chile were able to come to a workable compromise over agricultural trade, an issue that nonetheless delayed the conclusion of this one of the Asia-Pacific's original new FTA projects.[11] In other sectors the United States took Singapore (often portrayed as the paragon of free trade virtue) to task over services trade protectionism during FTA negotiations. The final sticking point, however, was the United States' contentious demand upon the Singapore Government to relinquish its contingent use of capital controls, utilised in the event of a financial crisis. Washington also made the same demands in its FTA deal with Chile.[12] In another instance of US neo-liberal conditionality that extended beyond trade liberalisation, President Bush made it clear in his recent EAI proposal states that FTAs would only follow if ASEAN member states committed themselves to a programme of (neo-liberal) economic reform.[13] This approach may prove problematic given residual suspicions and criticism in many parts of post-crisis East Asia of the US's ardent neo-liberal advocacy.

More generally, textiles, footwear, petrochemicals, steel and other sensitive trade sectors represent additional 'hard rocks' in the path of concluding bilateral FTA deals in the Asia-Pacific. Another problem is that FTA projects require a proportionately high level of diplomatic resources, especially in comparison to multilateral trade negotiations where diplomatic economies of scale are realisable. While this partly explains the slow progress made in the new FTA policies of many Asia-Pacific states, many governments have been willing to prioritise diplomatic resources to their development. For instance, Japan, Singapore and other countries have increased recruitment in their foreign affairs and trade ministries to facilitate this. But these bilateral agreements are not just about trade liberalisation. In keeping with an emerging global trend they are invariably 'broad band' in nature, incorporating a range of trade and investment facilitation measures, economic co-operation initiatives and so on. The formal names of these agreements (e.g. Japan–Singapore Economic Partnership Agreement, New Zealand–Singapore Closer Economic Partnership, Japan–Korea Economic Agenda 21) are indicative of this. For example, the JSEPA comprises establishing mutual recognition agreements on rules and standards, the use of a commercial dispute resolution mechanism, as well as measures on government procurement, competition policy, e-commerce, multi-media, science and technology, investment promotion, tourism and educational exchange. Such measures aim to cultivate a wider *micro-networking* between policy-makers, business communities and other societal groups from the participating countries through broadening the points of network contact between them. Another reason for this FTA-plus approach is that most bilateral FTA perpetrators retain only single-digit average tariff rates on imported industrial products, and therefore the actual benefits of duty free trade are relatively marginal. Thus, additional measures make them more worthwhile to bilateral partners in pure economic terms.

3. The ASEAN Plus Three (APT) framework

The APT framework consists of the ten member states of ASEAN and the three Northeast Asian states of Japan, China and South Korea. It is historically significant as APT represents the first real coalescing of an East Asian economic grouping. The framework was established in December 1997 at its inaugural summit convened in Kuala Lumpur, during the height of the region's financial crisis. Much of the academic literature on APT tends to concentrate on background context analysis and what the regional grouping could potentially become, rather than the actual substance of the framework and its achievements to date (Tay 2001, Webber 2001, Stubbs 2002). This is to some extent understandable given the long-standing interest and speculation concerning East Asia's regional identity and relative position in an international economic system that itself has become increasingly defined by deepening regionalism. Thus, questions about where APT has come from and where it could go are critically important for many.

The usual starting point in addressing the first of these questions is to make the links between the APT and the East Asian Economic Grouping (EAEG), a precursorial failed venture into East Asian regional bloc-building first proposed by Malaysia's Prime Minister Mohammed Mahathir in December 1990.[14] This was soon revised to the East Asian Economic Caucus

(EAEC) in an attempt to make the initiative look less 'bloc-like'. Malaysia presented the EAEC initiative to fellow East Asian countries as an informal consultative mechanism for discussing matters of policy that may in turn have led to consensus-building on trade and economic issues. It was intended that the strategic value of such an arrangement would be particularly revealed in multilateral fora, notably at the time of its conception in asserting the region's collective interests at the Uruguay Round of the General Agreement on Tariffs and Trade (GATT). The EAEC initiative was tabled at the 1992 ASEAN summit in Singapore and at the 1993 APEC summit in Seattle. However, the United States and Australia were particularly hostile to any attempt to create an exclusivist Asian trade grouping, and moreover that undermined the fundamental integrity of APEC. Indonesia and Thailand were also suspicious of Malaysia's geo-strategic motives behind the initiative, and other East Asian states responded in a generally lukewarm or circumspect manner to the EAEC concept.

In the immediate years that followed, ASEAN member states focused on launching their AFTA project, and East Asian states in general looked to APEC's new grand vision of creating a 'free trade and investment zone' across the Asia-Pacific in accordance to the previously noted 'Bogor goals'. Yet, these were essentially sub-regional and trans-regional ventures from an East Asian perspective. The next step towards a coalescent East Asian economic grouping came when the region's ten representing states of the Asia-Europe Meeting (ASEM) framework assembled to conduct preparatory talks during the latter half of 1995 before the inaugural ASEM summit itself held in March 1996 at Bangkok.[15] Similarly arranged ASEM-related meetings between East Asian government officials continued after this, and social constructivists have particularly argued that the ASEM process played a vital role in East Asian regional identity-formation, and hence East Asian regionalism *per se*[16] (Gilson 2002). Around this time, Japan, China and South Korea all expressed their interest in establishing regularised summits with the ASEAN group. Southeast Asian states' positive response to this interest led to the first APT summit in December 1997. This, of course, coincided with the outbreak of the region's financial crisis, and the APT framework was thus inevitably forged by crisis-related events and subsequent developments.

In the run up to the inaugural APT summit, Japan had proposed the idea of creating an Asian Monetary Fund (AMF) in September 1997 as a response to the unravelling currency crisis in Southeast Asia. The AMF was conceived as a standby fund of US$100 billion to provide emergency financial assistance to East Asian countries whose currencies were subject to disruptive speculative pressures. Taiwan also backed this Japanese initiative, whereby the two offered to pool their considerable foreign exchange reserves in order to operationalise the AMF. However, the United States was opposed to the idea because of concern over how the AMF would undermine the multilateral competence of the IMF, and hence indirectly lead to a loss of American structural power and influence over the international financial system (Rapkin 2001). This was despite Japan's argument that the AMF would be a new facility to provide additional resources to supplement those of the IMF, if required. China was against the AMF proposal too, mainly because of Taiwan's involvement but also owing to this perceived hegemonic manoeuvring of Japan's within the East Asian regional political economy. Consequently, other East Asian states proved reluctant in backing the AMF initiative.

While this first attempt at developing regional financial governance mechanisms in East Asia failed, other more acceptable proposals from Japan followed, and this whole process was to later converge with the APT process. In October 1998, Japan unilaterally launched its New Miyazawa Initiative (NMI, named after Japan's then finance minister), which was primarily based on US$30 billion of extended liquidity provision for East Asian economies if they again found themselves in financial crisis. Half of this amount involved a commitment by Tokyo to guarantee sovereign bonds issued by crisis-afflicted governments (Indonesia, Malaysia, the Philippines, South Korea and Thailand) on international capital markets. This would assist the recapitalisation of failing banks and corporations, and constituted the NMI's long-term financial support facility. The other half was dedicated to facilitate shorter-term financial support, involving in effect bilateral currency swap arrangements that were offered to those same countries. A currency swap is an agreement to exchange one currency for another and to reverse the transaction at some later date. The intention here was for Japan to swap its US dollar reserves for under pressure local currencies in an attempt to head off a full-blown financial crisis. However, only Malaysia and South Korea took up Japan's offer, entering into respective US$2.5 billion and US$5 billion agreements under the NMI.[17] Other measures introduced by the NMI included a US$3 billion Asian Currency Crisis Support Facility (established at the Asian Development Bank, and designed to support East Asian countries raise funds through guarantees, interest subsidies and other means), a US$1.1 billion Trade Insurance Facility (offered to Malaysia and Thailand) and US$1.2 billion of trade credit guarantees offered by the Export–Import Bank of Japan to the Philippines and Malaysia.

East Asian countries generally welcomed the NMI, especially after how the crisis had by this time revealed the IMF's failures and inadequacies in dealing with the region's financial problems[18] (Hughes 2000). Indeed, some similarities may be drawn between the perceived multilateral institution failure of the IMF and the emergence of new regional financial governance mechanisms in East Asia on the one hand, and the WTO's own perceived failures and the growing FTA trend in the Asia-Pacific on the other. With both multilateral institutions failing to meet certain East Asian expectations, the region's states looked to alternative routes at the regional level. The NMI both provided a foundation stone for later developments in East Asian financial co-operation, as well as helped catalyse discussions on regional finance at the second APT summit, convened at Hanoi in December 1998. Here, East Asia's leaders agreed under the 'Hanoi Plan of Action' to develop new methods for improving regional financial stability. Also at Hanoi, Japan announced the introduction of another financial support scheme, its US$5 billion Special Yen Loan Facility, whereby it would offer low interest, long-term loans for the purpose of assisting infrastructure developments in East Asia's crisis-afflicted economies. In addition, China's proposal for regularised APT finance meetings at the vice-ministerial level was accepted and operationalised in March 1999. This was upgraded to full ministerial level the following year at Chiang Mai, Thailand, where APT finance ministers met at the sidelines of an Asian Development Bank (ADB) meeting in May 2000 and proposed the Chiang Mai Initiative (CMI).

A few months later at the Fourth APT summit held in November 2000 at Singapore, East Asian leaders formally endorsed the CMI plan, which essentially constituted a more regional approach to averting another financial crisis. At its centre are a series of bilateral currency swap agreements between APT member states. As Ravenhill (2002) is keen to point out, the CMI is not an 'AMF mark II' because it rests upon a combination of bilateral agreements rather than the creation of a regional institution. Moreover, the liquidity provision involved is nowhere near as large as that proposed under the ill-fated AMF. Within the CMI, the core ASEAN economies agreed to raise their contributions to their own pre-existing ASEAN Swap Agreement (ASA) facility from a total of US$200 million to US$1 billion.[19] Additional currency swap deals were initiated across APT's wider membership, with a total of 14 bilateral arrangements either signed or to be concluded by May 2003 – the date set for completing the whole CMI swap network[20] (Figure 5.6). Taken together with the ASA, these currency deals amounted to US$36 billion. This represents a mere fraction of the combined foreign exchange reserves at the disposal of East Asian states, which together would total at around US$1 trillion.[21] According to many analysts, such low swap arrangement sums are likely to prove insufficient to fend off a major speculative 'attack' on an unstable currency (Chalongphob 2002), a point similarly made by Jürgen Rüland in Chapter 4.

There are a number of possible reasons why the CMI does not involve more ambitious levels of currency swap funding. First, there are competing demands upon East Asian forex reserves, and substantial shares of them may be tied up elsewhere.[22] Second, the CMI is still a relatively young arrangement and it was perhaps politically expedient to start with relatively small sums at the outset. In the event of further financial turbulence, or warning signs of another full-blown crisis, we may expect the CMI's bilateral currency swap network to be accordingly fortified at relatively short notice. Thus, what is more important at this stage is the initial trust-building exercises that these swap agreements represent. Following on from this is the

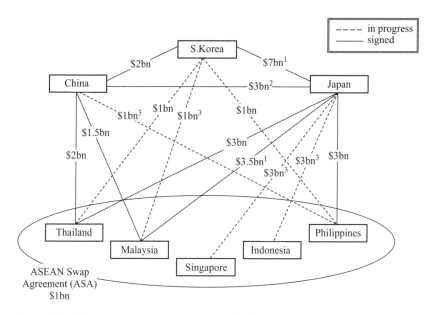

Figure 5.6 APT currency swap agreements under the Chiang Mai initiative (by end of 2002, to be concluded by May 2003).

Notes: 1. Extension of previous swap arrangement negotiated under the New Miyazawa Initiative (NMI); 2. The Japan–China swap is denominated in yen-renminbi, the only agreement not US dollar-based; 3. Provisional figures.

Sources: Henning (2002), various news media reports.

third main reason, which relates to lessons learnt from the AMF episode. The APT member states are wary of the CMI being perceived as a challenge to the IMF's multilateral competence, and therein posing a threat to US foreign economic policy interests. Not only may the relatively small sums involved in the bilateral currency swap agreements be partly intended to allay any AMF-related anxieties, but more importantly operationalising the agreements themselves are subject to IMF conditionality. Under the CMI, only 10 per cent of the initial swap arrangements can be released unconditionally: thereafter beneficiaries must reach an agreement with the IMF on a programme of economic reforms before further assistance is conferred. As Ravenhill (2002) observed, then, 'rather than an alternative to the IMF, the swap arrangements provide a modest, albeit useful, supplement to the Fund's resources and largely subject to its approval' (p. 188). He further notes that APT's Northeast Asian members were particularly keen to demonstrate the CMI's deference to the IMF regime.

Malaysia, though, has maintained vocal opposition to IMF conditionality on the CMI currency swap issue, and will undoubtedly argue for its withdrawal when the whole swap system is reviewed in 2004. Moreover, this review process may present an opportunity for APT member states to fortify the whole CMI system in general. Additional aspects of the CMI currently include: (i) an agreement to exchange information on short-term capital movements in East Asia, including the establishment of an early warning system to monitor signs of emergent financial crises; (ii) the exchange of views among APT members on reforming the international financial architecture; (iii) regularised meetings between deputy or vice-ministers of finance to review all CMI-related developments. Notwithstanding the limited regional ambition demonstrated by the CMI thus far, it nevertheless marks a significant step forward in East Asian financial co-operation, not least because of the almost complete lack of region-wide co-operation in this field before the 1997/98 crisis[23] (Henning 2002).

While the CMI represented the centrepiece project of the APT framework by early 2003, other initiatives and ideas on regional economic co-operation and integration had emerged by this time. There have been projects on promoting small and medium-sized enterprises, the provision of training courses on using environmental technologies, annual APT Ministerial Meetings (e.g. Economic, Labour), discussions on food security issues, and various other programmes such as APT Young Leaders and the e-APT Working Group (Stubbs 2002). In terms of overall practical achievement, the APT framework has thus made advances in regional *co-operation* rather than *integration*. Ideas on how to proceed to the latter have, though, been proposed at recent APT summits. For example, there has been talk of creating an East Asian Free Trade Area or Zone, common market and even full monetary union. These are bold objectives for a young regional framework like APT to aspire, and more generally for a region characterised by 'complex diversity' to achieve. Yet East Asia's leaders understand that these are extremely long-term goals. As Chinese Premier Zhu Rongji commented November 2000 summit, APT is a channel through which to 'gradually establish a framework for regional financial, trade and investment co-operation, and furthermore to realise still greater regional economic integration in a step by step manner'.[24] It is also worth noting that in the EU's antecedent founding Treaty of Rome of 1957 lay the long-term vision of one day establishing a European common market. The point here is that although over-ambitious objectives can prove counterproductive – especially if scheduled deadlines for realising them are missed – longer-term goals provide critical direction and purpose to a regional framework. Moreover, as Hubert Hess, former head of the IMF's East Asia department commented in May 2001 with specific regard to the CMI, 'the announcement of a few swap arrangements may not seem that exciting and their importance can be exaggerated. But if you take the longer-term view of this process, it is clear that East Asia's governments are seeking much greater financial and economic co-operation that will lead ultimately to regional integration.'[25]

The issue of future APT economic integration is connected to how the APT process itself and the new FTA trend have become increasingly conflated. This particularly relates to matters of trade, whereby the APT framework has helped facilitate the development of *bilateral* free trade agreement projects between East Asian states, as well as become the natural forum to discuss *regional* trade integration. On the first of these matters, China and the ASEAN group have especially used APT in every stage of the development of their FTA project: agreement on launching a joint feasibility study was announced at APT's 2000 summit at Singapore; a year later at the 2001 summit in Brunei, both sides came to a general agreement about the terms of the FTA; finally, at the 2002 summit in Phnom Penh, the ASEAN–China FTA was formally signed. At least partly in response to these manoeuvrings by Beijing, Tokyo decided to use APT's 2002 summit to formally launch its Japan–ASEAN Comprehensive Economic Partnership (JACEP) initiative, which could include a FTA element at its centre to be implemented like its ASEAN–China counterpart by 2010.[26] On the very same day, South Korean Prime Minister Kim Suk-soo, announced his country's interest in also signing a FTA deal with ASEAN.[27] This was followed up a few days later, and just after the Phnom Penh summit, with South Korea's proposal for a bilateral FTA project with Singapore.[28]

What is clear is that new FTA projects involving East Asian states exclusively are increasingly converging around the APT process. Moreover, in the APT's East Asia Study Group report[29] – submitted at the 2002 Phnom Penh summit and which examined possible ways to further strengthen economic relations between the region's states – the possibility of creating an East Asia Free Trade Agreement (EAFTA) was included. A feasibility study into establishing an EAFTA is already underway, although the report stated this was, 'a long-term goal', and should, 'take into account the variety of differences in developmental stages and the varied interests of the countries in the region'.[30] This constituted an acknowledgement of the East Asian region's own 'complex diversity', and summed up the challenge of realising such an objective. The following section discusses how an EAFTA may be established through a bilateral-to-regional evolutionary process, whereby such a regional trade arrangement may emerge from a 'latticed' foundation of dense bilateral trade agreements. For example, an FTA network based on eventually realised ASEAN–China, Japan–ASEAN, South Korea–ASEAN, AFTA, and Northeast Asian (see later discussion on this) arrangements would more or less create an EAFTA by a *de facto* process.

Recent developments within APT are indicative of another key dimension of this book, namely the conflation between economic and security co-operation. As Jürgen Haacke explains in more detail in Chapter 7, the 12 October 2002 Bali bomb attacks served to focus East Asian leaders' minds more sharply on dealing with terrorism and new security threats generally. This, combined with the US's revelations that North Korea was pursuing a nuclear weapons programme, were major agenda items at the 2002 APT summit in Phnom Penh. A more formalised broadening of APT's remit into the security domain may well transpire in the near future. For instance, the East Asia Study Group report also recommended that an 'East Asian summit' framework be established, in which it was foreseen that political and security fields would be firmly incorporated into the APT framework (see also Chapter 4). In sum, the APT process in general has approached a series of critical junctures in its still relatively young development.

4. Conclusion: new economic bilateralism, new regional political economy?

The main purpose of this section is to discuss the extent to which the twin processes of new economic bilateralism embodied in the new FTA trend and the APT framework provide some form of sub-structural foundation for economic regionalism to develop in East Asia and the Asia-Pacific. We should initially point out that of the two trends studied, trade bilateralism is far more salient than finance bilateralism. First, the former involves a far greater number of participating states than the latter, and also constitutes a much denser pattern of economic co-operation arrangements. Second, and following on from this, the former is extant over the Asia-Pacific and the latter within East Asia only. Third, and perhaps most critically, the new FTA trend is an 'active' form of co-operation in contrast to the 'dormant-until-activated' nature of the CMI currency swap network. Despite these notable differences, useful parallels can be drawn between these respective trends of bilateral economic co-operation, as well as conclusions made on their twinned impact on the Asia-Pacific regional political economy.

In each case, bilateralism seems to have supplanted preceding regionalised ventures at advancing certain aspects of economic co-operation. Both the new FTA trend and the CMI arrangement within APT emerged out of perceived or demonstrated failures of incumbent regional (as well as global-multilateral) organisations to offer at least East Asian states a sure and trusted passage out of the region's financial crisis. As noted earlier, APEC's and ASEAN's inadequacies to provide substantive crisis management solutions were clearly exposed in the late 1990s (Webber 2001, Dent 2003). In relation to Asia-Pacific trade diplomacy, bilateralism has emerged as the preferred mechanism for realising market access objectives, and consequently made APEC virtually redundant on advancing trade liberalisation in the trans-region. With regard to regional financial co-operation, Japan's ill-fated AMF project proved to be too diplomatically, and perhaps also technically, ambitious. Again, a bilateral approach was deemed more practical on both these accounts. Returning to trade, 'one-on-one' (i.e. bilateral) agreements to some degree negate the 'complex diversity' predicament in that resolving problems at the domestic political level (e.g. over agriculture) becomes easier if just a couple of countries are involved in the 'two-level game' dynamic rather than a multiple, asymmetric set of trade partners. This essentially explains why bilateral FTAs have flourished and why the EVSL scheme under APEC abjectly failed. The proliferation of bilateral FTAs may seem a rather messy and diplomatic resource-intensive method of forging trade agreements but they can be more easily brokered within a region as diverse as the Asia-Pacific than plurilateral or regional accords.

A similar principle is at work within the current trade agreements sought by China, Japan and the United States with the ASEAN regional group. Although the ASEAN–China FTA is supposed to be implemented on a 'country-to-subregion' basis, Singapore, Thailand and the Philippines have expressed an interest in negotiating implementation by bilateral means with China.[31] Likewise, the United States intends to eventually establish bilateral FTAs with ASEAN states that are WTO members within its recently proposed Enterprise for ASEAN Initiative. Similarly, the JACEP project could involve Japan negotiating a series of bilateral agreements negotiated separately with ASEAN countries. Japan already has a FTA with Singapore, and JACEP is further reinforced by recent parallel initiated FTA projects with Indonesia, Malaysia, the Philippines and Thailand. In addition, Japan's earlier attempts at regional financial diplomacy (e.g. the NMI) were essentially founded on a comparable hub-and-spoke bilateralism approach, which has been effectively extended within the CMI bilateral currency swap arrangements with China and South Korea acting as additional but more minor 'hubs' within the region-wide system. More generally, bilateral agreements tend to pose less of a threat to outsiders than regional 'bloc-type' agreements, even if they are supposedly based on 'open regionalism'. This principle may be applied to financial diplomacy as well as trade: the CMI's bilateral currency swap network may be perceived by some as a stealthy means to forge closer regionalised ties without offending or confronting the United States with an AMF-style scheme (Bowles 2002).

There is also the matter of bilateral-to-regional evolution to consider. Bilateralism may be the preferred means to foster economic co-operation in East Asia and the Asia-Pacific but this process may eventually lead to the development of new regionalist forms of co-operation and integration as the pattern of bilateral links matures and becomes increasingly dense. The *micro-networking* principle outlined earlier under the new bilateral FTA trend plays an important part in this 'lattice regionalism' process, whereby the 'broad band' nature of the FTA bring different policy-making, business and civil societal communities into closer network contact with the others across the Asia-Pacific. This is accompanied by a *macro-networking* dynamic operating at the inter-state level. For example, there has been recurrent talk of 'rationalising' bilateral FTA subsets into plurilateral FTAs, and this bilateral-to-plurilateral trend has already begun. In October 2002, Singapore, New Zealand and Chile announced plans to establish a 'Pacific-3', or P-3 trilateral

FTA by 2004. Singapore and New Zealand have already signed a bilateral FTA, and Chile has bilateral FTA projects in progress with both (Figure 5.5). Notwithstanding the challenge of harmonising customs procedures between all three economies, a trilateral arrangement offers significant advantages over a series of separate bilaterals, not least for firms trading across all three markets that now only have to comply to the customs procedures and rules of one unified, *macro-networked* system. This represents an achievable objective for a small subset of already well-established bilateral FTA protagonists, and thus the 'complex diversity' predicament far more manageable than a larger plurilateral arrangement would present at this stage. Another trilateral FTA project was recently proposed by Chinese Premier Zhu Rongji at the 2002 APT summit, which would involve China, Japan and South Korea. Zhu more specifically suggested that a feasibility study be first conducted into the establishment of a Northeast Asia Free Trade Area (NEAFTA), although at the time of writing Beijing had yet to receive an official response from either Tokyo or Seoul regarding this proposal.[32] This is primarily because the domestic politics calculus of a NEAFTA is far more complex than its P-3 counterpart. Further evidence of macro-networking includes the CER–ASEAN Closer Economic Partnership initiative launched in September 2002, although as yet it does not comprise a FTA element.[33] It is conceivable that the other forms of bilateral-to-plurilateral FTA evolution may evolve in the future, as suggested by Figure 5.7.

In sum, the new FTA trend and the CMI currency swap network is indicative of new 'thinking regionally, acting bilaterally' approaches to co-operation in the Asia-Pacific. Thus, the new economic bilateralism is significantly shaping both the discourse and practical development of new and prospective forms of regional economic co-operation and integration between Asia-Pacific states. Yet, caution is warranted. Despite the further intensification of the bilateral FTA project trend, only seven new agreements have actually been signed between Asia-Pacific states since the late 1990s. The remainder have mostly taken much longer to develop than expected. A much higher number of bilateral FTA deals must first be concluded, implemented and then evaluated before Asia-Pacific states are likely to commit themselves to progressing to plurilateral, sub-regional or wider regional trade deals based on 'latticed' bilateral foundations. Regarding APT and regional financial co-operation, it has been noted that the CMI bilateral currency swap network essentially rests on 'dormant' co-operation arrangements: that is co-operation itself will only be truly activated in the event of another financial crisis emerging. Chalongphob (2002) has suggested that the best strategy for progressing regional financial co-operation beyond the current CMI system would be to develop longer-term sources of financing for those countries facing short-term debt problems. For instance, the creation of East Asian bond market within the APT framework would be a means to achieve a long-term recycling of funds from surplus countries to deficit countries in the

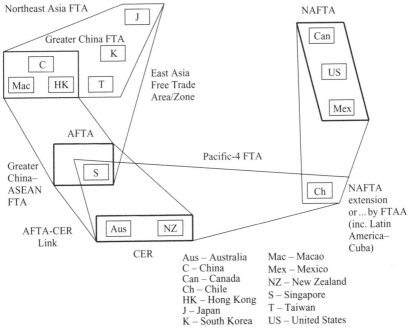

Figure 5.7   Bilateral-to-plurilateral FTA evolution?

region. The development of some form of exchange rate system or mechanism between APT member states is another option, as practised by the European Union before the introduction of the euro, although East Asian states will probably not be ready for this level of policy co-ordination and co-operation for some years, or even decades. In conclusion, then, while various obstacles lay in the path of deepening regional economic co-operation and integration in the Asia-Pacific, the new trade and finance bilateralism as embodied in the new FTA trend and the APT framework has at least shone some light upon possible and most practicable ways forward.

Notes

This chapter is partly based on research funded by an ESRC grant (award number: R000 223 715).

1. The term 'regional political economy' is a derivative heuristic device stemming from international political economy (IPE) analysis. By regional political economy, we are thus referring to the social, political and economic arrangements affecting a region's systems of production, exchange and distribution and the mix of values reflected therein, thus drawing upon Strange's (1994) definition of IPE but with 'region' substituted for 'global'. This study focuses on how recent trends in

economic bilateralism are shaping new arrangements and systems of regionalised co-operation, as well as future scenarios of regional integration, and hence the specific preference for 'regional' political economy over IPE.

2. After TPA was secured, USTR Robert Zoellick announced a series of new free trade initiatives. New FTA projects were proposed not just with Asia-Pacific states but also to 'strategic partner' states in Africa (e.g. Egypt, Morocco, South Africa) and Central America (Costa Rica, El Salvador, Guatemala, Honduras, Nicaragua). In addition, the progress was made in late 2002 on progressing the Free Trade Area of the Americas (FTAA) project, and around the same time Zoellick announced a proposal for global tariff-free trade to be achieved by 2015.

3. *ABC News Online*, 13.12.2002.

4. For the purposes of this analysis, PTAs refer to various forms of trade agreements where preferential access has been conferred, and hence include FTAs, custom unions, common markets, etc.

5. Developed country members of APEC were supposed to meet the 2010 deadline while the group's developing members were given until 2020 to meet these goals as set out at Bogor in 1994.

6. This has been acknowledged by a good majority of interviewed trade policy-makers from around the Asia-Pacific in interviews conducted over 2002 by this author.

7. He later seemed to ignore this idea in a later 'strategy' paper (Bergsten 2002).

8. APEC member states are supposed to unilaterally liberalise their trade policy regimes on a non-discriminatory, 'most favoured nation' (MFN) basis, thus being closely compliant to the WTO's multilateral approach. While there has been much debate about the exact implications of APEC's diffuse reciprocity method (i.e. whereby signed up member states profit over time from the aggregated benefits expected from combined total liberalisation), it could in theory mean that APEC member states are supposed to lower their trade barriers against all WTO members and not just on an intra-regional group basis, hence the term 'open regionalism'.

9. *ABC News OnLine*, 27.10.2002.

10. *Blue News World English*, 25.10.2002.

11. This project was first proposed in November 1998 and was eventually signed in October 2002.

12. *Straits Times*, 12.12.2002.

13. Those interested in free trade talks with the United States would first have to sign a trade and investment framework agreement, or TIFA, covering a range of areas, such as regulatory transparency and intellectual property protection. By February 2003, the United States had signed TIFAs with Brunei, Indonesia, the Philippines and Thailand.

14. Earlier, South Korea had called for an Asian Common Market in 1970, and Japan later proposed in 1988 that an Asian Network be established (Stubbs 2002: 441).

15. These ten states were Japan, China, South Korea and the ASEAN-7 (Brunei, Indonesia, Malaysia, Philippines, Singapore, Thailand and Vietnam), who came together with the 15 member states of the European Union within ASEM.

16. As Japanese finance minister Miyazawa himself commented, 'these talks with Europe are helping us build up our own Asian identity' (*Financial Times*, 16.01.2001).

17. As Figure 5.6 shows, these agreements were later upgraded to US$3.5 billion and US$7 billion respectively under the Chiang Mai Initiative.

18. In a November 1997 meeting between officials from 15 Asia-Pacific states, the 'Manila Framework' reaffirmed the principle that funding would only be conferred to crisis-afflicted countries after they had agreed on a 'bailout' agreement with the IMF. In the months that followed, South Korea, Indonesia and Thailand accepted IMF 'bailout' loan programmes that amounted to around US$100 billion. The Philippines – another crisis-afflicted country – was already in an IMF programme by the time of the regional crisis, while Malaysia famously refused IMF assistance. According to Feldstein (1998), the IMF view that the South Korean, Thai and Indonesian Governments would not be able to service its debts unless a broad programme of structural reform is implemented only served to undermine investor confidence still further, resulting in bond-rating agencies downgrading Korean debt to junk bond status. He further argued that the IMF's macroeconomic austerity measures killed off both sick and healthy firms alike.

19. This ASEAN scheme had been established back in 1977.

20. *Reuters*, 27.11.2001. May 2003 was the planned date for the then next APT finance ministers meeting that was again to take place at the sidelines of an ADB meeting, this time at Istanbul.

21. By October 2002, Japan's forex reserves stood at US$461 billion, China's at US$266 billion, South Korea's at US$117 billion and ASEAN had a combined total of US$204 billion (*Korea Economic Update*, December 2002). These were comparatively very large sums. For example, at the same time the United States' forex reserves stood at around US$60 billion.

22. For example, Ravenhill (2002) notes that a sizable share of Japan's forex reserves is tied up in US Treasury securities.

23. See Chapter 2 for more discussion on this issue.

24. *International Herald Tribune*, 27.11.2000.

25. *Financial Times*, 14.05.2001.

26. *Asahi Shimbun*, 05.11.2002.

27. *Korea Times*, 05.11.2002.

28. *Straits Times*, 08.11.2002.

29. The Study Group was launched in March 2001.

30. *Japan Times*, 14.10.2002.

31. *Business Times* (Singapore), 'Bilateral talks with Beijing if Others do so', 14.12.2002.

32. *Japan Times*, 05.11.2002. The three states had already initiated a new Northeast Asia summit framework earlier in 2002, and have increased co-operation on trade, environment protection, information technology, and other miscellaneous areas in recent years. It should also be noted that South Korea has traditionally been the strongest advocate of a Northeast Asian FTA in the past. Indeed, leading up to the 2002 APT summit, South Korea's Finance Minister, Jeon Yun-churl, suggested that such a trilateral arrangement be considered. *Financial Times*, 29.10.2002.

33. *Straits Times*, 14.09.2002.

References

Bergsten, C.F. (2000) 'Back to the Future: APEC Looks at Subregional Trade Agreements to Achieve Free Trade Goal', speech given at *PBEC luncheon*, 31 October, Washington DC.

Bergsten, C.F. (2001) 'Brunei: A Turning Point for APEC?', *International Economics: Policy Briefs, No.01–1*, Institute for International Economics, Washington DC.

Bergsten, C.F. (2002) 'Globalisation and Shared Prosperity: The Role of APEC', presentation to the *Dialogue on Globalisation and Shared Prosperity*, Merida, 26 May, Mexico.

Bowles, P. (2002) 'Asia's Post-Crisis Regionalism: Bringing the State Back In, Keeping the (United) States Out', *Review of International Political Economy*, Vol. 9(2), pp. 230–56.

Chalongphob, S. (2002) 'East Asian Financial Co-operation: An Assessment of the Rationale', paper presented at the *East Asian Cooperation* conference, Institute of Asia Pacific Studies/Centre for APEC & East Asian Cooperation, Chinese Academy of Social Sciences, August 22–23, Beijing.

Dent, C.M. (2003) 'Networking the Region? The Emergence and Impact of Asia-Pacific Bilateral Free Trade Agreement Projects', *The Pacific Review*, Vol. 16(1), pp. 1–28.

Dobson, W. (2001) 'Deeper Integration in East Asia: Regional Institutions and the International Economic System', *The World Economy*, Vol. 24(8), pp. 995–1018.

Feldstein, M. (1998) 'Refocusing the IMF', *Foreign Affairs*, Vol. 77(2), pp. 20–33.

Gilson, J. (2002) *Asia Meets Europe: Interregionalism and the Asia-Europe Meeting*, Edwin Elgar Cheltenham.

Henning, C.R. (2002) *East Asian Financial Co-operation*, Institute for International Economics, Washington DC.

Hughes, C.W. (2000) 'Japanese Policy and the East Asian Currency Crisis: Abject Defeat or Quiet Victory?', *Review of International Political Economy*, Vol. 7(2), pp. 219–53.

Lloyd, P. (2002) 'New Bilateralism in the Asia-Pacific', *The World Economy*, Vol. 25(9), pp. 1279–96.

Mahani, Z.A. (2002) 'ASEAN Integration: At Risk of Going in Different Directions', *The World Economy*, Vol. 25(9), pp. 1263–77.

Rapkin, D. (2001) 'The US, Japan, and the Power to Block: The APEC and AMF Cases', *The Pacific Review*, Vol. 14(3), pp. 373–410.

Ravenhill, J. (2002) 'A Three Bloc World? The New East Asian Regionalism', *International Relations of the Asia-Pacific*, Vol. 2, pp. 168–95.

Ravenhill, J. (2003) 'The New Bilateralism in the Asia-Pacific', *Third World Quarterly*, Vol. 24(3).

Scollay, R. and Gilbert, J.P. (2001) *New Regional Trading Arrangements in the Asia-Pacific*, Institute for International Economics, Washington DC.

Strange, S. (1994) *States and Markets*, Pinter, London.

Stubbs, R. (2002) 'ASEAN Plus Three: Emerging East Asian Regionalism?', *Asian Survey*, Vol. 42(3), pp. 440–55.

Tay, S. (2001) 'ASEAN Plus 3: Challenges and Cautions about a New Regionalism', *Singapore Institute of International Affairs Reader*, Vol. 1(1), pp. 21–44.

US Department of State (2002) *Free Trade, Free People*, Washington File, 4 November 2002.

Webber, D. (2001) 'Two Funerals and a Wedding? The Ups and Downs of Regionalism in East Asia and asia-Pacific After the Asian Crisis', *The Pacific Review*, Vol. 14(3), pp. 339–72.

6
Sea Power in the Asia-Pacific at the Turn of the Millennium

Eric Grove

1. The ocean planet

'Earth' is a very bad name for our planet; 'Oceania' would be better. Two thirds of it is covered by sea and although the world's inhabitants live on that relatively small part of the surface that is above water, most live close to the ocean, some 70 per cent of the world's population living within 100 miles of a coastline. The historic importance of water transport as, until the last century and a half, the only effective long-distance medium has had indelible effects on patterns of trade and population distribution, not least in the Asia-Pacific. Moreover, sea transport still has vital advantages over other modes for the carriage of all but those items with the highest value to weight ratios. It is cheaper to transport a tonne of coal 5000 miles in a bulk carrier than 500 kilometres by rail. Shipping dominates world trade, some 90 per cent by volume going by sea (US Office of Naval Intelligence 1997). Although Paul Kennedy's neo-Mackinderite analysis of the declining utility of sea power dominated discourse on the subject until recently mature consideration leads one to question it, especially after victory in the Cold War can be added to World Wars One and Two as 'three in a row' for maritime against continental coalitions. Thanks to Sumida (1997) we know that Mahan must not be bowdlerised and misinterpreted as he so often was from 1890 onwards. The latter's ideas were richer and more diverse than implied by the first section of *The Influence of Sea Power Upon History*, a section that it turns out was forced on him by his publishers. Mahan soon recognised that naval power did not necessarily depend on a large merchant fleet. Moreover, he argued for a naval consortium of like-minded states (as we have today, based around the US Navy) rather than solely based *on* an American naval monopoly. One must be careful now to use the term 'neo-Mahanian' paradigm, referring to those classical and oversimplified tenets that have been understood to stem from Mahan's writings by generations of navalists.

2. Globalisation versus neo-Mahanianism

The mercantilistic identity of state, merchant ship and warship that lay at the heart of 'neo-Mahanianism' was one of the first victims of globalisation. As an American source has put it: 'Maritime commerce today means multinational corporations, multiple countries, owners, crews, cargoes, and insurers. Over 90 000 merchant ships ply the world's oceans, flying 197 separate flags, a number greater than the total number of countries recognised by the United Nations. Their decks are laden with millions of containers each filled with diverse cargoes. A merchant ship at sea today represents the ultimate "multinational". Finding out "who's in charge" can often take months of legal enquiry' (US Office of Naval Intelligence 1997: 8). This source quotes a notional tanker owned in Hong Kong SAR, insured in London, reinsured in Germany, managed in Singapore and flying the Panamanian flag. Chartered by an Iranian oil company its cargo is traded between US, Japanese and South Korean interests during its voyage, all under the legal title of a mortgagee, an offshore bank based in the Cayman Islands. The officers are Norwegian, the seamen Filipinos and Bangladeshis. It is a matter of debate whether this spreads interests so thin that it is impossible to decide whose are being threatened should something untoward happen or spreads the impact to involve many countries significantly. Certainly it makes the issue of naval protection somewhat problematic.

The major merchant flags are no longer the major naval flags. There is some, but limited overlap. The most significant navies are perhaps those of the United States, the United Kingdom, France, Russia, Japan, India, China, Taiwan, the Netherlands, Spain, Germany, Italy, Canada, Australia and Brazil. The largest merchant registers (over 10 million gross register tons) in the late 1990s were the Bahamas, Cyprus, Greece, Liberia, Panama, Malta, China, Japan, Singapore, the United States and Russia (Janes 1997). Of course this does not reflect beneficial ownership; indeed over half the world's shipping fly flags of a different nationality from that of the owner. The Liberian flag is in many ways an American offshore register: it is even administered from the United States. When countries are graded under beneficial ownership the leading countries are China, Denmark, Germany, Greece, Italy, Japan, Norway, Singapore, Taiwan, the United Kingdom and the United States (Janes 2002). Some countries, such as the United Kingdom, argue that beneficial ownership rather than flag entitles a ship to naval protection under the self-defence provision of the UN Charter. Others, such as the Americans and French will in certain circumstances defend any ship under attack. The situation, however, remains confused and the only certainty is the breakdown of the neo-Mahanian paradigm in its simplest form. Yet there are connections between the economic use of the sea and naval capabilities. The world's major trading nations are the United States, Germany, Japan, France, the United Kingdom, Italy, Canada, Russia, the Netherlands, Belgium, China and South Korea. All (even little Belgium in terms of the reach for its mine countermeasures forces) are significant naval powers. When one comes to sea use therefore Mahan (or his followers) may still be alive after all.

3. Asia-Pacific navies

They seem to be particularly alive in the Asia-Pacific. Only in this region is there a congruence of significant naval powers and large national mercantile marines. In part this is because of the rather selective application of free trade principles in the region, not least by the United States which imposes strict cabotage regulations forcing traffic between Alaska, Hawaii and the ports of the Western continental United States into ships flying more than one star together with the stripes. Yet even here there are key factors mitigating the neo-Mahanian model. Japan, historically one of the greatest naval powers and a nation crucially dependent on seaborne energy imports, is limited in her naval capabilities by the pacifist political culture inherited from the Second World War. Although she is beginning to view her Maritime Self-Defence Force (MSDF) in slightly more 'normal' terms, it will be some time before she will be willing to act, and equally as important be accepted and trusted by her neighbours as acting as a normal naval power.

China is also limited, this time by a culture that has historically downplayed maritime endeavour.[1] The Communist regime for a long time was as 'continentalist' as any preceding Imperial predecessor. Its 'peoples war' rhetoric was decidedly unhelpful to the development of naval forces whose essence has always been high technology. The PRC Navy, despite creditable attempts to increase its capabilities over the last two decades, is still more a coastal projection force than anything else. This may not matter so much in the short- to medium-term as its main areas of potential interest are around Taiwan and in the South China Sea. Yet China remains far from being a great naval power, and she will have great problems in mobilising her mushrooming resources to make herself one. The dependence of sea trade of the newly industrialised countries (NICs) of the region makes naval capabilities to maintain the free movement of shipping – if only in the near vicinity – very advisable. Not for nothing have Taiwan, South Korea and Singapore all invested heavily in naval forces in recent years and all deploy impressive fleets in capability, if not in reach. The Taiwanese Navy is especially impressive, at present the equal of its Communist rival in overall capability and perhaps even sheer size.

A major problem with all the navies of the western part of the region, however, is technology. There are two dimensions to this: electronic and mechanical. Naval forces pioneered both information warfare and the related 'revolution in military affairs' long before either term was invented. Led by the British in the 1950s, the major navies developed computerised combat data systems and electronic links to network them. An unseen revolution took place in naval warfare, a revolution as important as that from sail to steam that consigned to second-class status those that could not keep up. Only the United States and its 'Mahanian consortium' of British Commonwealth and NATO navies have kept up; even Japan has not fully adjusted to the information revolution and the PRC remains far behind. The NICs, Singapore in particular, have made some progress with data links and computerised command systems. The area remains a key one, however, and the lead of the United States is increasing to a point where there are even question marks over its closest allies retaining full interoperability (leaving aside questions of less trusted allies receiving full access to US networks).

Designing and building the assets themselves can also be a problem. At first sight this might be considered strange as the Asia-Pacific contains the world's leading mercantile shipbuilders but warships require special skills, especially submarines. The only country in Pacific Asia littoral able to build submarines without significant outside help has been Japan. China depended on the Russians originally for technology transfer and later for actual imports; her first generation nuclear-powered attack and ballistic missile submarines were indigenous but very troubled as a result, and Russians are assisting with the next generation. The Germans have assisted the Indians (who also use Russian expertise and hulls), the Indonesians and South Korea, while the Swedes are the submarine patrons of Australia and Singapore. Pressure from Beijing has prevented the Dutch from continuing their relationship with Taiwan but submarines are a key component in the latest US arms deal with Taipei. That such a developed country as Taiwan is so dependent on foreign sourcing is significant.

Even surface warships require rare design skills and technologies. Japan relies on US and British equipment to a remarkable extent, and China on the French and the Russians. Australia and New Zealand's new frigates are German in design (even down to their galleys optimised for the Turkish market) and their older units are American and British respectively. Malaysia builds in Britain and buys second-hand from Italy. Indonesia took the old GDR's fleet from off a reunified Germany. Singapore copied a German small corvette and has turned to France for stealthy frigate. Thailand gets surface ships from China and the United States, and has also bought a carrier from Spain. Taiwan buys frigates from France as well as builds them to American designs.

The only fully independent naval powers in the region are Russia and the United States, and even their unilateralism is limited, the former's by the catastrophic state of the Russian economy and fleet, and the latter by almost a decade's draw down in capability to the point where Allied assistance is expected in any serious conflict. Nevertheless, we should not underestimate the residual strength of the United States' Pacific assets. According to the 2002/03 edition of *Janes Fighting Ships*, these assets comprised: four 'Ohio' class ballistic missile submarines; 25 'Los Angeles' class nuclear-powered attack submarines; seven carriers (one forward deployed at Yokosuka, Japan); 14 'Aegis' class cruisers (three at Yokosuka); 13 'Arleigh Burke' class Aegis destroyers (two based at Yokosuka); 11 FFG7 frigates (two at Yokosuka), one fleet command ship (at Yokosuka), and 20 major amphibious ships (four based at Sasebo, Japan). By any standards this is an impressive fleet. The Japan based battle group is not an inconsiderable navy in itself. Supported financially by Japan, it is in a sense the 'sanitised' offensive arm of the Japanese Navy, one whose presence and capabilities are generally more welcome than they would be if the ships wore the Rising Sun ensign.

The Russian Pacific Fleet is but a shadow of its former self. It is primarily an extended defence of home waters and in 2003 the Russians were forced to accept with great reluctance that little else is possible. Despite Middle Eastern and Asian diversions the US Navy, albeit reduced, is thus left to occupy the theatre it conquered in the greatest maritime war in history from 1941 to 1945. If maritime power played an enabling and supportive role against Germany, it was the basic means of victory against the maritime Empire of Japan. Japan's superb three-dimensional fleet was repulsed at Midway, worn down around the Solomon Islands, and then decisively defeated in the Philippine Sea and around the Philippines themselves in 1944 before being finished off at sea and in harbour in 1945. American amphibious forces advanced to the gates of the home islands themselves. American submarines assisted by aircraft dropped bombs and mines sank almost all of Japan's merchant fleet and stopped traffic between Japan and mainland Asia. Finally, nuclear bombers flying from a Marianas air base captured by naval forces the previous year, using fuel brought in by sea and even, one of them, a bomb delivered to Tinian by a US Navy cruiser, delivered the *coups de grace*.

4. The Pacific maritime theatre

The US Navy from the Pacific War onwards has always been happier at power projection rather than defence of shipping and in its post-Cold War iterations of strategy. The main aim of the US Navy is the assertion of dominance in a multidimensional maritime 'battle space' that covers a littoral region. Littoral power projection operations are driving the procurement of the new surface combatants that will be orientated primarily for land attack. Even the submarine force is being forced to jump on the littoral bandwagon with a new emphasis on operations directly against the shore. To project power, however, one must possess sea control and its basic rules remain the same whatever the circumstances. The enemy's main forces must be neutralised by destruction or containment such that the escort and other enabling forces can protect mission essential units sufficiently for them to achieve their objectives. In certain circumstances, the escort and direct support forces can neutralise the enemy's sea denial forces without the cover of other forces. The fundamental part of any maritime operation is escort, although due to failure to understand key doctrinal lessons of the past, it remains amazingly difficult to establish this as a cardinal operational point. Discussions with more than one Asia-Pacific navy have revealed flawed thinking similar to that which almost caused disaster to the Allies in the two World Wars, and which did contribute to Japan's defeat at sea in 1941–45. Japan is understandably, but a little disturbingly, unwilling to learn the lessons of the traumas of those years, and this failure has been compounded by both American unsoundness on this issue and unwillingness on the part of ship-owners to contribute to convoy exercises. We therefore have the slightly odd situation of a fleet built around four impressive escort groups with little experience of escort operations. This, though, might be essential in the event of a serious challenge to the shipping upon which Japan depends. The MSDF would provide a major contribution to the escort force under the cover of allied battle forces.

These battle forces are primarily made up of air and subsurface platforms. Maritime aircraft are at their most flexible operating from floating platforms but land-based aircraft have an important part to play as surveillance, anti-air warfare and anti-surface warfare assets. Both the surface ship and the land-based launcher have potential as missile platforms in the anti-surface unit role but this is not the primary function of major surface combatants of above small corvette size. The stealthy surface ship may redress the balance a little but the main form of stealth at sea remains that obtained by submerging beneath the surface. Submarines therefore are primary battle forces, although the limitations of conventional power control the reach and mobility of those submarine forces that cannot deploy nuclear propulsion. Nuclear submarines are, however, clearly among the capital assets of those states that can afford them. Surface ships are best used to provide the direct protection both of the carriers and amphibious ships and merchantmen at risk.

5. The economic importance of the sea

Merchant shipping remains vital to the world economy in general and to that of the Asia-Pacific in particular. Although it is more than a decade ago that Admiral Sir James Eberle noted that international financial flows rather than trade flows dominate the international economy – something of which all in the Asia-Pacific are now acutely conscious after the 1997/98 East Asian financial crisis – the significance of international trade to the general economic well being of states and peoples has never been greater. Exports and imports form a very significant part of the economies of a large number of nations in this region. In 2000, exports comprised 25 per cent of the GDP of China, for Hong Kong and Singapore 150 per cent, Malaysia 125 per cent, the Philippines, Taiwan and Vietnam 55 per cent, Thailand 65 per cent, South Korea 45 per cent, New Zealand and Indonesia 35 per cent, and Australia 20 per cent (Economist Intelligence Unit 2002). Although Japan's exports were a relatively low 11 per cent of GDP in 2000, the value of that trade was enormous at around US$460 billion. She is the world's third greatest trading nation, after the United States and Germany. Moreover, the production of Japan's industry was crucially dependent on imports of energy, with well over 80 per cent of her net energy consumption being imported. The NICs of South Korea, Taiwan and Singapore maintain similar, and in some cases higher levels of energy import dependence – shared 'supply security' predicament as Dent (2002) has observed. Those imports must come by sea.

Even countries that are less dependent on international trade as a proportion of GDP, such as Japan and the United States,[2] still have a considerable interest in the free flow of shipping in order to import certain vital commodities at acceptable prices, and to maintain a healthy export market. The United States is the world's largest trading nation with about 20 per cent of world imports and 15 per cent of exports. Disruption of shipping could have a massive effect. As Weeks (1997) has put it in relation to shipping in the Asia-Pacific, 'clearly the US has a growing economic interest in the security of SLOCs [Sea Lines Of Communication] in this region, particularly in view of the impact of their disruption on US trading partners' (p. 4).

The oil trade is an especial feature of dependence on shipping. Crude oil exports increased from almost 800 million tonnes in 1991 to almost 900 million tonnes in 1995. Of the 1995 total 325 million tonnes went to the United States and Canada, and 220 million tonnes to Japan (Choi 1997). The trade in liquid natural gas (LNG) carried in large refrigerated specialist carriers is set to increase. Japan, South Korea and Taiwan, already major consumers will increase demand while Thailand and China are also expected to begin importing significant quantities. Total expected LNG demand is expected to rise from almost 60 million tonnes in 1996 to about 95 million in 2010 (Far Eastern Economic Review 1997). The next most important category of bulk cargo is coal and coke, used for steel making as well as an energy source. Almost 295 million tonnes were exported by sea in 1991 and over 330 million tonnes in 1995. About a third of the coal transported by sea goes to Japan, half from Australia and Australia provides over a quarter of the other third or so that goes to Europe. About the same amount of iron ore goes by sea. Over a third goes to Japan, and about a fifth to the rest of East Asia – a trade that has more than doubled since 1991. Australasia is by far the biggest producer of iron ore, over two thirds of it going to East Asia. It is worth saying, however that Australia imports ores also, a good indication of the need for a free flow of shipping if industries and companies are to operate at maximum efficiency. The export of finished steel is also now crucial to the supply structure of modern manufacturing given the closure of plants in high cost areas of the world such as Northern Europe. Substantial quantities of grain are also carried at sea, the major sources being both the United States and Australia with the Middle East being a major market (Choi 1997). Other bulk cargoes that traverse the Pacific in quantity are bauxite, phosphates, manganese, copper, nickel, zinc, chrome, sulphur sugar and chemicals.

High value cargoes are now largely carried in containers with the standard container, containing 1280 cubic feet of space and with a maximum capacity of about 18.5 tonnes; this unit of volume is known as the 'TEU' and is that by which container cargo capacities are measured. Annual growth in the world container trade fluctuated in the 1990s but at its lowest point it has never been less than 4.6 per cent (1993) and in some years it was over 11 per cent (1995). In 1994 some 14 million TEU were handled in European ports, 12 million in the United States, 6 million in Japan and 10 million in the rest of East Asia. By 1998, Northeast Asia (i.e. China, Hong Kong SAR, Taiwan, South Korea and Japan) had almost 30 per cent of the world's container traffic (Jon 2001). The ports of the Asia-Pacific are among the world's busiest. Of the top ten ports in the world (in terms of throughput of metric tons), six are from the trans-region: Singapore is the second largest, Shanghai the third, Hong Kong fourth, Nagoya fifth, Yokohama seventh, Pusan eighth, and Long Beach in the United States the ninth in the world rankings. As shown above, the ships that carry these massive trade flows have never been more internationalised. This trend is likely to continue because of a combination of globalisation-associated factors, namely increased capital mobility across borders, further reduced state subsidies, tighter profit margins, pressure to reduce costs and ensure tax avoidance, and expanding global trade and trade relationships.

6. The security of Asian 'Sea Lines of Communication'

Trade, and therefore shipping, has been vital to East Asia's economic expansion and recovery. If anything seriously interfered with the free flow of this shipping the results could be serious. Quite how serious has become a matter of interesting debate. At the Eleventh International Conference of the Sea Lines Of Communication (SLOC) Study Group, held in Tokyo in November 1997, American analyst Daniel Coulter (1997) threw down a challenge to the conventional wisdom. He argued that the economic value of keeping open specific sea-lanes was dubious and that the definition of SLOCs was 'confused and imprecise' (p. 1). He argued that modern shipping was much more independent of land than its predecessors and that 'sea lanes today are no longer dictated purely by the land-bound end points of their trades' (p. 2). Coulter cited an example from East Asia, quoting the 'shibboleth' that the South China Sea was one of the most 'strategic' stretches of water in the world, as it provides a pathway for the millions of tonnes of oil destined for Japan, South Korea and China. Quoting a National Defence University study, he argued that if all four straits – the Malacca, Sunda, Lombok and Makassar – were blocked and the South China Sea itself, the extra steaming costs would account for only US$8 billion a year based on 1993 trade flows, about half the losses suffered by the United States to a major hurricane. If all Arab crude oil had to divert around Australia some US$1.5 million would be added to Japan's energy bill; if only the South China Sea was closed the cost would only be US$200 million annually. Such figures are minor fractions of Japan's total energy bill of between US$50 billion to US$100 billion, with major fluctuations much larger than the costs of diversion being caused by routine oil pricing and exchange fluctuations. The costs to China, South Korea and the United States would be less still. Coulter (1997) concluded thus:

In assessing the criticality of SLOC, the responsiveness of the shipping community to a disruption determines whether the trade is merely delayed due to longer transit times or denied access to the markets. With the exception of the Hormuz, SLOCs generally fall into the former category. The methodical analysis of both trade and shipping through Southeast Asia's SLOCs and the Suez Canal suggests that as long as there is sufficient shipping capacity to accommodate the increased demand for tonnage in a diversion scenario, the impact of extra steaming costs is negligible on the economies outside the closure area. No instances could be found where economies would be denied access to the trade due to prohibitive transportation costs. This is further buttressed by the real world closures of the Suez Canal in 1956–7 and 1967–75. In both instances, pressures for outside intervention based on economic rationales did not occur. Why? The reason is simple: the shipping markets responded by providing the appropriate tonnage necessary to carry that trade at minimal cost, both financial and political, to the global economy (p. 7).

Coulter (1997) was trying to make the point that one should not overstate the global and wider regional impact of shipping disruptions. He admitted that, 'no one disputes that those nearest the SLOCs would certainly be affected' (p. 3). Indeed he used this to argue that those Southeast Asian countries that straddle the major SLOCs thus had a major interest in maintaining the free flow of shipping, as to do otherwise 'would be akin to cutting their own throat' (p. 4). Yet, there are many countries in the Asia-Pacific who would be deeply affected if someone less dependent on the free flow of shipping took measures to interdict it either in choke points or on the open sea. Coulter is right to point to the problematic nature of the concept of SLOCs and some of the rhetoric surrounding them. However, his thesis should not be interpreted as essentially downgrading the key importance of shipping arriving and departing in the ports of the region, and this could be attacked at many points, not least off the ports themselves. Ships can be diverted, and indeed one of the basic means of defending them from attack is to do so, as seen in both World Wars. But diversion has its limits and there are costs that could be significant. Coulter points to the potential winners in the case of increased costs, notably ship owners, but there would be losers too. Certain exporters might well lose markets if marginal costs showed only minor increases. This might not affect the global economy too much but its local effects could be catastrophic. Equally the local effects of loss of imports might be highly significant indeed.

Key factors in the Asia-Pacific region specific to this debate concern the relatively ill-developed networks of land transport available. With the exception of China and Japan, railway systems in East Asia are generally underdeveloped and inadequate in haulage capacity. Even Australia is limited in its land transport links and has more the character of an archipelago. There is less buffering effect from alternative transport modes than would be available in Europe and North America. The sea is therefore the basic means of transport in the Asia-Pacific in a way that is more the case than in other regions. Interfering with shipping is therefore of particular salience.

There are those, however, who argue that it is difficult to inflict serious damage on shipping. The events in the Iran–Iraq War during the 1980s are sometimes held to have demonstrated these problems. Much damage was inflicted (amounting to US$1 billion) and some ships sunk or damaged beyond repair in the 483 attacks carried out, yet the price of oil was largely unaffected. This maybe the case, but much of this occurred at a time when the price of oil was being kept low by the United States as a decisive Cold War tactic. The capabilities brought to bear in the Gulf were limited in power, the merchantmen were increasingly effectively defended by warships, and in the end a really serious threat to Iran's vital sea communications posed by the US Navy did indeed help bring her to the Conference table. Maritime pressure had worked with the United States threatening Iran's very economic survival. The same could happen in certain circumstances in the Asia-Pacific.

Merchant shipping might well suffer attack either because of its direct involvement in local conflict, or because it happens to have to pass through an area of conflict *en route*. Nations may well use the threat to shipping as an effective means of bringing pressure to bear upon a nation with which it has a dispute. This can take various forms, such as attack by missile or torpedo from a variety of maritime platforms, or perhaps more cost-effectively mining. The threat of ballistic missile bombardment may also be used in an intimidatory way to deter the free passage of shipping, as it has been by China against Taiwan. The best way of avoiding such threats is to use other routes that are often available. Sometimes, though, there may be no alternative and naval protection of some kind may well be required. This could be problematical to organise given the mismatch of flags between warships and modern merchantmen but the tendency has been to interpret association between the two in the liberal manner dictated by the economically liberal maritime environment.

7. Piracy

The threat of piracy may not be a fully official one and yet it remains a significant problem in the Asia-Pacific. In 2001, of the world's 335 recorded cases of piracy and armed robbery against ships, 196 took place in the trans-region. Of these, 91 occurred in Indonesian waters alone (ICC International Maritime Bureau 2002). There is much scope for co-operative measures to help deal with this problem, as was done with some success in the 1990s. In 1991, there were 32 piracy attacks reported in the Straits of Malacca, one of the world's busiest shipping routes and of great commercial importance to Singapore in particular given its regional entrepot role.[3] These attacks were reduced to seven and then to five or less in succeeding years by co-operative measures taken by Indonesia, Malaysia and Singapore within the ASEAN Shipping framework, which allowed for entry into each other's territorial waters. After an International Maritime Organisation (IMP) workshop in Singapore in 1999, a regional agreement was drawn for joint action to curb piracy and armed robbery on the high seas. Sadly the number of attacks soared suddenly to 75 in 2000 as the momentum of enforcement slackened (ICC International Maritime Bureau 2002). Only India, Singapore and Russia had responded to the IMP agreement but their action had been 'fragmented and uncoordinated' according to a major tanker operator.[4] Japan had been discouraged from sending down Coastguard units because of Chinese and others' concerns about a wider Japanese presence. Nevertheless, in 2001, Singapore and Japan announced their intentions to tackle the piracy issue, motivated by similar 'supply security' objectives. In that year cases in the Straits of Malacca showed a welcome reduction to 17, and September 11 and the resulting shipping movements in support of Operation Enduring Freedom in Afghanistan saw more systematic Indian patrols supplemented by American warships.[5] These patrols also had an anti-terrorist dimension given the strength of al Qaeda support in Indonesia.

Another regional trouble spot in the mid-1990s was in China's coastal waters, where Chinese customs and marine militia craft – in a long historical tradition – have been gamekeepers turned poachers. Piracy has always been a way of life in this region, a not dissimilar situation to that in Mediaeval European waters. In 1993, there were 37 reported piracy attacks from such sources in the East China Sea area. This number fell to 18 in 1994, two in 1996, none at all in 1998/99, one in 2000 and two in 2001. Meanwhile, a little further north around Hong Kong and Macau, the number of such attacks jumped to 31 in 1995 from six in 1994 but then came down to nine again in 1996, five in 1997 and two in 1998. There were two more in 2000 but none in 2001. There is some evidence that media coverage has forced Beijing to exert greater control, which could explain the general downward trend in the number of reported piracy incidents. One should not over-state the piracy problem (the global listings often cover relatively minor crimes carried out in harbour) but the tendency for acts against ships under-way to proliferate and escalate makes constabulary counter-measures an essential feature of the Asia-Pacific maritime scene. Co-operative measures have clear advantages – the operations of the Indian navy in the Straits of Malacca area are an interesting development – but the self consciously nationalistic attitudes in the area and the continued suspicion of Japan still create an unfavourable context for such empirically desirable measures.

8. Fishing

Although shipping is the most important economic use of the sea there are two others that are of considerable importance, not least in the Asia-Pacific. The first is fishing. More than half the world's fish are caught or bred in Asian waters, and about half the world's fish are consumed in the region. Six of the top ten fishing countries are Asian: China, Taiwan, South Korea, India, Japan and Thailand. Over 40 per cent of the world's fishing vessels are registered in these states. China has the world's largest catch, some 12 million tonnes. The world's largest fish buyer is Japan, responsible for a third of global imports and the largest fish seller is Thailand with almost US$3.5 billion worth of fish exports in the early 1990s. In Asia, fish provides about 30 per cent of daily animal protein, more than anywhere else in the world, and fishing as an activity sustains more jobs than in any other region.[6] Demand is beginning to outreach supply. All Southeast Asian stocks are fully exploited, if not over-fished and the value of such fisheries as the Gulf of Thailand and around the Philippines has declined.

Given both increasing competition and the enclosure of the world's oceans with the general adoption of national fishing jurisdiction out to 200 miles – a measure that brought 90 per cent of the world's fish within the control of the coastal state – there is much scope for conflict. Japanese boats fish in Russian waters, Chinese boats in South Korea's, and South Korean boats in the waters of Japan, Burma, Thailand, Malaysia, Cambodia, Indonesia and Vietnam.[7] In the words of one Thai based journalist, 'Thailand's trespassing fishing fleet and the fishermen and navies of neighbouring countries are turning the seas of Southeast Asia into a battleground.'[8] He quoted cases of armed clashes between fishery protection vessels from Myanmar and armed Thai fishermen, as well as Burmese, Malaysian and Vietnamese seizures of Thai vessels. Thai warships were reported to be reluctant to get involved but in 1995 there was a serious clash with Vietnamese patrol boats in the Gulf of Thailand in which three men were killed.

Clashes between other states' craft have occurred. The Malaysians have seized various nations' boats in the Straits of Malacca, and Vietnamese boats in the South China Sea. Vietnamese and Philippine vessels have seized PRC fishermen in the South China Sea, Indonesians have seized Taiwanese fishing boats in the Arafura Sea and around Taiwan there have been clashes between Taiwanese boats and those from China and the Philippines. He concluded that given the problems of illegal fishing, especially by the Thais, 'the risk of maritime conflict in Southeast Asia will continue to grow'.[9] Certainly there is a major enforcement task for regional navies and coast guards, especially as states reach agreement on common approaches on the exploitation and management of diminishing stocks. Only through co-operative measures can this problem be addressed.

9. Seabed hydrocarbons

The other major economic use of the sea is as a source of hydrocarbons for fuel. According to a mid-1990s study, of the Southeast Asian states Indonesia had the largest oil stake in the seabed with almost 60 million tonnes being produced. Next came Malaysia with just over 35 million tonnes, Brunei with 7.5 million tonnes, Vietnam with 5 million tonnes, Thailand with 2 million tonnes and the Philippines with 1.25 million tonnes. Malaysia led with natural gas with almost 20 billion cubic metres, followed by Vietnam with over 8 billion cubic metres coming from off-shore, then Brunei, Indonesia and Thailand each with about 7 billion cubic metres. Japan's offshore oil production was small, less than 0.7 million tonnes with only a million metric tonnes of proven reserves. China was in a much healthier state with over 2 million tonnes of annual oil production from offshore and about 560 million tonnes of proven reserves. Vietnam and Malaysia had proven reserves of a similar size, 544 million and 530 million respectively. Myanmar, which had not yet started producing, also had significant oil reserves under the sea of over 100 million tonnes, almost comparable to Brunei's.

The increased demand for energy expected in the early years of the new century (which should see China importing energy in 2015 to the same extent that the United States does today, and both Indonesia and Malaysia becoming net oil and gas importers by 2003 and 2012 respectively) puts more of a premium on these undersea supply sources. China increased the production of its oil rigs in the South China Sea by 31 per cent in the first half of 1997 to 6.8 million tonnes. Natural gas is also receiving a new emphasis. Indonesia is developing two huge gas fields, the Natuna and the Wiriagar, and Australia is developing new fields in the Timor Sea. It is this demand for offshore energy that provides the real motive in the South China Sea conflict. As long as the area seems to provide a hydrocarbon bonanza there will be tension between the local claimants. A co-operative solution will be at a discount, despite rhetoric to the contrary.

10. Conclusion

The sea thus remains *the* key element in the Asia-Pacific. It is the basic form of freight transport, a key source of food and an increasingly important source of oil and gas. Conflict over its use has led to violence in the past and may lead to more in the future. If international violence erupts it will also be the primary medium by which military power is thrust ashore. Maritime forces are thus the keys to security in the region and it is not surprising that local capabilities are improving. Yet, despite Middle Eastern and Central Asian diversions, the United States remains the dominant military sea power in the region. It will retain this dominance that also implies a general strategic hegemony, for the foreseeable future.

There are possibilities for local co-operation, especially in the constabulary and benign applications of maritime power, for example, anti-piracy operations and search and rescue. This kind of co-operation has been successful in the past, and could be again, but the momentum must be maintained. Maritime co-operation is a good idea in circumstances where the seas unite. The Maritime Co-operation Working Group of the Council for Security Cooperation in the Asia Pacific Region has made several constructive suggestions for such co-operation. Search and rescue combined exercises have taken place. The Western Pacific Naval Symposium also provides a high level means of bringing navies together. There is a long tradition of local suspicion that still puts a premium on unilateralism but the logic of the maritime environment is to co-operate. The opposition to greater Japanese constabulary action in the Straits of Malacca is a classic case in point. But the opportunities are there if the local actors wish to take them up. Maritime activities by their own logic ought to be a primary focus of regional co-operation.

Notes

1. For a good historical survey of China's uncertain quest for sea power see Swanson (1982).
2. The US's trade/GDP ratio is similar to Japan's. Larger economies, with substantial domestic markets, tend to be less trade dependent obvious reasons of relative self-sufficiency.
3. Singapore intersects with almost 400 shipping lanes and has links to over 600 ports worldwide.
4. 'Piracy Figures Slow Down in East Asia', NAVINT, *The International Naval Newsletter*, 01.03.2002, p. 2.
5. *Straits Times*, 09.08.2002, *Navy Times*, 28.01.2002.
6. *Far East Economic Review*, 13.03.1997.
7. Ibid.
8. *Far East Economic Review*, 13.03.1997, p. 53.
9. Ibid. p. 54.

References

Choi, J.H. (1997) 'Projections of Shipping Patterns in East Asia', paper presented at the *NEACD Workshop on Maritime Trade and Transportation* conference, Arden House, 4 April, New York.

Coulter, D.Y. (1997) 'The Economics of SLOC Protection: An Overvalued Mission', paper presented at the *Sea Lines Of Communication* conference, 17–18 November, Tokyo.

Dent, C.M. (2002) *The Foreign Economic Policies of Singapore, South Korea and Taiwan*, Edward Elgar, Cheltenham.

Economist Intelligence Unit (2002) *Pocket World in Figures 2003*, EIU, London.

Far Eastern Economic Review (1997) *Asia 1998 Yearbook*, FEER, Hong Kong.

ICC International Maritime Bureau (2002) *Piracy and Armed Robbery Against Ships: Annual Report*, ICC International Maritime Bureau, London.

Janes (1997) *Janes Fighting Ships, 1997–8*, Coulsdon, London.

Janes (2002) *Janes Fighting Ships, 2002–3*, Coulsdon, London.

Jon, J.S. (2001) 'Maritime Transportation Situation in East Asia', paper presented at *The Strategic Importance of Seaborne Trade and Shipping – A Common Interest of the Asia Pacific* conference, 3–4 April, Canberra.

Swanson, B. (1982) *Eighth Voyage of the Dragon*, Naval Institute Press, Annapolis.

Sumida, J. (1997) *Inventing Grand Strategy and Teaching Command: The Classic Works of Alfred Thayer Mahan Reconsidered*, Johns Hopkins University Press, Baltimore.

US Office of Naval Intelligence (1997) *Worldwide Maritime Challenges, 1997*, USONI, Washington DC.

Weeks, S.B. (1997) 'Sea Lines of Communication- Security and Access', paper presented at the *NEACD Workshop on Maritime Trade and Transportation* conference, Arden House, 4 April, New York.

Part IV
Sub-Regional Studies

7

The War on Terror: Implications for the ASEAN Region

Jürgen Haacke

1. Introduction

On 11 September 2001, a stunned world watched as terrorists flying hijacked civilian aircraft jets erased the twin towers of the World Trade Centre in New York City and seriously damaged the Pentagon in Washington DC. Slightly more than a year later, on 12 October 2002, almost two hundred lives were lost in bombings on the island of Bali, Indonesia. This chapter examines the nature of the challenge posed by the terrorist attacks for the Association of Southeast Asian Nations (ASEAN) and discusses the implications of ASEAN's role in the war on terror. It is generally argued here that ASEAN's participation in the campaign against terrorism in Southeast Asia and beyond has been characterised by significant ambiguity. On the one hand, the war on terror has offered ASEAN governments the opportunities to extract and draw on external assistance to deal with domestic economic and transregional security challenges. On the other hand, regional governments have found it difficult to demonstrate their collective capacity to act as an effective diplomatic community and security regime, and their erstwhile hopes that ASEAN could yet emerge as a manager of regional order have once again been exposed as having only limited substance. This has not been without effect on its international standing. ASEAN is also facing up to the fact that security co-operation with the major powers to stem regional terrorism is a double-edged sword in part because such co-operation fuels an emerging struggle for regional influence by the major powers.

2. The challenge of 11 September 2001 and 12 October 2002

The challenges for ASEAN deriving from September 11 stem primarily from the US response to the events of that day. For US decision-makers, September 11 marked a watershed in the country's fight against international terrorism. This was evidenced by measures subsequently taken to protect the American homeland, the war in Afghanistan to root out al-Qaeda, and the efforts to engage in co-operation with allies, longstanding security partners and others to prevent another terrorist attack on the United States. The impact of September 11 on the Bush administration is visible not only in the many public speeches and pronouncements made since, but also in the formulations of Washington's new national security strategy. This strategy emphasises a doctrine of pre-emption and is unambiguous about the need to maintain American primacy in global politics (The White House 2002). As such, the events at New York, Washington and Pennsylvania clarified the Bush administration's thinking on competing US grand strategies (Posen and Ross 1996/97). The American re-assessment of challenges to its security has entailed Washington assigning greater strategic significance to Southeast Asia, which – in the minds of US analysts and policy-makers – the region had lacked for many years. Indeed, it has been suggested that the United States' post-September 11 approach towards Southeast Asia has resembled that adopted in the late 1940s when the region assumed increasing strategic importance in the context of the emerging Cold War rivalry (Hess 1987).

By contrast, notwithstanding the shock and revulsion widely shared over the terrorist atrocities committed in the United States, 'the 12th of September in Southeast Asia was pretty much like the 10th of September had been'.[1] That said, ASEAN governments did of course consider September 11 to have thrown up a stark challenge: to offer a meaningful contribution to the international war against terrorism. After all, the Bush administration had vowed to make no distinction between the terrorists and those that harbour them, a point of major relevance given the existence of groups in several ASEAN states with proven or presumed links to al-Qaeda (Abuza 2003). As George W. Bush put it unequivocally: 'Either you are with us, or you are with the terrorists.'[2] For individual ASEAN countries, President Bush raised the question of how they might assist in the war on terror. For the Association as a whole, the challenge was to make ASEAN reaffirm its role as a diplomatic community and a meaningful regional security actor backing the United States in the global campaign against terrorism.

In the event, however, to fashion an appropriate individual response was considered by many ASEAN member countries to be more important than to articulate and implement a collective position. The reason for this was three-fold. First, it was clear that member states would respond to September 11 with different concerns and agendas in mind. This was inevitable due to the differing security arrangements between individual ASEAN countries and Washington, a huge disparity in national security capacities, variant perceptions of threat and numerous domestic constraints. Second, individual member countries – but not necessarily the Association – stood to gain in multiple material ways by supporting Washington diplomatically and militarily. This had been the perceived message of the US$600 million in economic assistance that the United States offered Indonesia's President Megawati when she visited the White House about a week after September 11 and the substantial pledges of economic and military support extended to Philippine President Arroyo in November. Third, in view of the lingering intramural suspicions within the Association and remaining external security challenges, several ASEAN countries had an incentive to support the war on terror to promote the economic and security relationship with Washington and to avoid all that potentially would undermine it. To be sure, although member states have regarded their collective response to September 11 in this sense as secondary in importance to their individual responses, co-operative action at the intramural level was considered necessary. Indeed, ASEAN decision-makers widely agreed that failure to demonstrate collective support for the war on terror was likely to damage the Association's image and credibility irrespective of any individual contributions. This was of some concern as the Association has been keen to reverse the loss of standing that it suffered as a consequence of its perceived incapacity to respond to the 1997/98 East Asian financial crisis (Ganesan 1999, Henderson 1999).

The Bali explosions have posed a further threefold challenge. First, in the light of the substantial loss of life among foreign tourists and the immediate upgrading of travel advisories for Indonesia and the wider region, including Singapore, the Philippines, Thailand and even some of the Indochinese states, the bombings have represented a potentially major economic threat to ASEAN countries. Early indications are that the tourism industry, which generally accounts for several percentage points of GDP not only in Indonesia, but also in Thailand, Malaysia and Singapore, has been seriously shaken even though the medium and long-term trends remain unclear. The Bali bombings have, second, also challenged ASEAN to re-assess the effectiveness of their counter-terrorism efforts undertaken since 11 September 2001. Third, the Bali terrorist incident has once again highlighted the limited influence that the Association has on its members, particularly Indonesia, raising the question of what the Association might do when members take or fail to take action that undermines regional security. This challenge had in previous years already presented itself on several occasions, not least with respect to the East Asian financial crisis, the haze problem and East Timor.

3. Responses within the ASEAN region to the attacks of September 11

3.1. Introductory comments

This is not the place to chronicle in minute detail the decisions and actions taken individually and collectively by regional states or institutions after September 2001 to confront the terrorist challenge. However, it is important to describe key features of ASEAN's response before we can discuss the implications of that response in the fourth section. This response has in part been reactive as well as pro-active. It has involved individual ASEAN governments' decisions *vis-à-vis* domestic exponents of terrorism, international co-operation (particularly with the United States), and intramural inter-state co-operation within the Association.

Domestic political reasons have led individual contributions of ASEAN states to vary in terms of their nature, quality and effectiveness. The new ASEAN entrants, for example, all expressed support for fighting terrorism, but their practical input in the campaign against terror has been marginal at best. Their effective non-participation, particularly in the early phase in the war against terrorism, was a consequence not only of limited state capacities, but also of historical experiences and perceptions of an unwarranted double standard in the US counter-terrorism campaign as regards the distinction between freedom fighters and terrorists. In contrast, four of the five original members have consistently and actively participated in the struggle against international terrorism in ways compatible with their national and regime security interests. As regards the national measures adopted, Kuala Lumpur for instance used its Internal Security Act (ISA) to detain more than 60 suspects over a period of more than a year. Also invoking its own ISA, Singapore conducted arrests of suspected members of Jemaah Islamiyah in December 2001 and August 2002. A crackdown on suspects has also occurred in the Philippines, although under a different type of legislation. Thailand has been very cautious in its dealings with its Muslim population, as testified by the length of time it took for Bangkok to admit to the existence of a Thai branch of Jemaah Islamiyah and its insistence that the group has not been penetrated by religious and political extremists. Among the original members of ASEAN, Indonesia for long was the most reluctant to take unequivocal action against a known or suspected presence of extremists or terrorists. Indeed, notwithstanding her initial pledges in Washington in September 2001, President Megawati frustrated both her neighbours and the United States by failing to confront and detain those alleged to bear responsibility for regional and international terrorism, most notably Abu Bakar Bashir, the presumed spiritual leader of Jemaah Islamiyah. This stance was significantly reversed only after the explosions of October 12 in Bali.

Until then, Jakarta had instituted administrative changes, such as the establishment of an interdepartmental Task Force, to deal with the challenge of terrorism. In May 2002, the authorities had also detained the leader of the Laskar Jihad, Jafar Umar Thalib, for inciting supporters to commit criminal acts and insulting the President. However, concerns about the political repercussions of cracking down on suspected representatives of domestic and regional terrorist networks for a long time constituted a chief reason for Indonesia's leadership not to pursue the war on terror with greater vigour. Megawati has been politically vulnerable among others because she does not command a parliamentary majority, leaving her exposed to political machinations by her political opponents, not least her own Vice-President,

Hamzah Haz. Haz has gained a measure of notoriety among Western analysts, especially after he suggested that the attacks on New York and Washington would 'cleanse the US of its sins' (Huxley 2002: 77). Indeed, Vice-President Haz until very recently consistently rejected with contrived outrage any suggestion that Indonesia was potentially facing a serious domestic terrorism problem. In making such claims he, like others, took cognisance and could appeal to the fertile ground of widespread conspiracy theories and a strong suspicion among the Indonesian public of foreign moves against the Republic. Having briefly outlined some of the differences concerning the national responses of individual ASEAN countries to September 11, the focus now shifts to two other dimensions in ASEAN members' role in the war on terror, namely (i) bilateral co-operation with the United States; and (ii) multilateral or bilateral intramural co-operation.

3.2. Bilateral co-operation with the United States

ASEAN states' respective bilateral co-operation with Washington in counter-terrorism has taken many forms in the aftermath of September 11. At its most basic level, it has involved member states stepping-up security for US interests, and the upgrading of intelligence exchanges. Washington also received from ASEAN states logistical support for operations in Afghanistan and offers for the provision of humanitarian assistance. By submitting their respective reports, all ASEAN states also complied with important UN Security Council Resolutions such as Resolution 1373, notwithstanding continuing problems in implementing this resolution. In some cases, ASEAN countries in 2002 detained and deported non-nationals to the United States for further questioning. One very prominent case has been Omar al-Faruq, allegedly a Kuwaiti citizen, who has been linked to the radical Laskar Jundullah, which is known for conducting sweeps against Christians, and has been accused of planning to assassinate the then presidential candidate Megawati. Al-Faruq was apprehended in Indonesia in June 2002 and handed over to the United States only days later.[3] Responding to Washington's requests, several ASEAN countries, for example, also signed the Container Security Initiative (CSI) that will allow American customs officials to inspect US-bound cargo containers at their point of shipping.

Not surprisingly, however, the reasons underpinning differences in national level responses have also shaped the context and contours of co-operation between member states of the Association and the United States. Without question the Philippines has to date offered the United States the most enthusiastic support in the war on terror generally and for US military operations in particular. In anticipation of the Afghanistan campaign, US forces were allowed access to Subic Naval Base, Clark Air Base and Mactan Air Base (now Benito Ebuen Air Base) in Cebu. Following the initial thrust of the military campaign against the Taliban and al-Qaeda in October 2001, Manila quickly reached agreement with Washington on US training that would help the Armed Forces of the Philippines (AFP) to locate and eliminate terrorist cells and networks within its national borders. Within weeks of a visit to Washington by President Gloria Arroyo in November 2001, US Special Forces assumed a key role in meeting the longstanding security threat posed by the Abu Sayyaf group (ASG). During the Balikatan 02-1 exercises from late January to July 2002,[4] US forces provided training and tendered tactical advice, helped with intelligence gathering, and took on infrastructure construction projects which allowed the AFP to move around better, re-supply and conduct medical evacuations. US forces also assisted in successful military operations to secure the release from capture of US citizen Gracia Burnham and to hunt down ASG leader Abu Sabaya. In late June 2002, Admiral Fargo, newly appointed Commander of US Pacific Command, and AFP chief of staff General Cimatu discussed the transition from Balikatan 02-1 to a sustained programme focusing on counter-terrorism training and assistance in the southern Philippines and Luzon as part of strengthening the broader security relationship. This reached a further high in November 2002 in the signing of a five-year Mutual Logistic Support Agreement that is intended to facilitate the exchange of military supplies during exercises and to enhance the effectiveness and interoperability of joint US–Philippine military operations. Notably, the assistance the United States has extended is not confined to counter the Muslim terrorists. Just a week after visiting Manila in August 2002, US Secretary of State Colin Powell announced the designation of the Communist Party of the Philippines and its military wing, the New People's Army (CPP-NPA), as a foreign terrorist organisation (FTO). Manila seems very happy to continue to draw on Washington's assistance as testified by President Arroyo's request, in November 2002, for police training along the lines of the military training already received.

In contrast, Jakarta has been much less eager to adopt decisive steps to support Washington as unreservedly as Manila, US incentives notwithstanding. Indeed, co-operation schemes that to Philippine leaders have made make good political and strategic sense, particularly the deployment of US troops, remain anathema to Indonesian leaders. Of course, as Secretary of State Colin Powell has made clear that Washington is not in the business of forcing the hand of ASEAN countries. As he put it: 'We are looking for opportunities to train and cooperate with other nations as they desire and at their invitation.'[5] That said, the George W. Bush administration has found that irrespective of Jakarta's dependence on international financial institutions, Washington has only been able to exert limited leverage over the Megawati government. In this context, it is noteworthy that at least parts of Indonesia's military would appear to have calculated that greater recalcitrance on its part might lead to greater US willingness to re-assess recent US sanctions, and herald the restoration of military-to-military relations. Only in May 2002, during a visit to Washington, did Indonesia's

Defence Minister Matori Abdul Djalil explore this possibility. With Philippine–US co-operation and Indonesian–US co-operation forming two apparent poles along a continuum of counter-terrorism co-operation, other ASEAN countries from among the original members have pursued bilateral co-operation in ways that fall between the very enthusiastic and the very reluctant.

3.3. Bilateral and trilateral co-operation by ASEAN states

The Philippines has not only enthusiastically supported the US war on terror, but also played a key role in instigating anti-terrorism co-operation among the maritime ASEAN states. In the light of experiences of transnational terrorism and crime in the Sulu Sea and the all too apparent problems even before 11 September 2001 in guarding porous land and sea boundaries, Manila, within days of the attacks, re-articulated ideas about sharing intelligence and conducting joint border patrols with Malaysia and Indonesia. Over the next few months, their senior officials finalised the details of a draft framework agreement on how to facilitate co-operation and interoperability among participating countries to address border and security incidents. The relevance of striking such an agreement became clear once again in late 2001 when Nur Misuari, leader of the Moro National Liberation Front and governor of the Autonomous Region of Muslim Mindanao, staged a bloody but failed insurrection to prevent his political ouster and then fled for Sabah. This prompted the foreign ministers of the Philippines and Malaysia to release a joint communiqué that addressed their understanding about the implications of this insurrection for Filipino Muslims and the peace process in Mindanao. By the end of December 2001, Malaysia, the Philippines and Indonesia had formulated their first draft accord to fight terrorism and border crime. The draft was revisited in February 2002, and in May that year the three states signed the Agreement on Information Exchange and Establishment of Communication Procedures. This trilateral agreement covers an array of transnational security threats including terrorism, drug trafficking, money-laundering, illicit trafficking of arms, theft of marine resources, smuggling, piracy, hijacking, intrusion and illegal entry. Cambodia acceded to the Agreement in July 2002, and Thailand joined around the time of the 8th ASEAN Summit held the following November.

Bilateral efforts at counter-terrorism co-operation have again involved in particular the five original ASEAN members. This co-operation has included above all intelligence exchanges, some of which have resulted in the arrests of suspected terrorists. Singapore, in particular, has been keen to promote the sharing of intelligence. Again, Indonesia was, at least for a while, least amenable to following up such co-operation among the original members. The Megawati government did not act on the intelligence made available by the city-state, and some politicians within and outside the administration reacted angrily when Singapore's Senior Minister Lee Kuan Yew commented publicly on this fact. When Singapore proposed that suspected ringleaders of Jemaah Islamiah resident in Indonesia might be extradited to the city-state, Jakarta refused point-blank.

3.4. ASEAN's collective response

Compared with some of the responses by individual members, or even the aforementioned trilateral sub-regional initiative, diplomatic efforts designed to allow ASEAN to build its anti-terrorism profile initially looked the most hesitant. The Association first stated its consensual position on the war of terror at the Third ASEAN Ministers Meeting on Transnational Crime, organised in Singapore on 11 October 2001. Under point 18 of their joint communiqué the ministers 'strongly condemned all acts of terrorism, in particular the terrorist attacks of 11 September 2001 on the US' (ASEAN 2001a). To be sure, ministers also 'agreed to work closely with the international community to strengthen co-operation in preventing and combating terrorism' and stated their commitment to 'enhancing co-operation among our law enforcement agencies to combat terrorism'. A month later, on the occasion of the 7th ASEAN Summit in Brunei Darussalam, ASEAN leaders issued the 2001 ASEAN Declaration on Joint Action to Counter Terrorism. This declaration was something of a hard-wrung compromise that reflected the delicate situation in which some regional governments saw themselves not least in view of domestic political opposition to the prosecution of the war in Afghanistan at the time. It described the attacks on New York City and Washington DC as an 'assault on all of us' but equally emphasised (again) that ASEAN opposed 'terrorism in all its forms and manifestations committed wherever, whenever and by whomever' and repudiated the idea that terrorism was linked to Islam (ASEAN 2001b). The declaration also included pledges on exchanging information and intelligence as well as on advancing national capacities in the fight against terrorism.

ASEAN's joint co-operative endeavours really only gained momentum between the Informal Foreign Ministers' Retreat, organised in Phuket in February 2002, and the Special ASEAN Ministerial Meeting on Terrorism convened in Kuala Lumpur over 20–21 May 2002. As perhaps its most significant achievement, ASEAN officials during this time succeeded in formulating and finalising in May 2002 a concrete work programme to implement its plan of action against transnational crime including international terrorism. The commitment to the adoption of this work programme was no doubt the consequence of the discovery – prior to the February Phuket meeting – of terrorist cells in Singapore and Malaysia comprising members of Jemaah Islamiah and Kampulan Mujaheddin Malaysia (KMM) respectively.[6] Although successful anti-terrorism operations in themselves, the detection of such cells suggested that Southeast Asia had a more serious terrorism problem than hitherto admitted and perhaps anticipated. Indeed, the region arguably deserved being represented as a 'second front', as had been claimed by the Bush administration after the Afghanistan operations, much to the chagrin of ASEAN governments. Primarily in view of the dearth of previous experience in counter-terrorism, ASEAN's work programme identifies six basic issues for intramural co-operation. Three involve respectively the exchange of information, the compilation and dissemination of relevant laws and regulations of ASEAN Member Countries; and the compilation and dissemination of bilateral and multilateral agreements and information on relevant international treaties where feasible. The fourth goal is the development of multilateral or bilateral legal arrangements to facilitate apprehension, investigation, prosecution, extradition, inquiry and seizure in order to enhance mutual legal and administrative assistance among member countries where feasible. The final two objectives concern the enhancement of co-operation and co-ordination in law enforcement and intelligence sharing and the development of regional training programmes (ASEAN 2002a). The Chair of the ASEAN Standing Committee has been tasked to oversee the liasing with other members in the implementation of the work plan.

Having outlined ASEAN's counter-terrorism agenda in this manner, the 35th ASEAN Foreign Ministers' Meeting in Bandar Seri Begawan in late July 2002 signed a joint anti-terrorism declaration with the United States. Although a political, non-binding declaration it is meant to express ASEAN commitment to 'prevent, disrupt and combat international terrorism through the exchange and flow of information, intelligence, and capacity-building' (ASEAN 2002b). Building in part on the previous counter-terrorism discourse of the Association, the signatories once more reiterated their opposition to 'terrorism in all its forms and manifestations committed wherever, whenever and by whomever' (ibid), as they had previously done in the 2001 ASEAN Declaration on Joint Action to Counter Terrorism. At the same time, they also restated the validity of the principles of sovereign equality, territorial integrity and non-intervention. The declaration also politically commits both sides to practical steps. It was agreed that Washington strengthen Southeast Asia's anti-terrorism capacity-building efforts in relation to the ability to block terrorist funds, to enhance transportation, border and immigration controls, and to help engender practical counter-terrorism regimes. The declaration also calls upon ASEAN members to become a party to all United Nations protocols and conventions on terrorism, and suggests the need for greater efficacy on their part in combating terrorism.

Member states of ASEAN have also promoted a collective stance on the war on terror within the ASEAN Regional Forum (ARF). While ARF activities in the context of the war on terror developed as of January 2002, to date the ARF's major counter-terrorism measure is the Statement on Measures against Terrorist Financing. Having been worked out in a Workshop on Financial Measures against Terrorism hosted by the United States and Malaysia in Honolulu in March 2002, the ARF statement (ASEAN Regional Forum 2002) obliges members to deny terrorists access to funds. For ASEAN the statement is congenial in two ways. First, it allows member countries to argue that, under its guidance, the ARF has embraced a practical form of preventive diplomacy long called for by its critics. Second, the statement serves as an appeal to non-ASEAN members to grant practical and financial support to ASEAN countries in implementing UN Security Council Resolution 1373. ARF participants have also established an Inter-sessional Meeting on Counter-Terrorism and Transnational Crime (ISM on CT–TC) whose activity will be based upon a Concept Paper drawn up by Washington and Kuala Lumpur, who will be Co-Chairmen of the ISM on CT–TC in the 2002/3 inter-sessional year.

3.5. ASEAN's response to the Bali bombings

The blasts at Kuta beach resort on the island of Bali came only days after US Ambassador in Jakarta suggested that non-essential embassy personnel might have to be withdrawn in the light of the failure by the Indonesian authorities to pursue a vigorous investigation into a bomb near diplomatic premises used by his staff. Contrary to the attacks of 11 September 2001, the Bali bombings propelled the government of President Megawati into immediate action. Within days the administration initiated emergency regulations that allowed the authorities not only to pursue the investigation into the Bali blasts, but also to act decisively against those suspected of involvement in other terrorist acts. Within days, Jemaah Islamiyah's alleged spiritual leader, Abu Bakar Bashir, was detained, albeit not under the new anti-terrorism regulations but the existing criminal code. Significant efforts have moreover been extended to apprehend and bring to justice the perpetrators of the Bali bombings. In this context, Indonesia's bilateral co-operation with the United States and other Western states has markedly picked up and made good progress.

By comparison, ASEAN's collective response to the Bali atrocities has remained subdued, even though immediately after the bombings ASEAN Secretary-General Rudolfo Severino, in a letter of condolence addressed to President Megawati, had publicly called upon the Association to further intensify its solidarity and co-operation in countering terrorism. Cambodia, as chair of the ARF, had soon thereafter issued a similar statement on the Bali terrorist bombings. In the event, ASEAN member states used the occasion of the 8th ASEAN Summit in Phnom Penh in early November 2002 to resolve to intensify their efforts, collectively and individually, to prevent, counter and suppress the activities of terrorist groups in the region. They also pledged to continue with practical co-operative measures among themselves and with the international community. At the same time, ASEAN governments also strongly criticised the Western governments' practice of 'indiscriminately advising' their citizens to refrain from visiting or otherwise dealing with the ASEAN countries, 'in the absence of established evidence to substantiate rumours of possible terrorist attacks' (ASEAN

2002c). These threatened to spell at least temporary hardship if not havoc for their respective tourism industries and their economies at large.

4. Implications of the war against terrorism for the ASEAN region

Having outlined the main contours of ASEAN's response to the war on terror and noted the spread of motivations underpinning members' individual positions, this section will analyse three important implications of ASEAN's anti-terrorism stance. It will discuss, in turn, the repercussions of ASEAN's response to the war for the Association's standing, its effectiveness as a diplomatic community and security regime as well as the meaning of September 11 for ASEAN's longstanding aspiration to play a key role in managing its regional affairs. The section will also explore how ASEAN's anti-terrorism co-operation with the United States is influencing the dynamics of great power relations.

4.1. Standing

Ever since the dramatic decline of its members' economic fortunes in the aftermath of the 1997/98 financial crisis, which saw ASEAN register a concomitant drop in its standing as a cohesive regional organisation not least as a consequence of fierce extra-regional criticism, the Association has struggled to restore its image. ASEAN governments have sought to improve the collective image in two principal ways. The first has focused on developing ASEAN's diplomatic and security culture, the so-called 'ASEAN way'.[7] The second has centred on the pursuit of an ambitious agenda of regional and economic integration in the form of the ASEAN Plus Three (APT) process involving China, Japan and South Korea (see Chapter 5), and the promotion of economic development in the Mekong Subregion (see Chapter 9) to overcome the divide between new and old members. Particularly the APT process has proved important to ASEAN to recover some of its standing after 1998. However, the events of September 11 as well as any response the Association would give in the war against terror always had the potential to inflict renewed damage on ASEAN's standing. This would be the case, it was widely feared, if the Association's counter-terrorism response was deemed ineffective by foreign governments and media, especially if ASEAN's intramural and international co-operation was considered to be inhibited, not least by the Association's continued regard for its diplomatic and security culture.

The purpose of this section, then, is first to establish whether ASEAN has succeeded in avoiding a further drop in its standing. This question might be answered in the affirmative if running commentary by foreign governments and media reporting on the Association's anti-terrorism efforts has not been overly negative. In this context, it should be noted that ASEAN governments have paid particular attention to the public diplomacy of the United States and Western public opinion. Although there is no direct linkage between US public diplomacy and Western media or public opinion *per se*, regional leaders in Southeast Asia appreciate the influence that US government diplomacy often has on shaping the mainstream views about other international actors. This mainstream view is important to ASEAN governments insofar negative media images of ASEAN may pose a threat due to the way in which they could influence trading and investment decisions affecting the region. For these reasons, and in view of the structural power of the United States, ASEAN governments have generally been particularly eager to avert being criticised, implicitly or explicitly, by Washington.

In the event, ASEAN's international standing did not immediately take a major hit in the first few months following September 11. This was surprising as ASEAN initially failed to produce little more than an ambivalent response in the international war against terrorism, as illustrated by the 2001 ASEAN Declaration on Joint Action to Counter Terrorism and further months of collective inaction. However, as previously noted, the majority of the original ASEAN countries, particularly the Philippines, Singapore, Malaysia and Thailand all contributed, within days, more or less unambiguously and effectively to the war on terror through an array of measures. The George W. Bush administration has been very appreciative of the assistance extended, even when not fully satisfied, and policy-makers at all levels as well as government officials used all available opportunities to publicly thank their counterparts in the ASEAN for their support. Arguably, Washington's official rhetoric is a key factor in explaining why ASEAN's standing in the first few weeks after September 11 did therefore not suffer a dramatic decline as a consequence of intramural difficulties to provide more unambiguous diplomatic and military succour. ASEAN did not have itself to thank for this development, but was happy to see both international attention largely focused elsewhere and no significant criticisms of its own role in the war on terror.

Very soon, however, some ASEAN members became ever more acutely aware of the possible repercussions for their collective standing of the failure by Jakarta to tackle seriously the problem of regional terrorist networks with alleged roots in Indonesia. Their careful prodding in Jakarta's direction remained without effect, however. Their concern about this was matched by that in Washington, and growing frustration over the extent to which President Megawati proved incapable or unwilling to meet the challenge of confronting suspected regional terrorists based in Indonesia soon led American officials to vary the tone of their official rhetoric. By early spring 2002, it was clear that Washington regarded Jakarta's stance as essentially unhelpful. Enhancing ASEAN's collective co-operation with Washington therefore ranked as a priority among the region's influential regional decision-makers outside Jakarta. As Malaysia's Foreign Minister, Syed Hamid Albar, put it before the signing of the joint US–ASEAN anti-terrorism declaration: 'There

is no better way of showing our willingness and seriousness of combating international terrorism than ... entering this US–ASEAN joint declaration.'[8]
The decision to release a joint statement with Washington proved important in temporarily lifting ASEAN's overall standing somewhat, judging by the coverage of the 35th ASEAN Ministerial Meeting. ASEAN also managed to win plaudits for its role in making the ARF – often perhaps unfairly considered a mere talk-shop – assume a concrete agenda at its Ninth Ministerial Meeting. That said, ASEAN's standing remained under threat due to Jakarta's procrastination and obstinacy, and vicious exchanges between Jakarta and Washington played a key part in this during September 2002. Consequently, the events of October 12 resembled for ASEAN a sword of Damocles descended. In the most horrific fashion, the high-handed rhetoric of some Indonesian politicians was exposed as naïve if not downright negligent. The travel advisories issued by Western governments in the aftermath of the bombings added, rightly or wrongly, to the impression that Southeast Asia was simply not the place to be. Implicit was the notion that the Association had, once again, mismanaged its regional affairs. Hence, although it happened more than a year after September 11, ASEAN had failed to avert a renewed plummeting of its international standing.

4.2. ASEAN as a diplomatic community, security regime and manager of regional order

There is wide agreement that ASEAN has for many years functioned as a diplomatic community and at least as a limited security regime.[9] As regards intramural relations, the Association has been credited in particular with successfully promoting mutual confidence and security among its members. ASEAN's diplomatic and security culture has played an important role in mediating historical differences, grievances and suspicions, irrespective of the fact that some of the region's longstanding conflicts have not been resolved and intermittent instances of mutual estrangement between some leaders have been the norm (Haacke 2003a). ASEAN can also be seen as an aspirant manager of regional order in so far as its members during its organisational existence have sought to address jointly a variety of challenges affecting Southeast Asia. To be sure, as Southeast Asian states possess a far better record in promoting bilateral defence co-operation among each other than at a multilateral intramural level, analysts have shied away from also invoking, say, the label of defence community to characterise the Association.

In the wake of September 11 ASEAN has continued to function as a diplomatic community in fighting regional and international terrorism even if its performance in this capacity was mired by substantial divergences among members. Jointly working out appropriate responses, developing work plans and putting these into practice, as well as the co-operation with the United States in particular, has clearly brought together an array of national institutions charged with combating the international aspects of terrorism.

ASEAN's performance as a security regime has been less inspiring, however. This is not to say that one should have expected September 11 to override longstanding dynamics of intramural conflict. However, it is notable and perhaps indicative that some bilateral relationships suffered various degrees of renewed damage in the post-September 11 period, not least due to the perceived disregard of aspects of ASEAN's diplomatic and security culture and lack of restraint in their respective pursuit of foreign policy objectives. For example, the challenges associated with September 11 have had no impact on the recent strife between Myanmar (Burma) and Thailand. In fact, Rangoon and Bangkok were again locked in a bitter diplomatic feud as of late May 2002 over a border violation, which was accompanied by the use of force, resulting in a five-month long border closure until mid-October 2002 (see Chapter 10). A second illustration is the fiery rhetoric emanating from Indonesian officials in reaction to Singapore Senior Minister Lee Kuan Yew's remarks in February 2002 that the city-state would remain at risk from terrorist attack as long as extremist elements in Indonesia were on the loose. More cynically inclined analysts would, of course, argue that in so far as ASEAN has been unable to quell bilateral feuding nothing at all has changed. Indeed, some might rightly stress that the key norms underpinning ASEAN co-operation such as non-interference or quiet diplomacy have for decades been practised with a certain degree of ambiguity.

September 11 has also again exposed the Association as an unlikely manager of regional order. This goal has always been pursued with different enthusiasm by member states. Indeed, members have long agreed on the importance of external powers in addressing external security threats. Still, ASEAN states have for some years hoped to win greater recognition as a manager of regional order. To promote this objective the Association among others agreed in July 2000 on the establishment of an ASEAN Troika. The Troika was 'to enable ASEAN to address in a timely manner urgent and important regional political and security issues and situations of common concern likely to disturb regional peace and harmony'. In view of the security challenges in the ASEAN region, the Troika concept would in theory appear to have allowed for its practical invocation both before and after September 11.[10] Although feeble attempts were made in this direction in relation to Myanmar, the Troika has yet to be convened. The issue of religious extremism and terrorism in Indonesia has also not been seen as an appropriate starting point for the Troika. Consequently, this new addition to the armoury of ASEAN as a manager of regional order has remained blunt, leaving the Association exposed to charges of inaction and ineffectiveness, similarly to those when the environmental, economic and political crises descended on ASEAN in the wake of the 1997/98 financial crisis.

The main reason for ASEAN's inability to project itself as a manager of regional order is not necessarily that the means available to ASEAN are *per se* deficient. However, its diplomatic instruments are subject to political agreement; as all of ASEAN's decisions in political-security matters are taken by consensus, they are also subject to the assent of its members. This implies that ASEAN has found it difficult to put on its agenda many issues even though they, as in the case of secessionism, religious extremism and terrorist activities, pose serious threats to regional security. In the case of Indonesia, which has traditionally firmly opposed outside intervention in its domestic affairs, the application of mechanisms such as the Troika has proved particularly difficult. Indeed, some newly shared understandings about ASEAN's diplomatic and security culture notwithstanding, the Association *de facto* remains impotent when it comes to dealing with security challenges emanating from within its membership. Worried about the consequences for regional security stemming from developments in Indonesia – but unable or unwilling to confront Jakarta on the underlying issues, or meeting with little success when doing so at the bilateral level – ASEAN states have left it to outsiders to apply the necessary political pressure. It is notable of course that this strategy too largely failed and that it was only the Bali bombings that rattled the Megawati administration sufficiently to join the war against terrorism in a more serious and sustained manner.

ASEAN has also been incapable of assuming the role of manager of regional order because it has to rely on peer pressure to address relevant issues even when a consensus has emerged that ASEAN should become involved. It is ironic that while close co-operation between ASEAN member states and the United States at regional and bilateral level is politically desirable and adept, this feature of ASEAN's post-September 11 stance may further undermine its attempt to win recognition as an aspirant manager of regional order. There is of course no intrinsic incompatibility between member states enhancing their respective bilateral security co-operation with the United States and effectively functioning as a diplomatic community and operating as a manager of regional order. Throughout ASEAN's organisational existence members have always retained their individual security and defence policies. Regional consent to the pursuit of defence ties with external powers was explicitly covered by ASEAN's Treaty of Amity and Co-operation as far back as 1976.

The point instead is that the decision by several ASEAN countries to considerably reinforce their political and security relationship with Washington demonstrates that members see a new need to provide an operational response that could otherwise not be met as effectively. In other words, post-September 11, several ASEAN states consider bilateral security co-operation with Washington necessary to meet both conventional security challenges and non-traditional security threats facing ASEAN states. For example, Manila's decision after September 11 to advance as much as possible bilateral security relations with Washington was motivated by a genuine concern for terrorism as perpetrated by the Abu Sayyaf group. Manila's interest in developing closer military co-operation with Washington should, however, also be understood against the background of continuing suspicions of China and the lack of an adequate national defence capacity. Singapore's interest in expanding military and intelligence co-operation with Washington serves both to deter regional neighbours and to make a contribution to confronting the new security challenges posed by international crime, including terrorism. This gives the United States an even bigger role in regional security than before the terrorist attacks and arguably diminishes the role of the Association.

Here one might interject that bilateral anti-terrorism co-operation within among ASEAN members will pick up, and that historically bilateral counter-insurgency co-operation produced a cobweb of regional security ties that helped to build intramural confidence and regional stability. However, post-September 11, it is not clear that in security terms the Association will benefit in the same way from bilateral or sub-regional anti-terrorism co-operation among members as has already been initiated or is still planned than it did from previous bilateral security co-operation. First, the pursuit of anti-terrorism co-operation has been subject and may remain subject to more political stresses than the shared struggle against insurgents involved. Also, turning to (sub-) regional mechanisms is also not necessarily considered helpful. Singapore has thus far, for example, rejected joining the sub-regional Agreement on Information Exchange and Establishment of Communication Procedures. That said, given the differential relevant institutional anti-terrorism expertise available among its membership the Association is likely to serve at least as a limited vehicle to help advance the coping capacity of individual member countries.

If ASEAN's future as a manager of regional order is hence doubtful, it should not be assumed that the institution into which its operating norms have been transposed to deal with the immediate post-Cold War challenges will remain relevant either. In other words, the question is whether the ARF, through which ASEAN has sought to mediate the differences among the major powers and between the major powers and itself, can also demonstrate relevance in meeting the new transnational security challenges. While the ASEAN Regional Forum has embraced the challenge of dealing with international terrorism, not least by committing itself to address the problem of terrorist financing, its relevance – at least for now – hangs in the balance. At least four factors are relevant. First, the ARF's relevance in anti-terrorism co-operation is limited by the nature of the Forum's past activities and working practices, that is, the focus on confidence building among its officials from the ministries of foreign affairs, and the limited involvement of defence officials. Put differently, the ARF has since its inception only been more of a first stop for members to engage in operational co-operation at working level. Second, the ARF's relevance is circumscribed by practical security co-operation already achieved between some ASEAN members and the United States in so far as this makes duplication unnecessary. And, third, the ARF's future relevance in the regional war on terror may also be compromised by attempts of other major powers to pursue regional counter-terrorism measures in co-operation forums that exclude the United States. The role of the ASEAN Regional Forum in the struggle against regional terrorism may, fourth, also be limited by the longstanding concerns that Western countries in particular have expressed about the division of labour, responsibility and influence within the Forum. In accordance with its aspiration to assert itself as manager of regional order in Southeast Asia, the Association upon the ARF's establishment assumed the role of 'primary driving force' in the latter. However, for some years now criticisms about ASEAN's leadership of the ARF have multiplied. Tellingly, several governments in the Western Pacific region, not least the United States, welcomed the first regional conference of defence ministers co-sponsored by the International Institute for Strategic Studies in Singapore in May 2002. This conference, to be repeated in 2003, is likely to become an institutionalised dialogue that may in some respects in future rival the ARF process. The increasing number of its bilateral military-to-military contacts will also reinforce the longstanding security role played by the United States and raise further questions about the contemporary relevance of the institutional settings through which ASEAN has in the past sought to win political recognition and influence and to build mutual confidence.

4.3. Accelerating great power competition in the ASEAN region

ASEAN has for years sought to establish a balance-of-power among the major regional states and between these countries and ASEAN that would allow the Association to prosper in a peaceful and stable environment. The creation of the ASEAN Regional Forum was very much guided by such considerations (Leifer 1996, Emmers 2001). In effect, the ARF involved a policy of multiple engagement whereby China in particular but also Japan was to be tied to regional processes of norm elaboration. The United States was equally to be engaged, not least in view of its market, its potential investments and the security it provided by dint of America's regional posture. Following September 11, however, ASEAN's relations with the great powers appear to be increasingly informed by a competitive struggle for influence by the United States, China, Japan and even India. To be clear, this chapter does not assert that what would seem to amount to a pattern of great power competition in Southeast Asia is a consequence of the events of September 11 or the ensuing war against terror. Instead, it is merely suggested that developments in members' bilateral security relations with the United States in the context of the multifaceted war against terror have accelerated and perhaps intensified the momentum and stakes of the great powers' multi-dimensional struggle for influence in the ASEAN region.

As previously noted, September 11 proved for the United States to be a catalyst for reinforcing its existing alliances and security relations with ASEAN states. The Bush administration has taken forward the agenda pursued by the (former) Commander of the US Pacific Command, Admiral Dennis Blair, who strove to establish and/or deepen military-to-military contacts to build trust among the region's armed forces by developing bilateral contacts, and proposing multilateral approaches to regional security. The objective of American military diplomacy has been to win for US forces even better access to regional ports and other infrastructure in Southeast Asia, a step designed to enhance Washington's overall regional military posture in the Asia-Pacific. In this context, the US government has recently successfully concluded a Mutual Logistics Support Agreement (MLSA) with Manila and held, albeit so far still unfruitful, discussions about future possibilities for access to Cam Ranh Bay. The MLSA, concluded in November 2002, allows for the 'reciprocal provision of logistic support, supplies and services' between Manila and Washington in a number of situations: joint military exercises, national emergencies and actual hostilities involving either party.[11] The objective of deeper military-to-military diplomacy and exchanges is also of course to win greater influence over present and future decision-makers in Southeast Asia. Recent steps by the Pentagon towards normalising military relations with Indonesia need to be seen in this context.

As regards Washington's economic diplomacy, a key objective has been to expand and deepen open trading and investment regimes to the advantage of US commercial interests. In this context, the United States not only worked hard to complete the United States – Singapore Free Trade Agreement, which was basically agreed by the end of November 2002, but also offered new commercial incentives to other ASEAN states. Just prior to the 8th ASEAN Summit in early November 2002, the President announced the Enterprise for ASEAN Initiative (EAI) that is designed to eventually create a regional network of bilateral free trade agreements (FTAs) between individual ASEAN states and the United States.[12] On the way towards such agreements Washington has offered to support WTO membership of Vietnam, Cambodia and Laos, and established precursory trade and investment frameworks agreements, or TIFAs. ASEAN's economic ministers and the United States Trade Representative are in the process of considering the development of an ASEAN-wide TIFA.[13]

Washington's decision to upgrade security and defence relations with ASEAN countries has followed the attempts of other major regional states to defend or extend their own influence in Southeast Asia. China's decision to strengthen bilateral relations with individual ASEAN states and the grouping as a whole after the region's financial crisis of 1997/98 is particularly noteworthy in this regard. Indeed, defence officials have indirectly alluded to China as a motivation for promoting regional security co-operation with ASEAN countries. As Admiral Blair (2000) contended, the fundamental security challenge for the United States in East Asia is to 'transform the balance of power approach proposed by those who advocate a multipolar global power structure into one where the prospect of using armed force to resolve disputes never arises' (p. 4). To be sure, the United States has seen China's efforts to promote relations with ASEAN not solely through the lenses of regional stability and military security, but also with the future political fungibility of increasing regional economic interdependence in mind. And in this context, US officials have duly noted Beijing's efforts to enhance its regional stature *inter alia* through accelerating economic interaction with the ASEAN states. These attempts gave rise in November 2000 to the proposal by Prime Minister Zhu Rongji to create within ten years the afore-mentioned ASEAN–China FTA (see Chapter 5).

Washington's success in using September 11 to reinforce its regional security role and working towards deeper political and economic co-operation with the Association has in turn been interpreted in China as rendering less significant Beijing's diplomatic gains made in the aftermath of the 1997/98 East Asian financial crisis. The dynamics of the emerging competition for influence are well illustrated by events in the lead-up to and at the 8th ASEAN Summit in Phnom Penh in November 2002. China's government was keen, for example, to use the Ninth ARF Ministerial Meeting as an occasion to re-emphasise its own new security concept in contra-distinction to the alliance concept and the US focus on military security. During the summit, China and ASEAN signed a joint declaration on the further strengthening and deepening of co-operation in the field of non-traditional security. Perhaps in a further indication of the increasing concern about Washington's influence across the maritime heart of the ASEAN region after September 11, Beijing also proposed to ASEAN to deal with transnational threats to security (including terrorism) within the APT framework, which of course excludes the United States. All these proposals show that Beijing is keen to remain relevant in Southeast Asia, including in the war on terror. At the time of their summit in November 2002, China has moreover sought to reassert its regional influence by extending a hand of partnership to the Association in their joint efforts to forge compromise deals in working towards the world's most populous FTA, formally embedded within the ASEAN–China Economic Co-operation Framework agreement. Meanwhile, Japanese policy-makers and business interests have become increasingly concerned about Beijing's push for the rapid development of its political-security and economic relations with the Association. The PRC's success in winning ASEAN's assent to the establishment of an ASEAN–China FTA in particular has been interpreted as an indication of China's growing influence in Southeast Asia and hence been perceived as potentially threatening Tokyo's own regional position and standing.

ASEAN is naturally keen to exploit the attention that it is given by the great powers, both to promote deeper economic integration with both Northeast Asia as well as the United States and to address issues or resolve disputes that have a bearing on regional stability and security. Its members have evidently also felt sufficiently comfortable to forge links with China, as demonstrated by the aforementioned ASEAN–China joint declaration on non-traditional security issues and the ASEAN–China Economic Co-operation Framework, both agreed in November 2002. The diplomatic outcome having fallen short of their initial negotiating position, ASEAN governments sought to compensate by moving forward their relations not only with China but also with Japan, indeed with all of the other major regional powers. Hence, within hours of the aforementioned agreements, the heads of government of ASEAN and Japan signed a Joint Declaration on a Comprehensive Economic Partnership, which is also to be realised within ten years and may include elements of a FTA. The extent and accelerating tempo of attempts to forge closer relations between ASEAN and the major powers is illustrated further by ASEAN's decision to exploit India's eagerness to explore with ASEAN the long-term objective of a regional trade and investment area and the decision to hold annual ASEAN–India summits. This follows practical input to the war on terror by both Tokyo and New Delhi, which has seen both win a larger security role than they enjoyed before the terrorist attacks.

5. Conclusion

The terrorist attacks of 11 September 2001 and 12 October 2002 have presented major challenges to ASEAN, particularly as regards the image of the Association as a diplomatic community and security regime. In some ways, the challenge of September 11 was in fact less serious than that which emerged on the back of the Bali bombings of October 12. If anything, Indonesia's decisive political and law enforcement response testifies to this. Whether or not ASEAN will ultimately rid itself of the scourge of terrorism is of course an open question. However, it is already clear that the implications of September 11 and October 12 can only be described as serious. ASEAN's international standing was hurt, not because the Association necessarily failed in its response to the war on terror after September 11, but because ASEAN and the United States achieved very little in persuading Indonesia to deal with religious extremism and suspected terrorists before the Bali bombings. The robust participation on the part of the Philippines, Singapore and Malaysia in the global war on terror during the first that followed September 11 does not alter this assessment.

Another major implication of the terrorist attacks on September 11 and October 12 is that these events have done little to strengthen ASEAN as a security regime and further undermined any pretensions some members may still have had for it to assume the mantle of manager of regional order. ASEAN's response to the terrorist attacks again highlighted how the strict adherence to members' diplomatic and security culture might impact on regional security in less than sanguine ways. While important to mediate a diverse set of interests as well as intermittent estrangement between members, even new shared understandings relating to the 'ASEAN way' do not offer an operational response to the threats posed by regional and international terrorism. Such a response can instead be crafted only by drawing at least partially on the knowledge and capacities of external powers, particularly the United States. The chapter suggested that ASEAN has little alternative but for co-operation with the major powers to be expanded to address not merely the old conventional security challenges, but equally the new transnational ones. The drawback for ASEAN states is that the focus on bilateral security co-operation with an external power, which involves both more and deeper intelligence co-operation and direct military-to-military ties, may yet render existing regional institutions in the ASEAN region less relevant.

Finally, the chapter showed how by supporting and inviting the United States to address trans-regional threats to security, individual members of the Association have accelerated the competition for influence among the major powers in the ASEAN region. Although at this point in time the great powers' competition for influence in Southeast Asia seems benign and ASEAN members' economic and national security may well receive a boost by virtue of the parallel pursuit of closer interactions with the major powers, a more precarious scenario is also possible. This would see ASEAN being exposed to a struggle for influence with a sharper and darker competitive edge, which would perhaps see its members increasingly placed under pressure by the major powers to act in ways that do not disadvantage their respective position and objectives *vis-à-vis* the other powers. However, how such competitive dynamics might be played out in future months and years is difficult to say. Indeed, the decisions taken by the great powers in the context on the war against terrorism as well as domestic factors in the ASEAN states may yet lead to unforeseen developments. Some believe, for example, that a sustained focus on military measures in the war on terror, linked to what some have termed 'praetorian unilateralism' may undermine the legitimacy of US action and lead to 'civilizational enmity' (Ramakrishna 2002). This would also see Muslim opinion in Southeast Asia inflamed in ways that would have implications for US–ASEAN ties. Having recently described its own system as the 'single surviving model of human progress', one should also not be entirely surprised if at some point the Bush administration was tempted to put greater stress on the promotion of American values and institutions in its foreign policy towards the region. Such an eventuality would probably be viewed as a renewed attempt at US interference and force regional governments to adopt a more ambivalent attitude in their relations with Washington. After all, many ASEAN governments are not only concerned with external or transnational security challenges but also questions of regime survival.

Notes

1. From statement made by Donald Emmerson, 'Southeast Asia and the United States Since 11 September', hearing on Southeast Asia and 9/11: Regional Trends and US Interests, Subcommittee on East Asia and the Pacific, Committee on International Relations, US House of Representatives, Washington, D.C., 12 December 2001, http://www.house.gov/international_relations/emme1212.htm.
2. 'Address to a Joint Session of Congress and the American People', Washington, D.C., 20 September 2001, http://www.whitehouse.gov/news/releases/2001/09/20010920-8.htm.
3. Another case has been Ahmed Ibrahim Bilal who was deported to the United States by Kuala Lumpur.
4. Balikatan means 'shouldering the load together'.
5. Remarks made by Powell at Roundtable with ASEAN Journalists, Washington, D.C., 25 July 2002, http://www.state.gov/secretary/rm/2002/12207.htm.
6. *Bangkok Post*, 22.02.2002, 'ASEAN to unite against terror'.
7. For an in-depth discussion of the development of the 'ASEAN way', see Haacke (2003a). See also Chapter 8 in this volume by Alan Collins.
8. *BBC World Service*, 24.07.2002, 'Terror tops agenda of Asian forum'.
9. On this point see Leifer (1989) and Huxley (1993). For the view that ASEAN has come close to being a security community, see Acharya (2001). For a critical assessment of ASEAN, also see Narine (2002).
10. For more details on the subject see Chapter 8.
11. *Straits Times*, 22.11.2002, 'Pact allows US military to stay in Philippines'.
12. See White House, Fact Sheet: Enterprise for ASEAN Initiative, 26 October 2002, http://www.whitehouse.gov/news/releases/2002/10/20021026-7.html.; US–ASEAN Business Council, 'Announcement on "Enterprise for ASEAN Initiative" Marks New Chapter in US–ASEAN Relations', 26 November 2002, http://www.us-asean.org/Press_Releases/EAI.htm.
13. See Chapter 5 for a detailed discussion on new FTA projects in the Asia-Pacific.

References

Abuza, Z. (2003) *Tentacles of Terror: Al Qaeda's Southeast Asian Network*, Lynne Rienner, Boulder, CO.

Acharya, A. (2001) *Constructing a Security Community in Southeast Asia: ASEAN and the Problem of Regional Order*, Routledge, London.

ASEAN (2001a) *Joint Communique, ASEAN Ministerial Meeting on Transnational Crime*, Singapore, 11 October 2001, http://www.asean.or.id/5621.htm.

ASEAN (2001b) *ASEAN Declaration on Joint Action to Counter Terrorism*, Bandar Seri Begawan, 5 November 2001, http://www.asean.or.id/5620.htm.

ASEAN (2002a) *Joint Communique of the Special ASEAN Ministerial Meeting on Terrorism*, Kuala Lumpur, 20–21 May 2002, http://www.asean.or.id/5618.htm.

ASEAN (2002b) *ASEAN–United States of America Joint Declaration for Cooperation to Combat International Terrorism*, Bandar Seri Begawan, 1 August 2002, http://www.asean.or.id/7424.htm.

ASEAN (2002c) *Declaration on Terrorism by the 8th ASEAN Summit*, Phnom Penh, 3 November 2002, http://www.asean.or.id/13154.htm.

ASEAN Regional Forum (2002) *ARF Statement on Measures Against Terrorist Financing*, ASEAN Secretariat, Jakarta, 30 July.

Blair, D.C. (2000) 'The Role of the Armed Forces in Regional Security Co-operation', 25 August 2000, *PacNet Newsletter* no. 34, 25 August 2000.

Emmers, R. (2001) 'The Influence of the Balance of Power Factor within the ASEAN Regional Forum', *Contemporary Southeast Asia*, Vol. 23(2), pp. 275–91.

Ganesan, N. (1999) *'Bilateral Tensions in post-Cold War ASEAN'*, Institute of Southeast Asian Studies, Singapore.

Haacke, J. (2003) *ASEAN's Diplomatic and Security Culture: Origins, Development and Prospects*, RoutledgeCurzon, London.

Henderson, J. (1999) *Reassessing ASEAN*, Adelphi Paper 328, Oxford University Press/ Institute for Strategic and International Studies, Oxford.

Hess, G.R. (1987) *The United States' Emergence as a Southeast Asian Power, 1940–1950*, Columbia University Press, New York.

Huxley, T. (1993) *Insecurity in the ASEAN Region*, Whitehall Paper 23, Royal Institute Services, Institute for Defence Studies, London.

Huxley, T. (2002) *Disintegrating Indonesia? Implications for Regional Security*, Adelphi Paper 349, Oxford University Press/International Institute for Strategic Studies, Oxford.

Leifer, M. (1989) *ASEAN and the Security of South-East Asia*, Routledge, London.

Leifer, M. (1996) *The ASEAN Regional Forum: Extending ASEAN's Model of Regional Security*, Adelphi Paper 302, Oxford University Press/ International Institute for Strategic Studies, Oxford.

Narine, S. (2002) *Explaining ASEAN: Regionalism in Southeast Asia*, Lynne Rienner, Boulder.

Posen, B.R. and Ross, A.L. (1996/97) 'Competing Visions for US Grand Strategy', *International Security*, Vol. 21(3), pp. 5–53.

Ramakrishna, K. (2002) *911, American Praetorian Unilateralism and the Impact of State–Society Relations in Southeast Asia*, Working Paper No. 26, Institute of Defence and Strategic Studies, Singapore.

The White House (2002) *National Security Strategy*, Washington DC.

8

ASEAN: Challenged from Within and Without

Alan Collins

1. Introduction

The clouds of the financial storm that raged in 1997–98 continue, metaphorically, to envelope Southeast Asia. Although the region is showing signs of financial recovery it is tentative and remains vulnerable to shocks in the international political economy. The loss of financial confidence in the American market following a series of scandals in 2002, coupled to the threat of war against Iraq, has begun to impact upon the economic recovery of Southeast Asia. Singapore, the region's economically most secure state, recorded only a 3.7 per cent rate of growth between July and September 2002. This was considerably less than the 7 per cent estimated rate of growth for the third quarter, and whereas this quarter was expected to show a levelling out on a quarter-on-quarter basis, it actually dropped by 10.3 per cent. The literal clouds that float over the region are no less threatening. With the forest-fires on Kalimantan and elsewhere in Indonesia sending pollutants now annually into the atmosphere, the euphemistically named 'haze' remains a significant economic and environmental problem. On the ground a variety of transnational problems are threatening the stability of the region. These include drug trafficking, which in 1999 the Thai government identified as the number one threat to national security. Other forms of international crime (people-smuggling, money laundering), and since 11 September 2001 global terrorism, are also causing tensions in the region.

The picture of Southeast Asia is thus a far cry from that of the first-half of 1997. Prior to the financial crisis that began in Thailand, the region's international organisation, the Association of Southeast Asian Nations (ASEAN), had good cause to celebrate its thirtieth birthday.[1] Born during the troubled times of *Konfrontasi* and the Malaysian–Philippine dispute over Sabah, ASEAN by the summer of 1997 could boast a membership of 'tiger economies' that were courted by the major powers. Confidence was high with ASEAN assuming the primary role in the new regional security body – the ASEAN Regional Forum (ARF) – and expanding to incorporate the remaining states of Southeast Asia. Eighteen months later, at the end of 1998, this picture of ASEAN was hardly recognisable. At the 33rd ASEAN Ministerial Meeting (AMM) held in Bangkok in July 2000, the Singaporean Foreign Minister, S. Jayakumar, even called on ASEAN to reinvent itself (Tay 2001). The response of ASEAN members to these various challenges has, though, failed to impress. Commentaries on Southeast Asia, and ASEAN in particular, have been downbeat. Narine's (1999) view that the prospects for ASEAN's 'growth and development are, at best, discouraging', and the most likely outcome is that 'ASEAN will become increasingly irrelevant', are widely shared (p. 375). The challenges that ASEAN face come from within and without the Association. From within there are worries that with Indonesia – the *primus inter pares* of ASEAN – focusing on internal problems, ASEAN is adrift and without clear leadership. While this is an important factor, it is perhaps also pertinent to note that the two previously reform-minded ASEAN members, Thailand and the Philippines, have also become more preoccupied with domestic affairs. The current Thai government of Thaksin Shinawatra has no interest in pursuing the progressive proposals of its predecessor, such as 'flexible engagement'. Meanwhile economic and domestic strife, especially in Mindanao, have taken centre stage in the Philippines. There are also concerns about certain members taking unilateral actions that are undermining ASEAN's concerted approach. Singapore's and increasingly Thailand's interest in pursuing bilateral free trade agreements, and the implications of this for the ASEAN Free Trade Agreement (AFTA) is a prime example.[2]

From without the impact of globalisation has increased the interaction between Southeast Asia and the rest of Asia and the Pacific. The ASEAN goal of creating a Zone of Peace, Freedom and Neutrality (ZOPFAN) that would limit the influence of extra-regional powers in Southeast Asia has been exchanged for engagement with them. The establishment of the ARF and the ASEAN Plus Three (APT) talks indicate an appreciation among the ASEAN members that Southeast Asian security and economic problems cannot be considered separately from the rest of East Asia. The inaugural meeting of the South-West Pacific Dialogue Forum in October 2002 also revealed that some problems facing ASEAN members are best dealt with in a multilateral forum outside the ASEAN framework. If the solutions to Southeast Asian problems are to be found in the other forums of East Asia or the wider Asia-Pacific, then this begs the question, what is the purpose of ASEAN? At the turn of a new century, ASEAN is thus faced with challenges from within and without.

2. Setting the scene: achieving security via national and regional resilience

The Association of Southeast Asian Nations (ASEAN) was established in 1967 with five founding member states (Indonesia, Malaysia, the Philippines,

Singapore and Thailand), and since then its membership has expanded to ten states. Brunei joined in 1984, and with the original five comprises the more developed ASEAN members, or 'ASEAN-6'. Vietnam became ASEAN's seventh member in 1995, and in 1997 Laos and Burma (Myanmar) joined. In 1999, after its admission had been postponed in 1997, Cambodia became ASEAN's tenth member. The four members to join in the 1990s are collectively known as the 'CMLV' members, and are less developed than the ASEAN-6. By the end of the twentieth century the goal of an ASEAN-10 had been achieved. In time it is expected that ASEAN will enlarge again and welcome East Timor as its eleventh member.

Since it was first created, ASEAN has been primarily concerned with establishing stability in Southeast Asia. This stability comes from two sources: first, the establishment of strong nation-states, and second, limiting, or at least directing, the involvement of external powers in the region. ASEAN has thus been, and indeed continues to be, first and foremost an Association of states engaged in nation and region-building. In its formative years this was known as 'national and regional resilience'. National resilience, or nation building, entailed each member developing national economies, strengthening the sense of national identity among their diverse ethnic peoples and safeguarding the political regime and state borders from insurgency movements. Of equal importance was that these goals were to be achieved without interference from neighbouring states or states external to Southeast Asia. The attainment of state security was thus dependent upon the successful achievement of a strong nation-state, with state sovereignty respected from within and without the state. It becomes evident, therefore, why security in Southeast Asia is conceived of as comprehensive, and amounts to much more than purely military and external threat concerns. It also explains why non-interference and regional autonomy (regional solutions to regional problems) have been important elements in attaining state security.

National resilience led to regional stability, it was argued, because by addressing the dangers of subversion the state remains a viable entity and prevents the contagion of communist insurgency and ethnic separatism from infecting neighbouring states. Consequently, if all states adopted national resilience they would provide regional stability, or regional resilience. Regional resilience has been likened to a chain in which the chain derives its strength from its constituent parts. Regional resilience would likewise support national resilience by creating stable external relations that would enable the regimes to concentrate on national development. Leifer (1990) captures the logic of the process when he writes, '[b]y cultivating intra-mural accord and so reducing threats among themselves, the ASEAN states would be able to devote themselves through the instrumentality of economic development to the common cause of political stability' (p. 2). In practice this meant that the state elite would be allowed to engage in what were often brutal policies against their own people in the knowledge that their neighbours would not interfere. Political stability was thus achieved by removing alternative sources for the people's loyalty. ASEAN publicly endorsed regional resilience in the 1976 Treaty of Amity and Cooperation in Southeast Asia (TAC) and the 1971 ZOPFAN.[3] The ZOPFAN declaration captures the second element of achieving regional stability: minimising the influence of external powers. With the British announcing their withdrawal of forces east of the Suez in 1968, and Nixon announcing at Guam in 1969 that the United States would not continue to carry the burden of fighting communism abroad, a power vacuum appeared to emerge. A power vacuum that communist China or the Soviet Union might fill. The Indonesian Foreign Minister, Adam Malik, in September 1971 articulated ASEAN's response to the changing international environment:

> I strongly believe that it is only through developing among ourselves an area of internal cohesion and stability, based on indigenous socio-political and economic strength, that we can ever hope to assist in the early stabilisation of a new equilibrium in the region that would not be the exclusive 'diktat' of the major powers...In fact, I am convinced that unless the big powers acknowledge and the Southeast Asian nations themselves assume a greater and more direct responsibility in the maintenance of security in the area, no lasting stability can ever be achieved.[4]

The failure of the United States in South Vietnam confirmed Malik's opinion. American intervention led to an increase in violence that also spread to neighbouring countries, and not only did it fail to increase, it actually undermined, the legitimacy of the Saigon regime. This is not to suggest that ZOPFAN led Southeast Asian states to isolate themselves from external powers, indeed with the exception of Indonesia they maintained defence ties with the Western powers. Rather, it sought to put ASEAN members in the driving seat when it came to discussions on the region's stability. In 1971, this was more an ambition for the future than a reflection of the present circumstance. In this chapter, the challenges that ASEAN have faced since the 1997/98 financial crisis will be assessed in terms of which challenges emanate from within ASEAN and from external bodies.

3. The challenge from within

At the Sixth ASEAN Summit held in Hanoi in December 1998 ASEAN announced its Hanoi Plan of Action (HPA), which was essentially ASEAN's first collective response to the 1997/98 financial crisis. Writing within a year of the HPA, Ramcharan (2000) concluded that at 'the Hanoi Summit in 1998...a consensus seemed to have been reached on a clear differentiation of politico-security issues and issues on political economy: in the former case, the ASEAN way applies; in the latter it no longer does' (p. 81). What led Ramcharan to this conclusion, and is it possible for ASEAN to operate in accordance with the 'ASEAN way' in politico-security issues and not on issues in the political economy? Indeed, what is the so-called 'ASEAN way'? This essentially refers to both the principles that act as a code of conduct governing the members' interactions and the processes through which the ASEAN members interact. The degree to which ASEAN member states act in accordance with the principles and processes is questionable, and thus it is a contentious issue as to whether the ASEAN way exists at all (Busse 1999, Nischalke 2000). The codes of conduct are the principles enshrined in the 1967 Bangkok Declaration: mutual respect for political independence, territorial integrity, and national identity; non-interference in the internal affairs of one another; peaceful settlement of disputes; renunciation of the threat or use of force; and effective co-operation. These principles are drawn from the UN Charter and not therefore peculiar to ASEAN. The norm of non-interference though has come to have a special meaning in the ASEAN context, and this will be the norm examined. The processes refer to the consensual, informal, decision-making process of ASEAN that takes place behind closed doors. There is no public shaming of a member that refuses to agree with the other members, indeed, pronouncements require all the members' support; ASEAN declarations create the impression of a co-operative body.[5] This process, coupled to non-interference, has created an organisation that supports its members by creating the impression of public unity.

The feature the 'ASEAN way' is most readily associated with what is often called the organisation's *cardinal principle* of non-interference. In the ASEAN context non-interference does not mean that members are indifferent towards one another; indeed the elites have aided one another (see also Chapters 7 and 10). This support for fellow elites can be seen as part of the nation-building process. In this instance it concerns assisting a regime to achieve legitimacy. When Corazon Aquino replaced Ferdinand Marcos in the Philippines, her position in power was threatened by both the communists and disgruntled military officers. Despite security concerns, other ASEAN member representatives attended the Manila summit in December 1987, and thereby manifest their willingness to endorse President Aquino's authority. During Vietnam's occupation of Cambodia, ASEAN supported a coalition of opposition of groups (CGDK–Coalition Government of Democratic Kampuchea) to the Vietnamese installed regime. Again in 1997, an ASEAN organised 'Troika' of foreign ministers was sent to Cambodia to mediate between the parties when intra-factional conflict arose.

By 1998 this principle of non-interference was under threat. In the summer of 1998, the Thai Foreign Minister, Surin Pitsuwan, had called upon ASEAN to adopt a policy of 'flexible engagement'. He was arguing that in the wake of the financial crisis, and specifically problems in Burma that were having an effect on Thailand, 'it is obvious that ASEAN countries have an overriding interest in the internal affairs of its fellow members and may, on occasion, find it necessary to recommend a certain course of action on specific issues that affect US all, directly or indirectly' (Haacke 1999: 585). Although other ASEAN members, with the exception of the Philippines, rejected flexible engagement and instead proposed enhanced interaction, late 1998 witnessed a series of public and critical comments directed against one ASEAN member by two others. These comments came from the then leaders of Indonesia, B.J. Habibie, and the Philippines, Joseph Estrada, regarding the arrest and detention of Malaysia's Deputy Prime Minister, Anwar Ibrahim. Both raised the prospect of boycotting the APEC summit to be held in Kuala Lumpur and both met Anwar's daughter, Nurual Izzah, who led protests against the Malaysian Prime Minister, Dr Mahathir Mohamad. Such actions are clearly at odds with the principle of non-interference. Not only were ASEAN members criticising another ASEAN member over its handling of an internal problem, but they were also giving tacit support to the opposition.

Had the Pandora's box of non-interference been opened? Not according to Ramcharan (2000), who considers the 'ASEAN way' to still be the *modus operandi* of the Association on politico-security issues. In this arena ASEAN has initiated a foreign ministers' retreat, created a Troika and adopted the procedures for its mechanism to resolve intra-mural disputes, namely the ASEAN High Council. Four ASEAN members even contributed to the peace-keeping force sent to East Timor. All four initiatives confirm Ramcharan's assertion. The ASEAN foreign ministers' retreat, which was initiated in July 1999, has become an annual event. Although foreign ministers can broach any subject for discussion this does not indicate an endorsement of flexible engagement. There is no suggestion that a topic can be discussed against the wishes of those directly involved, and, as the name 'retreat' suggests, the discussion takes place away from public scrutiny thus maintaining ASEAN's preference for closed-door discussions. The decision taken at the 33rd AMM in July 2000 to establish a Troika also confirms the continuation of the 'ASEAN way', and in particular the cardinal principle of non-interference. The Troika is an *ad hoc* body comprising of three ASEAN foreign ministers. It was established to 'address in a timely manner urgent and important regional political and security issues and situations of common concern likely to disturb regional peace and harmony', yet, it was to accomplish such a feat in accordance with 'the core principles of consensus and non-interference' (ASEAN Troika 2000). Unsurprisingly, the Troika has not initiated a host of issues that have disturbed the region's peace and harmony, the deterioration of Burmese–Thai relations in early 2001 being a case in point. Although relations between these ASEAN neighbours had worsened because of drug trafficking and the ongoing clashes between Burmese government troops and separatist forces that live along the Thai–Burma border, they reached such a low ebb in 2001 that when Burmese forces took over a Thai border outpost there followed an extensive exchange of fire between both sides. Despite the significance of two ASEAN members using force against one another, it was evident that neither wished for third-party intervention and the Troika was not convened.

The procedures adopted for the ASEAN High Council also reaffirm the importance of ASEAN's consensual decision-making process. If a member state decides to use the ASEAN High Council[6] to resolve a dispute, it can only be convened with the consent of the other party. Both parties are supposed to seek an accommodation through diplomacy prior to meeting in the High Council, and if they fail to find a solution then any decision taken by the High Council is based upon consensus. Non-interference thus remains at the forefront of ASEAN thinking, and this helps to explain the actions of some ASEAN members when they contributed to an international peace-keeping force for East Timor in 1999 – the International Force for East Timor (INTERFET). Four ASEAN members (Thailand, the Philippines, Singapore and Malaysia) contributed to INTERFET, with a Thai general holding deputy command. Invited to contribute by Jakarta – without such consent they would not have become involved – their presence was designed to support Indonesia in two ways. First, the then Indonesian President, B.J. Habibie, had come to resent Australia's leading role in the unfolding East Timor crisis. Thus, the presence of 'friendly' ASEAN states was welcomed. In this sense ASEAN was responding to a request for assistance by a fellow member. Second, ASEAN members were concerned that Indonesia's international standing, and by association ASEAN's image as a whole, was damaged by the violence in East Timor, especially given the complicity in that violence by the Indonesian army. By being seen to act, these ASEAN members were thus seeking to limit the damage done to Indonesia's reputation and indeed to their own. It is pertinent to note that ASEAN was sensitive to criticism of its record on human rights because only two years previously it had admitted Burma. Although it may seem odd that INTERFET is evidence of non-interference, such intervention was nevertheless sought by Jakarta and that by acting the members were seeking to assist a fellow member. As Funston (1998) argues, 'helping neighbouring governments and countries – acting as a mutual support group – is very much the essence of ASEAN' (p. 27).

While we should generally agree with Ramcharan's (2000) assessment on the prevailing 'ASEAN way' regarding politico-security issues, what of issues pertaining to the economic field, which as Ramcharan contends the 'ASEAN way' no longer applies? Here there has indeed been a frenzy of activity, with ASEAN producing a plethora of acronyms since the 1997/98 financial crisis. Since then, ASEAN has created an ASEAN Surveillance Process (ASP), is working towards an ASEAN Investment Area (AIA), has speeded up the implementation of the AFTA, and instigated an Initiative for ASEAN Integration (IAI) to prevent the CMLV members falling behind the economic advancement of the ASEAN-6 and hence to avoid a 'two-tier' ASEAN transpiring.

On the face of it, Ramcharan (2000) appears right in his judgement. The ASP, endorsed by ASEAN finance ministers on 4 October 1999, involves 'exchanging information and discussing [the] economic and financial development of Member States in the region'. It does this through 'a peer review process' designed to prevent another crisis by 'propos[ing] possible regional and national level actions' (Terms of Understanding on the Establishment of the ASEAN Surveillance Process 1998). To make this an effective monitoring body the ASP would require detailed information regarding each member's economy. Such intrusiveness into the economies of each member can be seen in the other programmes. The AIA is intended to encourage foreign investment in ASEAN by obliging member states to open their industries for investments by foreign and ASEAN investors by 2010, while the IAI framework calls upon the ASEAN-6 to assist in the development of the CMLV's economies. In other words, these programmes call upon the members to co-ordinate their actions and possibly, as Goh Chok Tong, the Singaporean Prime Minister has intimated, establish an ASEAN version of the European Economic Community of the 1950s.[7] Such close co-ordination and monitoring of their economies is certainly at odds with the non-interference principle.

The implementation of these programmes though indicates that the 'ASEAN way', and non-interference, remains very much in evidence. For example, while the ASP in theory has been established to monitor member's economies and act as an early warning mechanism if it detects worrying developments, this intrusiveness has left it moribund. Member states are not obliged to provide the economic data that the ASP needs, they instead agreed to submit the information on a voluntary basis. The details of each member's economy the ASP would require in order to act as a surveillance mechanism would be considerable. In view of the sensitivity of such data it is perhaps unsurprising that progress on the ASP has been slow and disappointing. ASEAN's Secretary-General, Rodolfo Severino, admitted this when he noted the 'reluctance by some member economies to reveal "too much" information and data' (Hund 2002: 110). Kraft (2000) also makes this point when he writes, it is the ASP's 'need for a degree of transparency that some members of the organisation have found objectionable. Malaysia and Singapore have opposed turning over the kind of macroeconomic data needed ... Laos, Myanmar and Vietnam have likewise been reported as registering their misgivings about it. The plan bogged down before it had a chance to be tested' (p. 458).

The ASP actually highlights the weakness of the 'ASEAN way's' informal procedures, since this is clearly not compatible with an intrusive surveillance mechanism that by scrutinising member's economic data could alert ASEAN to an impeding crisis. This reluctance to establish mechanisms that impinge upon member's sovereignty can also be seen in the AIA. The AIA is intended to encourage foreign investment in ASEAN by obliging member states to open their industries for investments by foreign and ASEAN investors by 2010. However, the institutional framework to ensure compliance shows reluctance among the ASEAN members to pool their sovereignty. The body established to oversee the project is the AIA Council, which comprises the ministers responsible for investment and the ASEAN Secretary-General. The AIA Council answers to ASEAN Economic Ministers (AEM). Hund (2002) thus argues the 'AIA Council is no independent body to oversee the unconditional implementation of the AIA, but merely represents the extended arm of the national governments' (p. 107). Hund also notes that there exist no punitive measures for penalising non-compliance.

In addition to these developments there are also signs that as the deadline for AFTA's implementation nears a degree of backsliding is taking place. The Malaysian government has already managed to defer tariff reduction from 2003 until 2005 for its automotive industries, and in 2002 the Philippines President, Gloria Arroyo, openly stated that she intended to 'slow the (tariff) liberalization program phase ... to the minimum and take full advantage of all accepted loopholes allowed'.[8] These deferments can occur because the regulations governing AFTA allow members to delay the transfer of a product to the Inclusion List (those products on which tariff reductions between 0 and 5 per cent will apply) or even withdraw it from the Inclusion List. In light of this the likelihood of AFTA being fully implemented is questionable. Hund (2000) argues, 'AFTA invites the continuous reassessment, renegotiation, modification and, eventually, dissolution, of the original consensus ... subjecting [AFTA] to the changing developments in, and power-play politics of, intra-ASEAN relations' (pp. 104–5).

ASEAN has thus rejected the opportunity to reinvent itself and has instead sought to maintain its *modus operandi* of non-interference. The problem for ASEAN is that while non-interference assisted in nation-building in the past, the current international environment requires ASEAN to rethink this principle. The transnational challenges that the Troika or the foreign ministers 'retreat' could help to resolve are only likely to work if the members pool their sovereignty and give them the power to co-ordinate members' actions. Such co-ordination will invariably require transparency and dialogue over domestic affairs, a co-ordination of activity that cannot be hostage to member state cries of non-interference if it is going to work. Likewise in the economic field, if the programmes involve monitoring member state economies, they will need a degree of intrusiveness that requires economic transparency. Commenting on the initiatives taken by ASEAN at the 2000 and 2001 AMMs, Nischalke (2002) dismisses them as producing 'meagre results' that have given 'further impetus to the notion of ASEAN's progressive marginalisation' (p. 90). If ASEAN is to reinvent itself and respond effectively to the challenges that have beset it, it will need to address the cardinal principle of non-interference. This is ASEAN's challenge from within.

4. The challenge from without

ASEAN was established to be a regional solution to regional problems, and in the spirit of the ZOPFAN declaration this was to be achieved by keeping external powers at an arm's length. This changed in the early 1990s as ASEAN members remained dedicated to Malik's appeal to be the ones holding the primary responsibility for the region's security, but now this was to be achieved through engagement with external powers. In the economic field this can be seen in the Asia-Pacific Economic Cooperation (APEC) forum, and in the security field in the ARF. In the latter especially, ASEAN members – buoyed by their economic success before 1997 – were able to assume the role of primary driver. Both, though, have proven a disappointment. APEC was widely perceived as inactive during the 1997/98 financial crisis (see Chapter 1), while the ARF has been hamstrung by the need to operate at a speed acceptable to its slowest member. Notwithstanding a recent burst of enthusiasm over the ARF's approach towards terrorism, the reaction to the ARF has been one of disappointment (Narine 1997, Lim 1998, Emmers 2001, Garofano 2002).

The period since the financial crisis though has witnessed the emergence of another forum through which ASEAN members are engaging with external powers. This process is known as the APT talks, which began in December 1997 when the heads of government from Japan, China and South Korea met with their ASEAN counterparts at the ASEAN Informal Summit held in Kuala Lumpur. A year later, at Hanoi, it was agreed that these meetings should become annual, and in 2000 finance ministers met in May and foreign ministers met after the annual July AMM; these meetings have also become annual. At the 35th AMM held at Bandar Seri Begawan in Brunei in July 2002, the foreign ministers of Japan, China and South Korea held their first three-way meeting, and it was agreed that this too would become an annual event alongside the APT talks. The Malaysian government is keen to create an APT Secretariat, and while this is currently regarded as premature, the view of Singapore's Foreign Minister, S. Jayakumar, is that the APT is 'here to stay', and the question now, 'is how to nurture it'.[9] The APT has thus emerged as a key forum through which the ASEAN members are engaging three East Asian states. This new framework also represents a nascent interest in the notion of East Asian regionalism and, as Chapters 4 and 5 discuss in more detail, its development may be broadly understood in a post-financial crisis context. The speed with which the 1997/98 financial crisis spread from Southeast Asia to Northeast Asia had revealed in a dramatic fashion the interdependence of East Asia's economies. Speaking in 1999 the Singaporean Prime Minister, Goh Chok Tong, said, 'you cannot talk about Northeast Asia and Southeast Asia. What happens in Southeast Asia will have an impact on Northeast Asia'. What is the consequence of such interdependency? Goh provided the answer when he concluded, 'now we are thinking in terms of evolving an East Asian community'.[10] In other words, providing an East Asian solution to East Asian problems.

Part of the motivation for developing the APT framework derives from a general disappointment felt by East Asian powers over the ineffectiveness of the multilateral economic institutions during the 1997/98 crisis experience. As the then Thai Deputy Prime Minister, and current director-general of the World Trade Organisation (WTO), Supachai Panitchpakdi, stated, 'we cannot rely on the World Bank, Asian Development Bank, or the International Monetary Fund but we must rely on regional co-operation' (Layador 2000: 439). There was certainly frustration felt at the perceived failure of the International Monetary Fund's (IMF) conditions it attached to its loans (i.e. tighter monetary controls, structural reforms), and the ineffectiveness of APEC and the WTO. Tied to this feeling that the Western-dominated institutions had failed them was the disappointment over the US's apparent indifference to their plight. The prevailing view was that the US response to the three previous major financial crises (the 1982 Third World debt crisis, the EU's Exchange Rate Mechanism crisis of 1992/93 and the 1994/95 Mexican financial crisis) had been immediate and appropriate. Coupled to these reasons, the APT also enables the ASEAN members, and Japan, to integrate the increasingly powerful Chinese economy into the regional environment. The first major accomplishment of the APT was the Chiang Mai Initiative launched in May 2000. One of the causes of the 1997/98 financial crisis was the attack on countries' currencies by currency speculators. The Chiang Mai Initiative commits the governments to review each other's financial policies, to exchange information and to allow members to 'swap' currency from one another in order to fend off currency speculators. By May 2003, up to 14 bilateral swap arrangements should have been either signed or concluded, which as Christopher Dent notes in more detail in Chapter 5 was the date set for completing the whole CMI currency swap network.

In addition to financial co-operation, a Chinese proposal for a ASEAN–China Free Trade Area (FTA) was endorsed by both parties at the Fifth APT summit in November 2001, and formally signed at the Sixth APT summit a year later in Phnom Penh, to be fully implemented by 2010. The Japanese expressed an interest in a Japan–ASEAN Comprehensive Economic Partnership (JACEP) when they concluded a bilateral FTA with Singapore in January 2002. In November 2002 the JACEP was agreed (Joint Declaration 2002). In May 2002, Japan also stated a preference for an East Asia Free Trade Zone, linking the APT members with Australia and New Zealand.[11] More fanciful ideas of a common currency, an East Asian Union or an Asian Monetary Fund have also been voiced.[12] In 2002, the APT framework extended its area of co-operation beyond the economic realm to include issues of security more readily associated with the ARF. In November 1999, the Philippines had proposed moving beyond economic concerns by establishing an East Asian Security Forum (Layador 2000), and while it was not agreed to establish such a forum at that stage, at the APT gathering in July 2002 in Brunei it was agreed to examine security matters. In 2003, the APT will convene in Bangkok to discuss transnational crime.

The APT represents a marked change for ASEAN, which had at the beginning of the 1990s given a cool reception to Malaysia's call for an East Asian Economic Grouping (EAEG). At that time ASEAN reconstituted the proposal as the East Asian Economic Caucus (EAEC) to operate within the APEC framework, as opposed to outside it as the EAEG proposal had sought. The APT thus represents an attempt by ASEAN to achieve economic security with other East Asian, as opposed to Asia-Pacific partners. It is not therefore surprising that it was Malaysia that proposed establishing an APT Secretariat. It is also not surprising that the emergence of the APT has raised doubts about the continuing validity of APEC, and since it is partly an East Asian solution to Southeast Asian problems, and hence ASEAN itself.

Since the APT framework is itself at an early stage of development, and various challenges exist to its continuing development, it would be imprudent to claim it will lead to ASEAN's decline. Nevertheless, the encouragement ASEAN members have given this process indicates a belief that economic development and prosperity (i.e. economic security) lies in closer economic and financial ties with China, Japan and South Korea. This clearly begs the question, what value does a sub-regional association have if the answers to Southeast Asia's problems lie in an East Asian forum? Should the APT process begin to establish mechanisms or meetings that either do not include ASEAN members, or appear to give the APT an institutional basis separate from ASEAN? This would further raise questions regarding ASEAN's role in such a process, and thus also the Association's continuing value. It is in this sense that the 2002 three-way meeting that only involved Chinese, Japanese and South Korean foreign ministers can be seen as a potential threat to ASEAN. Likewise, the Malaysian proposal for an APT Secretariat could undermine ASEAN's own secretariat, and indeed this is the reason that Singapore, Thailand and Indonesia remain opposed to the proposal. Although the Malaysians argue that the secretariat would help alleviate the burden on the ASEAN Secretariat, the very argument that the APT needs its own institutional base because its 'agenda will no doubt mount in the years ahead', envisions an active process separate from ASEAN.[13] At the eighth ASEAN Summit held in Phnom Penh in November 2002, Malaysia attempted to reassure its fellow ASEAN members that the APT Secretariat would not undermine ASEAN by reclassifying it as a Bureau, and stating it would be 'organically linked' to the ASEAN Secretariat.[14] However, Malaysia's proposal remained unacceptable and there was no mention of the APT Secretariat/Bureau in the final press statement. This has not ended the matter though, with Malaysian Foreign Minister Hamid Albar stating, 'if no decision is made, we will not stop there. We will continue with our efforts to explain our intention.'[15]

It could be argued that as with the ARF, ASEAN will co-ordinate the goals of its members so that in a forum with larger powers the combined voice of the smaller ASEAN members can be influential (Soesastro 2001). This though will be dependent upon a strong ASEAN, and as noted earlier this is currently not the case. In addition, the final press statement from the Sixth APT Summit noted a 'willingness to explore the phased evolution of the ASEAN Plus Three summit into an East Asian summit'. It also noted the efforts of the three partner states to achieve greater integration 'through their own efforts' ('Press Statement' 2002). Such statements do not therefore indicate that ASEAN is likely to remain central to this process of East Asian regionalism. Of course, whether the APT will eclipse ASEAN is dependent upon the APT overcoming a number of its own obstacles. Perhaps the greatest obstacle will centre on the Sino-Japanese relationship. In particular, whether the rise in Chinese economic and military capacity will eclipse the Japanese, and thus raise the prospect of Beijing challenging Tokyo for the role of regional hegemon; they are, in this sense, possible competitors. ASEAN members may also prefer not to deepen regional integration with China, who they compete with in low-wage, labour-intensive industries. Finally, the United States might raise the objections it had towards EAEC, and regard APT as undermining US economic interests by eclipsing APEC. At present, though, the APT process is emerging as a key forum. The extent to which it will represent a challenge to ASEAN is therefore dependent upon how the APT framework itself evolves. If ASEAN's malaise continues while APT progresses, dissenting voices regarding ASEAN's relevance are only likely to become louder.

Another challenger to ASEAN emerged in late 2000, although it did not have its first inaugural meeting until October 2002. The South-West Pacific Dialogue Forum (SWPDF), which comprises foreign ministers from Indonesia, the Philippines, East Timor, Papua New Guinea, Australia and New Zealand, and its remit is primarily concerned with security affairs. At its inaugural meeting, the SWPDF looked at various internal matters such as the troubles in Mindanao and the Indonesian province of West Papua/Irian Jaya. Abdurrahman Wahid proposed the SWPDF initiative when he was Indonesia's President at ASEAN's Fourth Informal Summit held at Singapore in November 2000. Although ASEAN rejected the proposal it is why Wahid proposed it that is most revealing. After the summit, he complained that the discussions had given little attention to the ASEAN members in the south and that Indonesia's problems had been largely ignored. Making reference to Singapore's defence arrangements with Western powers, he argued that if Singapore could have formal agreements with powers outside ASEAN then so could Indonesia.[16] While officials were quick to state that Indonesia was not going to withdraw from ASEAN, Indonesia nevertheless insisted it would establish the forum.[17] The implication for ASEAN is simple. If member states begin to consider their interests can best be achieved in an alternative regional grouping, then is not the relevance of ASEAN lessened? While this may be so, it is important to note that if it is premature to question the challenge to ASEAN from the APT process, which is in its infancy, then this is even more so for the SWPDF. It has, after all, only had one meeting. Whether the SWPDF will amount to anything will depend upon how Australia and New Zealand interact with Indonesia. It was for instance notable that the New Zealand Foreign Minister, Phil Goff, offered to mediate between the Indonesian government and Papuan independence leaders. Indonesia's rejection of the offer was hardly surprising. If the SWPDF is to amount to anything there will have to be agreement among the members over what is and what is not possible.

5. Conclusion

ASEAN is certainly not dying or about to whither away. Indeed, in terms of meetings and declarations it appears to be fit and active. ASEAN has, though, become incapacitated. The challenge from within is to grasp the opportunities presented by the plethora of acronyms that ASEAN has established in the politico-security and economic fields, and adopt the type of transparency over domestic affairs that these require in order to function. In so doing ASEAN will be able to reinvent itself, perhaps even become an Asian version of the European Economic Community as Goh Chok Tong suggested in late 2002. The current evidence however suggests that the elite are reluctant to abandon the cardinal principle of non-interference, and this does not bode well for ASEAN rising to the challenge from within.

From without the Association is challenged by the APT, which promises an East Asian solution to Southeast Asian problems. Here the challenge arises from which states are driving the process forward. If ASEAN is capable of acting as a driver, as it does with the ARF, the Association will be able to assume the responsibility that Malik called for in 1971 for its economic and, because the APT process is increasing its remit to examine transnational crime, its security environment. However, should the APT process develop independently of ASEAN this is likely to raise questions as to ASEAN's relevance with important Southeast Asian economic and security issues being decided by external powers (Japan, China and South Korea). It is the prospect of such a detrimental impact on ASEAN that has led some ASEAN members to so far reject the establishment of an APT Secretariat or Bureau. The prospect of the APT changing its name to an East Asian summit further raises doubts as to ASEAN assuming the direct responsibility that Malik sought. In addition to the APT, the inaugural meeting of the SWPDF is also, perhaps, an indication that for some Southeast Asian problems ASEAN is not the forum of choice through which to find a solution. The challenge from without is, though, at an early stage and ASEAN remains *the* Southeast Asian organisation. If it is incapable of reinventing itself however, these alternative forums may begin to more critically challenge it.

Notes

1. The celebrations themselves were marred by the internal problems of Cambodia. This led to Cambodia's admission to ASEAN being postponed and the Association was unable to celebrate its thirty-year anniversary by realising the goal of an ASEAN-Ten.
2. See Chapter 5 for further discussion on bilateral FTAs and ASEAN.
3. The Indonesian concepts of national and regional resilience are enshrined in articles 11 and 12 of the TAC (Fifield 1979: 16).
4. *Far Eastern Economic Review*, 25.09.1971, 'Southeast Asia: Towards an Asian Asia'.
5. Should a member not wish to pursue a particular course of action, but has no objections to others proceeding with it, then a consensus is said to have been reached via the minus-x principle.
6. This was established in the TAC but has never been convened.
7. *Straits Times*, 05.11.2002, 'Singapore's plan for single ASEAN market'.
8. *Agence France Presse* (26.09.2002) 'Philippines leader calls for slowdown of her tariff reduction policy'.
9. *Straits Times*, 31.07.2002, 'ASEAN Plus Three takes on security'.
10. *Straits Times*, 29.11.1999, 'ASEAN to push free-trade plan as part of recovery'.
11. In September 2002, ASEAN signed a 'Comprehensive Economic Partnership' declaration with Australia and New Zealand. *Straits Times*, 15.06.2002.
12. Again, see Chapter 5 for more discussion on such issues.
13. *Agence France Presse*, 06.10.2002, 'Malaysia pushes for ASEAN-plus-three secretariat'.
14. *Straits Times*, 02.11.2002, 'KL proposes ASEAN bureau with link to three North Asian states'.
15. *New Straits Times*, 04.11.2002, 'KL seeks to set up ASEAN+3 bureau'.
16. *Business Times (Singapore)* 27.11.2000, 'Will Indonesia break ranks with ASEAN?'.
17. *Straits Times*, 14.01.2001, 'ASEAN "cornerstone" of Jakarta's foreign policy'.

References

ASEAN Troika (2000) *Concept Paper Adopted at the 33rd AMM Bangkok*, 24–25 July, internet site http://www.aseansec.org/3637.htm.

Busse, N. (1999) 'Constructivism and Southeast Asian Security', *The Pacific Review*, Vol. 12(1), pp. 39–60.

Emmers, R. (2001) 'The Influence of the Balance of Power Factor within the ASEAN Regional Forum', *Contemporary Southeast Asia*, Vol. 23(2), pp. 275–91.

Fifield, R.H. (1979) *National and Regional Interests in ASEAN: Competition and Co-operation in International Politics*, Occasional Paper 57, Institute of Southeast Asian Studies, Singapore.

Funston, J. (1998) 'ASEAN: Out of its Depth', *Contemporary Southeast Asia*, Vol. 20(1), pp. 22–37.

Garofano, J. (2002) 'Power, Institutionalism, and the ASEAN Regional Forum: A Security Community for Asia?', *Asian Survey*, Vol. 42(3), pp. 502–21.

Haacke, J. (1999) 'The Concept of Flexible Engagement and the Practice of Enhanced Interaction: Intramural Challenges to the "ASEAN Way"', *The Pacific Review*, Vol. 12(4), pp. 581–611.

Hund, M. (2002) 'From "Neighbourhood Watch Group" to Community? The Case of ASEAN Institutions and the Pooling of Sovereignty', *Australian Journal of International Affairs*, Vol. 56(1), pp. 99–122.

Joint Declaration of the Leaders of ASEAN and Japan on the Comprehensive Economic Partnership (2002) ASEAN–Japan Summit, 5 November, internet site: http://www.aseansec.org/13190.htm

Kraft, H. (2000) 'ASEAN and Intra-ASEAN Relations: Weathering the Storm?', *The Pacific Review*, Vol. 13(3), pp. 453–72.

Layador, M. (2000) 'The Emerging ASEAN Plus Three Process: Another Building Block for Community Building in the Asia Pacific?', *Indonesian Quarterly*, Vol. 28(4), pp. 434–43.

Leifer, M. (1990) *ASEAN and the Security of South-East Asia*, Routledge, London.

Lim, R. (1998) 'The ASEAN Regional Forum: Building on Sand', *Contemporary Southeast Asia*, Vol. 20(2), pp. 115–36.

Narine, S. (1997) 'ASEAN and the ARF: The Limits of the "ASEAN Way"', *Asian Survey*, Vol. 37(10), pp. 961–78.

Narine, S. (1999) 'ASEAN into the Twenty-First Century: Problems and Prospects', *The Pacific Review*, Vol. 12(3), pp. 357–380.

Nischalke, T.I. (2000) 'Insights from ASEAN's Foreign Policy Co-operation: The "ASEAN Way", a Real Spirit or a Phantom?', *Contemporary Southeast Asia*, Vol. 22(1), pp. 89–112.

Nischalke, T.I. (2002) 'Does ASEAN Measure Up? Post-Cold War Diplomacy and the Idea of Regional Community', *The Pacific Review*, Vol. 15(1), pp. 89–117.

Press Statement by the Chairman of the 8th ASEAN Summit, the 6th ASEAN Plus Three Summit and the ASEAN-China Summit (2002) Phnom Penh, Cambodia, 4 November, internet site: http://www.aseansec.org/13188.htm

Ramcharan, R. (2000) 'ASEAN and Non-interference: A Principle Maintained', *Contemporary Southeast Asia*, Vol. 22(1), pp. 60–88.

Soesastro, H. (2001) 'ASEAN in 2030: The Long View', in Simon S.C. Tay, Jesus P. Estanislao and Hadi Soesastro (eds) *Reinventing ASEAN*, Institute of South East Asian Studies, Singapore.

Tay, S.S.C. (2001) 'Institutions and Processes: Dilemmas and Possibilities', in Simon S.C. Tay, Jesus P. Estanislao and Hadi Soesastro (eds) *Reinventing ASEAN*, Institute of South East Asian Studies, Singapore.

Terms of Understanding on the Establishment of the ASEAN Surveillance Process (1998) Washington DC, USA, 4 October, internet site http://www.aseansec.org/6309.htm

9
Sub-Regional Co-operation in the Mekong Valley: Implications for Regional Security

Jörn Dosch

1. Introduction

The Greater Mekong Subregion (GMS) covers some 2.3 million square km and a population of about 245 million (Figure 9.1). The post-Second World War history of GMS co-operation dates back to 1957 when the Mekong Committee was established at the initiative of the UN Economic Commission for Asia and the Far East (ECAFE) and four riparian countries of the Lower Mekong Basin (Cambodia, Laos, Thailand and South Vietnam). However, the process only gained momentum in 1992 when, with the assistance of the Asian Development Bank (ADB), the six riparian states of the Mekong river – Cambodia, Thailand, Burma (or Myanmar), Laos, Vietnam and China (Yunnan Province), entered into a programme of formalised sub-regional co-operation. Since then the ADB has been the 'catalysing force' (Hirsch 2001: 237) for most co-operative initiatives. Furthermore as Bakker (1999) comments, 'the river-as-resource, in a glibly bioregional metaphor, has been transformed from a Cold War "front line" into a "corridor of commerce", drawing six watershed countries together in the pursuit of sustainable development' (pp. 209–10).

The goal of the GMS project, with its seemingly unlimited financial resources, is to facilitate sustainable economic growth and to improve the standard of living in the Mekong region by means of factor input specialisation and greatly expanded trade and investment. One priority has been co-operation by public and private sectors related to transportation, especially cross-border roads, as well as power generation and distribution. In addition to and in support of GMS projects, in 1995 the lower Mekong countries, Thailand, Cambodia, Laos and Vietnam, set up the Mekong River Commission (MRC) to co-ordinate development efforts in the region. And in 1996, the ASEAN Mekong Basin Development Co-operation

Figure 9.1 Map of the Greater Mekong sub-region.

(ASEAN-MBDC) was founded to give attention to multilateral infrastructure projects and other cross-border activities.

Most actors involved, as well as observers, tend to stress economic incentives as the Mekong states' main motivation to intensify sub-regional co-operation. As Nguyen (2002) puts it, 'subregional co-operation is essential to facilitate co-ordinated sustainable economic growth and reduce poverty in the riparian countries' (p. 1). At the same time, however, security has been an equally if not more important dimension. In an early essay on Mekong co-operation and against the backdrop of the Vietnam War, Black (1969) argued, 'the most important aspect of the development of the Mekong Basin is to provide a means for inhibiting violence in the region, and evoking among the riparian countries a sense of what is possible if they cultivate the habit of working together' (p. 12). Three decades later, a volume published by the Cambodian Institute for Co-operation and Peace is based on a very similar premise. As Adam (2000) observed, 'given the history of wars, aggressions and instability, when the Mekong river functioned largely as a dividing line, there is a security dimension beyond economics that touches such issues as military build-ups, border disputes, migration, environmental degradation and resource management that need to be tackled in a spirit of co-operation and good neighbourliness' (p. 2). In a similar vein, Browder (2000) demonstrates that the establishment of the MRC was primarily guided by security considerations, namely Thailand and Vietnam's interest to build fruitful relations in the aftermath of the Cold War and to contain conflict on water resources and Laos' and Cambodia's motivation to reach an accord to help procure aid.

Using Deutsch's (1957) 'transactionist hypothesis' as a starting point – which posits that an increasing volume of economic, political and cultural transactions across national borders will result in the emergence of regional security communities if the process is accompanied by the growth of integrative institutions among the participating nations – this chapter will elaborate on the question whether GMS co-operation has resulted in more stable and peaceful sub-regional relations, as well to the emergence of what Dent (2002) labels 'political regionalism': that is, 'integral formations of transnational policy-networks, the expression of shared political interests amongst the region's leaders, advancements in policy co-ordination and common policy enterprises, and the creation of regional-level institutions to manage any common "political sphere"' (p. 2). The structure of this chapter is as follows. It first places the GMS within the academic debate on sub-regionalism before then proceeding to outline some security-related achievements and implications of sub-regional co-operation. Lastly, it assesses the level of security-building in the Mekong Valley.

2. Sub-regionalism: an overview of the academic debate

The massive structural changes in the aftermath of the Cold War not only provoked an extensive academic debate on the pros and cons of regional bloc-building but also ignited a discussion on sub-regionalism as either an alternative or a supplement to the former. In this respect, Taga (1994) distinguishes two different types of post-Cold War regionalism. The first of these is 'defensive type' regionalism, as represented by the European Union (EU) an the North American Free Trade Agreement (NAFTA). The second is 'positive type' regionalism that is commonly found in East Asia. He cites the Yellow Sea Rim region,[1] the Greater Hong Kong Area,[2] the Singapore–Batam–Johor Triangle (more commonly known as the Indonesia–Malaysia–Singapore

Growth Triangle, or IMSGT), and the Bath or Indochina Economic Zone[3] as examples. Others include the Brunei–Indonesia–Malaysia–Philippines East ASEAN Growth Area (BIMP-EAGA), the Indonesia–Malaysia–Thailand Growth Triangle (IMTGT), and the Japan Sea Economic Zone that comprises the coastal areas of Northeast China, the Russian Far East, South and North Korea and Japan. Sub-regional economic zones can be generally defined as 'a few neighbouring provinces of different countries interlinked closely through trade, investment, and personal movement across national borders' (Yamazawa 1994: 262). Others, such as Chen (1995), also subsume so-called special economic zones within state borders, city-states and free ports to the concept. For Ohmae (1995) these economic zones, or what he calls 'region-states', 'may or may not fall within the borders of a particular nation. Whether they do is purely an accident of history' (p. 81).

Apart from a series of studies that primarily intend to supply information on the respective sub-regional growth areas, the most ambitious strand of the debate from an academic point of view focuses on the role of government and private business interests on the emergence of sub-regionalism, often in the context of globalisation. There are broadly three lines of argumentation. The first posits that sub-regionalism has emerged in the 'post-nation state' context. As Ohmae (1995) further contends, 'there is not much evidence to support the notion that economic activity in today's borderless world follows either the political boundary lines of traditional nation-states or the cultural boundary lines of what Huntington calls "civilizations". But there is plenty of evidence that it does follow information-driven efforts' (p. 21). The second line of argumentation regards the role of the state as crucial to the evolution of sub-regionalism. According to this view, sub-regional co-operation schemes emerge as the result of deliberate government policy efforts to generate closer integration within a small regional area (Islam and Chowdhury 1997). For Thambipillai (1998), 'Governments play a crucial role in the planning, establishment and implementation of policies within growth areas. Growth areas are designated to exploit the existing natural cross-border economic and socio-political links, with the intention of extending the range and scope of activities' (p. 251). Moreover, according to Rocamora (1994), governmental actors perceive sub-regionalism as an increasingly attractive strategic alternative to larger or mega-regional integration schemes since growth areas 'bring together parts of countries without having to go through the laborious process of forming trade and investment blocs such as the European Union … which unite whole countries' (p. 33). The third line of argument constitutes a middle position that awards both nation-state and private sector an important role depending on the type of sub-regionalism. As Chen (1995) suggests:

The evolution of FEZs [Free Economic Zones] highlights the relative roles of the nation-state and private capital in global, national and local development. The evolution of intra-national FEZs reveals the interaction between government policy and the private sector in shaping local and regional development within the boundary of nation-states. The recent emergence of cross-national growth zones in the Asia-Pacific region offers a fresh and timely opportunity to examine issues regarding the changing relationship between the nation-state and global capital (p. 594).

In sum, three sets of variables can be identified describing different types of sub-regionalism arrangements, namely the: (i) *degree of institutionalisation*: formal or legally/morally binding versus informal or consultative in direction; (ii) *actors involved*: predominantly state actors versus non-state actors, particularly the private sector; (iii) *overall pattern*: co-operation is based on a long tradition of transborder contacts, has historically grown and/ or takes place within a narrowly defined geographical area (i.e. a 'natural' sub-region) versus co-operation as the result of political/social construction (i.e. a 'constructed sub-region'). The combination of these three sets of variables generates eight types of sub-regionalisms as Figure 9.2 shows.

The GMS approaches the type of A-D-F. The classification as such does not imply any assessment of the overall success of a certain type and the actual benefits for the actors involved in the respective scheme. Empirical findings do not generally indicate whether, for instance, formally institutionalised schemes are more beneficial than informal arrangements, or if the prominent involvement of state actors was more promising then non-governmental actors taking the driver's seat. In addition, most cases are not straightforward. Co-operation can be based on a large set of formal agreements without reaching deep institutionalisation because the respective treaties are not legally binding, leave loopholes or exit options or simply because actors decide not to play by the rules. At the same time, informal arrangements based on tradition, convention and unwritten but morally binding norms and procedures can work very well as a means of structuring inter-actor relations.

A comparison of regionalism in Latin America and Southeast Asia illustrates this point. Whereas co-operation in the Americas has always been formally rooted in a wide range of treaties and international law, regionalism in Southeast Asia is built on the 'ASEAN way' of informal consensus-building – an issue discussed by other chapters in this section. However, ASEAN has reached a higher degree of institutionalisation than any organised attempt to community-building in Latin America to date. Hence, in the context of this chapter 'formal institutionalisation' refers to legally or morally binding arrangements, while 'informal institutionalisation' means loose, non-binding co-operation or consultative intergovernmental interactions.

While it is difficult to *a priori* estimate the effectiveness or success of formal versus informal co-operation schemes, it can be assumed that

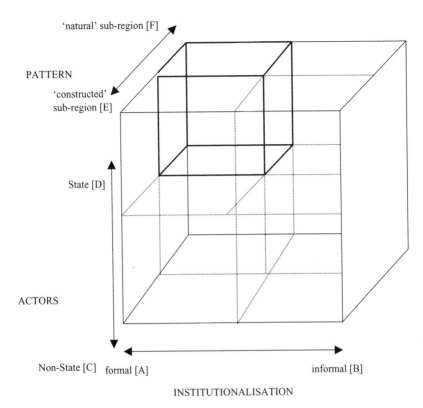

Figure 9.2   A typology of sub-regionalism.

'natural' sub-regions form a more solid basis for efficient co-operation than sub-regions that were constructed 'from above' to serve a limited political or foreign policy agenda. 'Natural' in this context refers to either: (i) a long history of political and economic transactions within a given area; or (ii) a natural resource area, such as river valleys or deltas, lakes and coastal zones. Often, both features are present as in the case of the IMSGT, for instance, which is deeply rooted in a centuries old tradition of intra-regional commercial activities dating back to the days of the Srivijaya trading empire. This ancient Kingdom was probably established in the third century and succeeded Funan as controller of the Malacca Straits in the seventh century. Centred on the island of Sumatra, Srivijaya dominated trade between the Indian subcontinent and China into the twelfth century. Despite Srivijaya's eventual demise, the sub-region surrounding the Straits of Malacca has remained Southeast Asia's main centre of economic gravity. Although not historically related, Singapore has often been described as a modern day Srivijaya and the ancient kingdom's legitimate successor.

In some contrast, the BIMP-EAGA represents a rather constructed pattern of co-operation that has lacked the success of more natural zones like the IMSGT. In 1994, BIMP-EAGA came into existence mainly on the initiative of the governments of the Philippines and Brunei who had previously not been involved in sub-regional co-operation schemes and tried to jump on the bandwagon at a time when the establishment of growth areas appeared to be a popular strategy to diversify foreign economic policies. To be sure, some places within the BIMP-EAEG (e.g. the Sulu Sea area), do indeed look back on a tradition of close political and economic contacts. However, the BIMP-EAGA as a whole is too diverse to be classified as a natural historic or resource area. Its map was drawn for political reasons and does not follow historically grown linkages. While the IMTGT is a twilight case, leaning more towards 'natural' though, the GMS can clearly be described as a natural sub-region. As Than (1997) comments, the 'history of the Mekong is the history of relationships among [the riparian] countries' (p. 41). The Chinese tribute system, early settlements on the river delta and the Ankor Empire contributed to the emergence of the Mekong basin as a 'natural economic area'. But it was particularly the French Mekong expedition of 1866, setting off from Saigon in the hope to reach China and to open vital new markets for the French colonial empire, that shaped the external perception of the Mekong valley as a region in its own right.[4] Table 9.1 briefly compares the main features of the four Southeast Asian sub-regional co-operation schemes.

The GMS and IMSGT are classified as formal schemes because in both cases co-operation is primarily based on binding arrangements, which, are either the result of inter-governmental negotiations or, as far as GMS is concerned, facilitated by the ADB. Since the involvement of the ADB is accompanied by extensive development assistance, it is easy for the participating actors to comply with the agreements and play by the rules. Here the ADB almost follows a policy of carrots without the stick. In addition, the 1995 Mekong Agreement, the founding document of the Mekong River Commission, lays out the basic principles, procedures and organisational structure for a water resource regime, including the management of the dry season water flows. It suffers, however, from the fact that China is not yet a member of the Commission. While sub-regional co-operation in the Mekong Basin is embedded in a set of formal rules, it goes without saying that informal procedures of policy co-ordination are present and do play an important part in intergovernmental co-operation.

3. Security implications

Table 9.1 shows that in addition to economic incentives, all four sub-regional 'growth area' projects have a security dimension. In the case of

Table 9.1 Sub-regional co-operation schemes in Southeast Asia

Scheme	Greater Mekong Sub-Region (GMS)	Indonesia–Malaysia–Singapore Growth Triangle (IMSGT)	Indonesia–Malaysia–Thailand Growth Triangle (IMTGT)	BIMP-EAGA
Founded	1992	1989	1993	1994
Population/Area	245 million people 2.3 million sq km	35 million people 334 000 sq km	25 million people 230 000 sq km	50 million people 1.56 million sq km
Type	Formal-State-'natural' (A-D-F)	Formal-Non State-'natural' (A-C-F)	Informal-State-'natural' (B-D-F)	Informal-State-'constructed' (B-D-E)
Central actors	• Governments → GMS Summit • ADB • GMS Business Forum	• initially governments (until 1994) • Private Sector	• Governments • ADB • Growth Triangle Business Council	• Governments • ADB • BIMP East ASEAN Business Council
Policy objectives	• realise and development opportunities • encourage trade and investment among GMS countries • resolve or mitigate cross-border problems • meet common resource and policy needs	Combine • the availability of low-cost land and labour in the Riau islands and semi-skilled labour in Johor • with capital from Singapore and other regions to manufacture and export goods • Creating a hinterland for Singapore	• promote foreign direct investment and facilitate economic development of the subregions • enhance international competitiveness for direct investment and export production • lower transport and transaction costs	• hasten, through regional co-operation, the development of the economy of Brunei and subregions of the three other countries

Table 9.1 (Contd.)

Scheme	Greater Mekong Sub-Region (GMS)	Indonesia–Malaysia–Singapore Growth Triangle (IMSGT)	Indonesia–Malaysia–Thailand Growth Triangle (IMTGT)	BIMP-EAGA
Founded	*1992*	*1989*	*1993*	*1994*
Achievements	• Implemented projects in the fields of infrastructure • hydropower energy • joint management of resources (Mekong navigation etc.) • co-operation on tourism	• about US$4 billion FDI and 100 000 new jobs in Riau alone • significantly improved infrastructure: new airports, ports and bridges • co-operation on tourism	• reduce production and distribution costs through economies of scale • some common policy proposals ↑ communications, human resource development, higher education	• Some modest joint investment (fisheries, tourism)
Security implications	Reducing tension between China and the lower Mekong states in general and China and Vietnam in particular	Creating a 'hinterland' for Singapore and reducing Singapore's (self-perceived) vulnerability	Reducing tension in bilateral relations between Thailand and Malaysia and Indonesia and Malaysia	Reducing tension in relations between the Philippines and Malaysia (over the long-standing Sabah issue) and contributing to the regional integration of Brunei

the GMS, 'the Mekong resource regime is linked to more general concerns for political security and stability and may in fact reflect political concerns for subregional neighborhood maintenance' (Makim 2002: 5). Many analysts seem to agree that the existence of sub-regional co-operation has *per se* contributed to a more peaceful and stable regional situation in the Mekong valley. As Than (1997) puts it, 'the political benefits of ADB-led GMS co-operation are enormous ... there is now peace and stability in most of the sub-region, where this has rarely existed. Formerly the source of conflicts among participating riparian countries, the Mekong has become a source of co-operation' (p. 45). However, just as in the case of ASEAN, which simply as a result of its very existence, seems to have significantly contributed to the avoidance of military conflict among its member states, it is difficult to establish a strong empirical link between co-operation in non-security areas and regional stability and peace. Then again, following Deutsch's (1957) work, historical evidence suggests that stable and peaceful inter-state relations are indeed the result of quantitatively and qualitatively increased transnational activities in multiple policy areas and related inter-governmental institution-building. ADB sponsorship of the GMS seems to exactly follow this logic as demonstrated, for example, by the latest infrastructure project – a road link that will connect central Thailand to southern Vietnam through Cambodia. As part of the US$77.5 million project, with the ADB contributing a 50 million loan, 350 kms of highway and almost 100 bridges will be reconstructed. As Albab Akanda, an ADB Principal Transport Specialist commented, 'Better roads will promote trade, tourism and economic development not only in Cambodia but in the GMS as a whole ... The increased tourism will in turn create more jobs and help in the drive to reduce poverty in the country. The project will also seek to reduce poverty through rural connectivity and accessibility.' Following Deutsch's (1957) assumption on the link between growing volumes of transactions and increasing prospects for peace and stability, most achievements of Mekong co-operation are likely to have an impact on sub-regional security. For example, consider the following transborder infrastructure projects and other initiatives and developments occurring within the GMS remit:

- The 400 km East–West Corridor project linking northern Thailand, central Laos and eastern Vietnam is due for completion at the end of 2003, and container traffic is expected to double to 1.6 million metric tons per year.
- In November 2001 Thailand, Vietnam and Laos agreed to build a major highway, including a bridge over the Mekong River, to connect the three countries in order to boost economic development. The bridge will link the Thai province of Mukdahan with Savannakhet in Laos. From there the existing road to the Vietnamese deep-sea port of Danang will be upgraded. The highway is due to be completed by 2006 and could later

be extended to Burma. The opening of Cambodia's first bridge across the Mekong, a massive one mile span, in December 2001 as part of the GMS scheme stands as a significant symbol for the political will to bring the countries and people of the region closer together.

- As a major step towards the joint management of the third largest international river, China, Laos, Burma and Thailand signed an agreement on commercial navigation on the Mekong River in April 2001. After the implementation of the treaty, commercial ships from the four countries will pass freely along an 893 km stretch of the 'golden waterway' from China's Simao to Louangphrabang in Laos. The agreement will open 14 ports and docks for commerce and will most certainly result in a further major increase in trade and tourism. In 2000, 200 000 tons of commodities were transported abroad from Yunnan Province on the Mekong, compared to only 400 tons in 1990.

- In 2000, Vietnam, Laos, Cambodia and Thailand signed an agreement to facilitate the movement of people and good across national borders. China and Burma are expected to join the treaty soon. The agreement simplifies and harmonises legislation, regulations and procedures governing cross-border transport.

- In the same year, the Mekong riparian states established a Business Forum to promote the role of private capital in spurring intra-regional investment. In April 2002, the Mekong Enterprise Fund (MEF) was launched. The US$13 million venture capital fund aims to invest in private companies founded and managed by private entrepreneurs, with a focus on export industries and local service providers.[5]

- The increasing trade between Thailand and China, partly as a result of GMS activities, is expected to boost intra-regional trade within the Mekong valley by 15 to 20 per cent in 2002 compared with the previous year.[6]

If we understand security in a broader sense not solely as hard or military security but also include the fields of soft security (i.e. the broad area of comprehensive security covering non-military areas such as economic security and environmental security), some recent achievements of Mekong-co-operation point towards growing sub-regional stability. Discussions on this matter are considered under the following three themes.

3.1. Institutionalisation of sub-regional relations and growing transparency

The GMS stands as a powerful international symbol for co-operation among former Cold War adversaries, particularly with respect to relations between Vietnam and China, and Thailand and Vietnam. It also represents a major pillar of Vietnam's new foreign policy outlook as outlined in the Politburo

Resolution No. 13 of May 1988 which prescribes a policy of 'diversification' and 'multilateralisation' of Vietnam's foreign relations. The implementation of the Resolution has resulted in a more transparent, predictable and responsible Vietnamese foreign policy. In a similar vein, GMS co-operation is a core element of China's foreign policy. According to Beijing's official perception, GMS serves China's interest of strengthening relations with ASEAN in the policy areas of political, social, economic and security co-operation and can be used as a vehicle to promote the development of the proposed ASEAN–China Free Trade Agreement (see Chapters 5, 7 and 8). Furthermore, co-operation within the GMS has channelled and institutionalised Thailand, Vietnam and China's respective decades-long attempts to pursue (sub-) regional leadership or even hegemonic ambitions. In other words, the multilateralisation of international relations in the sub-region has reduced the risk of the re-emergence of any hegemonic actor. The GMS states are also formally linked with other actors: Japan, South Korea, Australia, New Zealand, various EU states, ASEAN, ADB, the Economic and Social Commission for Asia and the Pacific (ESCAP), and the MRC. As a result, the formerly rather isolated and conflict-ridden sub-region is further integrated within the structures of global international relations. Today, sub-regional relations are more transparent and better monitored than during the Cold War period.

3.2. Environmental security

In November 2001, Cambodia, Laos, Thailand and Vietnam signed an agreement to deal with the annual flood problem in the Mekong area. In 2000 alone more than 800 people died and over US$400 million of property was damaged as a result of floods. Under the Flood Management and Mitigation agreement, the four governments will co-ordinate land-use policies, share water-management information and resources and intensify co-operation in cross-border flood-rescue operations. The Chinese government has agreed to provide the downstream countries with the information on river levels during the flood season. As marginal as it seems at first glance, 'with international conflicts over river water becoming more frequent, there is concern that the Mekong could become a serious source of tension unless the six states can agree on rules for developing the river. That is why China's agreement in April to send the readings from two monitoring stations on its section of the Mekong, more than 1000 kms upstream from Phnom Penh, is seen as a … significant improvement in managing one of Asia's biggest and least polluted rivers.'[7] In January 2002, representatives from Cambodia, Laos, Thailand and Vietnam together with donor institutions organised a workshop on sustainable development of the Mekong River Basin including the discussion of issues such as fish production, food security, irrigation, agriculture and agro-forestry.

3.3. Energy security

Compared with rivers of a similar size like the Nile and the Mississippi, the Mekong is still relatively untouched. The first Mekong bridge (between Thailand and Laos) was only opened in 1994 and the first mainstream dam, the 1500 Megawatt Manwan only completed in 1995 in Yunnan, China. Since then hydropower has been one of the main priorities of international river development in general and the GMS project in particular. One GMS infrastructure project, the 210 Megawatt Theun Hinboun Hydropower Project in Laos, was completed in 1998, and various others are under implementation or are being studied. However, according to Bakker (1999), 'the figures given for hydroelectric...potential vary widely, depending on the era, the institution, and the optimism of the consultant involved, but there is general agreement that Laos and Yunnan have the greatest hydropower potential. Figures on numbers of planned projects vary, due in part to the speed with which new sites are being added to the lists of feasibility studies' (p. 214). In the late 1990s, Laos had '60 dams planned or being built and Vietnam had 36. China planned 15 on the Mekong itself and an unknown number on tributaries. There are currently 17 hydropower dams under consideration for Cambodia on at least a dozen of its rivers, in addition to a number of energy, infrastructure, and telecommunications projects' (ibid).

4. Conclusion

While the GMS is unlikely to play any decisive part in shaping or altering regional *realpolitik* from the realist's point of view, any believer in liberal institutionalism will conclude that the wide range of co-operative efforts as part of GMS and related inter-governmental activities have had an impact on fostering sub-regional peace and stability. Indeed, the declaration that 'our most important achievement has been the growing trust and confidence among our countries' – from the Joint Statement at the first GMS Summit in November 2002[8] – is more than political rhetoric. However, the GMS has not yet developed into a pluralistic security community, which, according to Deutsch's definition, would be characterised by the general absence of military conflict as a possible means of problem solving in inter-member relations. As other chapters in this book testify, unresolved disputes in intra-regional relations within Southeast Asia remain. As a legacy of the colonial past the maritime boundaries between Vietnam and Cambodia are still not defined and parts of the land borders between Thailand and Laos, and between Thailand and Cambodia are indefinite. The most recent attempt to solving the long-standing Vietnamese–Cambodian border dispute failed in November 2001. In the next chapter, Anja Jetschke documents in some considerable detail the recent border conflict between Thailand and Burma. While military conflict seems to be unlikely among ASEAN member states, it cannot be ruled out in Vietnam–China relations given, for example, both countries' involvement in the dispute over conflicting territorial claims in the South China Sea. Most importantly, the unco-ordinated construction of power plants and irrigation systems by the upper Mekong countries, particularly China which plans to build more than a dozen power plants, poses a serious challenge to intra-regional co-operation since it could result in a potentially explosive competition between the upper and the lower Mekong states for water resources.

A further stumbling block for the emergence of a pluralistic security com-munity is the very limited societal involvement in intra-regional affairs. So far, GMS activities are predominantly centred on the rather small political elites of the Mekong riparian states. An Oxfam-sponsored NGO forum on 'Greater Mekong Sub-region and ADB', which took place parallel to the GMS Summit in November 2002, lays the charge that, 'Ten years into the ADB's GMS programme, more than 65 million people whose way of life is being radically changed are still shut out of the process. Despite all the claims, the GMS programme has brought little benefit to local people, but massive advantages to consultants, corporations and local elites.'[9] Furthermore, these elites do not seem to have developed extensive shared political inter-ests beyond the functional GMS agenda, which would justify the classifica-tion of Mekong co-operation as *political regionalism* as defined by Dent (2002). Then again, it seems safe to argue that the achievements mentioned above have made the sub-region a less conflictual place then it used to be a couple of decades ago. In sum, whether or not Mekong co-operation will evolve into a full pluralistic security community will depend on two main factors. First, the willingness of state actors to develop a wider set of inte-grative formal and informal institutions (e.g. agreements, treaties, codes of conduct, commissions, regular high level meetings on various issues and policy areas) using the existing and politically promising institutions built within the GMS framework as a nucleus. Second, a more prominent partic-ipation from societal actors, ranging from the private sector to NGOs. It remains to be seen whether these will transpire in a full and effective sense.

Notes

This chapter was written as part of an ongoing research project funded by the British Academy.

1. The coastal areas facing the Yellow Sea of North and Northeast China, North and South Korea and Japan.
2. Hong Kong and China's Guangdong and Fujian provinces.
3. Thailand, Laos, Cambodia and the Indo-Chinese Peninsula.
4. See De Carne (1995) for details on the French Mekong expedition.
5. *ADB News Release*, 22.04.2002, '$16 Million Mekong Enterprise Fund Launced'.
6. *Xinhua General News Agency*, 07.08.2002.
7. *International Herald Tribune*, 30.10.2002.
8. *Asia Pulse*, 07.11.2002.
9. Cited from Renton (2002).

References

Adam, E. (2000) 'Foreword', in K.K. Hourn and J.A. Kaplan (eds), *The Greater Mekong Subregion and ASEAN. From Backwaters to Headwaters*, Cambodian Institute for Co-operation and Peace, Phom Penh.

Bakker, K. (1999) 'The Politics of Hydropower: Developing the Mekong', *Political Geography*, Vol. 18, pp. 209–232.

Black, E. (1969) *The Mekong River: A Challenge in Peaceful Development for Southeast Asia*, National Strategy Information Center, New York.

Browder, G. (2000) 'An Analysis of the Negotiations for the 1995 Mekong Agreement', *International Negotiation*, Vol. 5(2), pp. 237–61.

Chen, X. (1995) 'The Evolution of Free Economic Zones and the Recent Development of Cross-National Growth Zones', *International Journal of Urban and Regional Research*, Vol. 19(4), pp. 593–621.

De Carne, L. (1995) *Travels on the Mekong – Cambodia, Laos and Yunnan* [reprint], White Lotus, Bangkok.

Dent, C.M. (2002) 'Introduction: Northeast Asia – A Region in Search of Regionalism?', in C.M. Dent and D.W.F. Huang (eds), *Northeast Asian Regionalism. Learning from the European Experiences*, RoutledgeCurzon, London.

Deutsch, K.W. (1957) *Political Community and the North Atlantic Area. International Organization in the Light of Historical Experience*, Princeton University Press, Princeton N.J.

Hirsch, P. (2001) 'Globalisation, Regionalisation and Local Voices: The Asian Development Bank and Rescaled Politics of Environment in the Mekong Region', *Singapore Journal of Tropical Geography*, Vol. 22(3), pp. 237–51.

Islam, I. and Chowdhury, A. (1997) *Asia-Pacific Economies: A Survey*, Routledge, London.

Makim, A. (2002) 'Resources for Security and Stability? The Politics of Regional Co-operation on the Mekong, 1957–2001', *Journal of Development & Environment*, Vol. 11(1), pp. 5–52.

Nguyen T.D. (2002) 'Vietnam's Interests in the Greater Mekong Subregions (GMS) and the Effect of GMS-Co-operation on Some Domestic and Foreign Policies in Vietnam', paper presented at the workshop on *Dynamics of Sub-regional Co-operation in the Mekong Valley, National Perceptions and Strategies*, Department of East Asian Studies, University of Leeds, 17 May, Leeds.

Ohmae, K. (1995) *The End of the Nation State: The Rise of Regional Economics*, Free Press, New York.

Renton, A. (2002) 'Whose Mekong Is It? NGOs Call on Region's Leaders to Open the Doors', *Oxfam GB (East Asia) Statement*, 11 November.

Rocamora, J. (1994) 'The Philippines and Competing Asian Regionalism', *Politik* (Ateno University Manila), Vol. 1(1), pp. 33–6.

Taga, H. (1994) 'International Networks Among Local Cities: The First Step Towards Regional Development', in F. Gipouloux (ed.), *Regional Economic Strategies in East Asia: A Comparative Perspective*, Maison Franco-Japonaise, Tokyo.

Thambipillai, P. (1998) 'The ASEAN Growth Areas: Sustaining the Dynamism', *The Pacific Review*, Vol. 11(2), pp. 249–66.

Than, M. (1997) 'Economic Co-operation in the Greater Mekong Subregion', *Asian-Pacific Economic Literature*, Vol. 11(2), pp. 40–57.

Yamazawa, I. (1994) *Economic Integration in the Asia-Pacific Region and the Options for Japan*, Japanese Ministry of Foreign Affairs, Tokyo.

10
Democratization: A Threat to Peace and Stability in Southeast Asia?

Anja Jetschke

1. Introduction

This chapter examines the question of how beneficial the democratization of some Southeast Asian states has been for the region as a whole. It will do so by comparing the implications of democratization for inter-state peace, which are currently being discussed in the literature with actual developments in the Southeast Asian sub-region. I particularly ask whether the democratization of key member states of the Association of Southeast Asian Nations (ASEAN) such as the Philippines, Thailand and most recently Indonesia has improved the prospects for regional stability in Southeast Asia. The reason for such an evaluation is twofold. First, it connects with the 'democratic peace' hypothesis, which essentially contends that democracies are unlikely to fight each other. While this might provide some positive signs for ASEAN in the sense that Southeast Asia might see an incipient zone of democratic peace, there is also cause for concern. Since not all ASEAN member states have experienced a transition to democracy, this leaves Southeast Asia as a zone of 'mixed state' dyads (i.e. democracies and non-democracies), which are more likely to fight wars than either 'democratic state' dyads or 'autocratic state' dyads. Moreover, statistical evidence suggests that it is states in transition to democracy that are the most likely to wage war. Second, there is a host of social constructivist analyses on ASEAN that have focused on the organization's specific culture of security to explain the long peace of ASEAN. These studies have mainly focused on the emergence and relevance of inter-subjective collective norms among ASEAN members (Busse 2000, Kivimäki 2001, Narine 2002, Nischalke 2002, Haacke 2003). Since these studies more or less explicitly view ASEAN's commitment to norms of non-interference, the non-use of force and sovereignty as stemming from their common domestic (autocratic) structures, the question emerges how the change in these structures affects ASEAN and hence stability in the region.

I will argue in the following that it is rather premature to claim ASEAN as a regional organization and the Southeast Asian region faces a major challenge due to democratization. While pressures to change ASEAN's principle of non-intervention come predominantly from the more democratic members, the observed changes in ASEAN's cardinal principle of non-interference do not stem from the new democracies in ASEAN alone (Indonesia, the Philippines and Thailand), but are in the interest of the autocratic members, too. In the face of a feared disintegration of Indonesia most importantly due to the separatist movement in Aceh, autocratic as well as democratic members have seen the need to depart from the principle of non-intervention to contain the conflict. In practice, however, all ASEAN members have maintained their policy of non-intervention. Similarly, while it might be claimed that especially the recent escalation of the border dispute between Thailand and Burma is related to their respective regime types (democracy vs. autocracy) (Owen 1994) and indicative of a destabilization of the region the available evidence suggests that Thailand is by no means on the way of being driven into an ideologically based war. Public opinion, which is for a tougher stance towards Burma, has not translated into a more offensive foreign policy and the Thai government has rather advocated taking a multilateral path to conflict resolution than outright military intervention or war.

In sum, the argument of this chapter is that ASEAN member states' interests might be a better predictor of prospects for future peace and co-operation than is the norms-based 'ASEAN way' of co-operation or the democratic peace theory. Co-operation in ASEAN has mainly been a function of the key interests of its member states in economic development, regime security and nation-building (Narine 2002). In the past, these interests have worked in favour of mutual acknowledgement of norms of non-interference, sovereignty and the territorial integrity of ASEAN member states. Yet, recent developments in ASEAN have provided a major challenge to these shared interests and therefore also question crucial principles of co-operation in ASEAN. As such, recent strains in ASEAN are only partly related to the democratization and stem largely from individual changes in cost and benefit calculations of non-interference.

The outline of this chapter is as follows. In the first part, I will quickly describe the current record of democratization in the ASEAN region. As will become evident, although the level of democratic freedom varies even among ASEAN members, the gap is especially large with regard to the new members Burma, Cambodia, Laos and Vietnam. The next section will summarize the current debate on democratic peace with regards to ASEAN. This debate basically argues that ASEAN might be seen as an example of 'dictatorial peace' with a normative posture, and views democratization as a potentially destabilizing element (Peceny *et al.* 2002). Proceeding from these explanations, I will ask what kind of predictions major theoretical approaches for co-operation within ASEAN make with regards to the future stability of Southeast Asia. As a baseline, it could be argued that social constructivist explanations would largely predict major challenges to the principles of ASEAN co-operation, and the region's destabilization as a whole as a consequence of democratization processes. This dynamic should be especially evident with regards to conflicts between democracies and autocracies, as in the case of the recent Thailand–Burma border conflict. As the case studies concerning the debate on intervention in Aceh and the Thai–Burmese border conflict demonstrate, however, these two cases point to causal factors which are largely unrelated to the factors social constructivists emphasize, common (authoritarian) identities. Although there are strong voices in Thailand who would like to promote freedom and democracy in Burma, they do not influence the foreign policy of Thailand. And while Aceh should provide a showcase for the democratic countries to promote human rights in Indonesia, both the Philippines and Thailand have officially announced their support for principles of non-interference.

2. Democratization in Southeast Asia

How do ASEAN states fare with regards to democratization and militarised inter-state disputes? Since 1986 there has been a gradual change in membership of ASEAN, with the number of states that are democratic continually increasing. Meanwhile, half of the original six member states of ASEAN have undergone a transition towards democracy (Indonesia, the Philippines and Thailand). This translates into approximately one third of ASEAN's current membership of ten states. Transitions to democracy have been revolutionary in these three ASEAN states. Indonesia and Thailand, but also the Philippines exhibited a high degree of autocracy before regime change. According to the Freedom House Index, Thailand was evaluated as 'not free' and had a combined score of 12 on a 14-digit scale in 1977 when undergoing transition, which brought the combined democracy score down to 7 from 1979 to 1986 before it was intermittently regarded as 'free' between 1989 and 1991. The democratic transition Indonesia faced after 1996 was equally revolutionary. Indonesia received the highest autocracy score between 1991 and 1995 (14 = 'not free'), and has subsequently received a higher democracy score since undergoing a democratic transition. In 2001, Freedom House judged Indonesia's political system to be 'partial free' with a combined democracy score of 7. The Philippines stands out as the only 'mixed regime' experiencing a transition. Its democracy/autocracy combined score was 10 ('partial free') during the whole Marcos dictatorship, and was down at 3 ('free') immediately after regime change in 1986 (Freedom House 2001). These shifts contrast markedly with the democracy score of the other ASEAN members, but especially with the newly admitted members Vietnam, Laos, Cambodia and Burma. Freedom House rated these countries as 'not free' in 2001.

Parallel to the democratization of some members, especially Thailand and Indonesia, significant changes have occurred. Most importantly, Thailand and Burma are currently involved in a militarised border dispute, the first serious conflict since ASEAN's inception, and this is examined in some detail later on in this chapter. Over the past years, a prolonged debate over ASEAN's cardinal principle of non-interference has taken place, which finally led to the establishment of an ASEAN Troika to intervene in specific conflicts in 1999. While the latter development does not necessarily give rise to concerns, it is the fact that non-interference was previously seen as causal in preventing war-like situations, which make the departure from it potentially irritating. As other chapters in this book have already acknowledged, increasing domestic instability generally in Indonesia has become a prime concern for other ASEAN countries, not least because of the potentially adverse transborder spillover effects that may arise from this development. Separation movements have been active in Indonesia's province of Aceh and in West Papua. However, the most serious inter-state conflict within ASEAN is that between Thailand and Burma.

3. Peace, democratization and the 'democratic peace' in Southeast Asia

Since the late 1980s, the literature on the so-called 'democratic peace' hypothesis has grown remarkably. Immanuel Kant's essay on the *Perpetual Peace* (1795) evolved around the question how an ever enduring international peace system could be established, and basically stipulated that such a peace system ultimately depended on the existence of democratic states in the international system, economic interdependence and an international federation of states. Kant's essay stimulated a variety of empirical and theoretical studies on the democratic peace. Largely due to the statistical analyses of Russett (1993) and various other studies,[1] we know today that democratic states have a much smaller probability of waging wars against another than non-democracies.

Yet, recent research has also focused on peace among authoritarian states and points to the relative stability of peaceful relations among these kinds of states, even if admitting, that peace among authoritarian states is less durable than the one among democracies (Gowa 1999, Peceny *et al.* 2002). The Association of Southeast Asian Nations is frequently cited as one of the most successful regional organizations in the developing world, which have preserved peace among them although its members have been predominantly authoritarian. In fact ASEAN's success in maintaining peace and stability in the wider region has caught the attention of practitioners and scholars alike, who have referred to ASEAN as an alternative model of co-operation by authoritarian states (Amitav 1995, Busse 2000, Haacke 2003). Before we turn to the impact of democratization on ASEAN's security culture, it is in order to look at how social constructivist approaches have explained the absence of war among ASEAN member states. In proceeding from these explanations ask how the democratization of three of ten ASEAN's member states affects the prospects for continuing peace and stability in the region. The interesting fact is that the previously mentioned studies basically agree that it was the like-mindedness of ASEAN member states (i.e. their common autocratic domestic structures and their construction of a collective identity) that ultimately facilitated the development of peaceful relations.

Kivimäki (2001) makes a strong argument in favour of a social constructivist explanation for peace among ASEAN member states, which focuses on the nature and strength of a normative community among them. Kivimäki argues that strong intersubjective norms of non-interference ultimately account for the fact that there have not been wars among ASEAN member states, although the existence of several territorial disputes makes war likely. He deduces this normative community from similar domestic structures. While Kivimäki focuses on intersubjective standards of appropriate behaviour, a second explanation leaves out this interaction level and focuses on similar norms of conflict resolution, which are being 'externalised'. The strongest explanation for democratic peace is that democracies tend to 'externalise' their largely peaceful domestic norms of conflict resolution when dealing with other democracies, and therefore are more peaceful towards likewise states than towards non-democracies (Russett 1993, Russett and O'Neal 2002). Busse (2000) makes a similar argument with regard to ASEAN by contending that the tendency to avoid open confrontations arises out of the political culture of Asian states. Because there has never been an enlightenment, or Roman system of law on which a Weberian-style bureaucracy can be founded, personal relationships among rulers have shaped the domestic political process and contributed to a personalized, patronage-network based policy style. This political culture has been externalized and led to an equally personalized foreign policy style and an emphasis on conflict avoidance. The lack of transparency in political institutions and decision-making processes of authoritarian states has been externalized on a sub-regional level. Just as the articulation of domestic political conflicts is being clearly circumscribed by the autocratic ruling elites and the military to suppress any challenge of their legitimacy, the open treatment of many inter-state conflicts has been avoided. A common denominator of both explanations is that similar states are likely to preserve peace among each other because they externalize the same norms of conflict management.

Given these approaches to explain the relative stability of the ASEAN sub-region, how would changes in regime type affect co-operation and peace among ASEAN states? If co-operation in ASEAN depended largely on the relative strength of intersubjective norms and were only loosely correlated to regime type, as some studies seem to suggest, we would expect these norms to be rather resilient towards change despite democratization. Intersubjective norms are also unlikely to change even if they are not in the interest of individual ASEAN member states. It could be argued that the more liberal ASEAN states would not try to change constitutive ASEAN principles. As we will see, there exist challenges to constitutive ASEAN principles by the more democratic ASEAN members. As such, there is some *prima facie* evidence that democratization and a change in these principles are related.

According to the 'externalization thesis' there is a direct correlation between regime types and foreign policy behaviour. Collective norms or institutions are largely neglected by this approach, and consequently it would predict that ASEAN norms and inter-state relations in particular would deteriorate after democratization. Mixed state dyads have a greater probability of war because they externalize different norms of conflict management. Support for this argument is Owen's (1994) study. Owen argues that the same features which produce peace among democracies – a liberal ideology and open debate guaranteed by democratic institutions – make war between democracies and non-democracies more likely because liberal states will regard non-democracies as unreasonable, unpredictable and potentially dangerous. As he comments, 'These states are either ruled by despots, or with unenlightened citizenries. Illiberal states may seek illiberal ends such as conquest, intolerance, or impoverishment of others' (p. 96). Consequently, the same constraints working in favour of a democratic peace are unlikely to work in the interaction between non-democracies and democracies. With regards to ASEAN, the democratization of the Philippines, Thailand and Indonesia will therefore change the relationship among the democratic and non-democratic ASEAN members, and is likely to lead to greater conflicts and probably war. We would also expect that especially the new democracies in ASEAN would challenge ASEAN's cardinal principle of non-interference (see Chapter 8), and promote a change of the group's consensual norms, for example, towards such issues as human rights. As discussed later, the current border dispute between Thailand and Burma provides an ideal test for this hypothesis, because it involves a new democracy and an autocratic state.

Kivimäki's (2001) approach similarly leads to the hypotheses that democratization provokes instability. He concludes that peace among predominantly autocratic or mixed (democratic and autocratic) states is possible, but that it is likely to be less stable than peace among democracies because it is not backed up by genuine objective structures of liberal democracy and economic interdependence. He more specifically argued that, 'It would seem that the construction of normative communities has not usually been independent of the material, objective realities. International perceptions of the division of interests could shatter the image of ASEAN interests more effectively than they could shatter the subjective sentiments of common interests of liberal democracies, which are based on positive objective interdependence' (p. 21).

These two hypotheses are backed up by statistical evidence indicating that states in transition from autocracy to democracy or vice versa, are the most likely to fight wars, and given this prospects for ASEAN may look rather bleak. Recent research indicates that it is democratizing states that are most prone to civil war and militarized inter-state disputes. As Hegre *et al.* (2001) observed, 'harshly authoritarian states and institutionally consistent democracies experience fewer civil wars than intermediate regimes' (p. 33). They further found that institutionally consistent democracies and stark autocracies are equally unlikely to experience civil war, and that an intermediate regime was estimated to be four times more prone to civil war than a consistent democracy. Furthermore, according to the statistical analysis of Mansfield and Snyder (1995), democratizing states are more likely to fight war than are states that had undergone no change in regime.[2] The relationship is weakest one year after regime change and strongest at ten years. With regard to the extent of regime change, Mansfield and Snyder also find a strong relationship between the previous degree of autocracy and the likelihood that states wage war after a democratic transition.

The following two sections explore cases in which a relationship between democratization and war could become obvious. The first concerns the Thailand–Burma militarized border conflict and assesses whether conflict escalation is related to Thailand's change in regime type. If this is so, we would find clear evidence that Thailand regards the conflict with Burma as a struggle of a democracy against an autocracy and therefore actively seek an escalation of the conflict. The Thai–Burmese border conflict is very relevant to these suggested hypotheses as it involves a democracy and an autocracy as geographical neighbours, and which involves a bilateral relationship with a history of past conflicts. The second case studies individual ASEAN members' reactions to the Aceh conflict in Indonesia to evaluate whether there is a difference in perception between the democratic and non-democratic among member states of ASEAN. Given gross and systematic human rights violations in Aceh by the Indonesian military, there has been a good opportunity for the more democratic members to promote human rights in Southeast Asia in response to this development. An important question will likewise be whether there is some support for non-interference on the part of the democratic members, and if yes, how this support is being motivated by commitment to ASEAN principles or to self-interest.

4. The recent Thai–Burmese border conflict

4.1. Introductory comments

The recent border conflict between Thailand and Burma might be considered a primary example to explore the effect of democratization on the probability of war. It is one of the most significant conflicts among ASEAN members in contemporary times, and according to Haacke (2003) constitutes a serious violation of ASEAN's principle of non-use of force. Conflicts along the common border between Thailand and Burma have erupted occasionally for the last 20 years or so. As the 'Correlates of War' database indicates, Thailand and Burma have had several border clashes since the formation of ASEAN (Jones *et al.* 1996). In fact, in this database disputes involving Thailand and Burma or Thailand and Laos are the most frequently cited militarized inter-state disputes in Southeast Asia. As such, the border clashes are by no means an exception from Thailand and Burma's relationship in the past. Yet, these conflicts have recently escalated and the military junta in Burma ordered the closure of all border checkpoints in May 2002. Both countries have since then increased their military presence along the border.

As the subsequent section will demonstrate, there is some evidence for the dynamics predicted by the externalisation hypothesis of an escalation of conflicts in mixed state dyads: the Thai public increasingly perceives the border conflict as a conflict between a democracy and an autocracy. As I will argue, though, public opinion has not influenced Thai foreign policy thus far. Instead of heading for an escalation of conflict, the Thai government has rather sought reconciliatory measures. There are attempts to change ASEAN's policy of 'constructive engagement' with Burma, which basically refers to a strict policy of non-intervention. But these efforts are rather related to the fact that Thailand experiences the negative effects of the policy of constructive engagement than to efforts to promote human rights change in Burma, such as the trade in narcotics and refugee flows (Bunyanunda 2001).

4.2. Historical precursors

In the 1970s and 1980s, Thai–Burmese border disputes occurred mainly as a side effect of Burma's fight against separatist movements along its Western border involving the Shan and Karen ethnic minorities. Since then, Burma has accused Thailand of assisting these ethnic minorities with weapons and by allowing them to operate from Thai territory. Although Bangkok has always officially denied these charges, there is some evidence for the claims, since in the past, Thailand has regarded the ethnic Shan and Karen minorities strategically as potential 'buffers' along its Western border. Thailand's 'buffer zone policy' is essentially a Cold War doctrine that was operative until the late 1990s, based on the rationale that the Eastern border needed military protection against the communist regimes of Laos and Vietnam, while the Western border with Burma could be effectively protected by using ethnic minorities on the Burmese side as such 'buffers'. The Thai military skilfully played out frictions among Burma's ethnically separated population, and made use of armed ethnic Karen standing between Burmese and Thai forces in order to limit the chances of a direct confrontation with Burma and to safeguard its own state.

Similarly, Thailand tried to use the Shan minority as a buffer towards China and clandestinely supported Shan struggles to seek an independent state. Since the border disputes were only short-lived and because during the Cold War the defence of the eastern border was not the Thai military's central concern, the border disputes were largely ignored. Moreover, due to Burma's strict policy of neutrality in Southeast Asia during the Cold War, it was neither regarded a military ally of China nor an ally of Vietnam, the two main military contenders of Thailand. As in earlier disputes along the border, in the latest dispute Burma has repeatedly accused the Thai government and military of supporting the Shan State Army (SSA) by providing them with weapons and ammunition, an allegation every administration in Bangkok has denied. On the other hand, due to the international sanctions regime due to Burma's gross and systematic human rights violations, Burma's strategic position has fundamentally changed. Burma is more and more perceived as an insecure ally in balancing China.

4.3. Chronology of the recent Thai–Burmese border conflict

The recent border conflict dates back to 1998. In September of that year, local Thai–Burmese Border Committee secretary, Lt Tae Aung, wrote a letter to Thailand's Chairman Colonel Chayuti Boonparn accusing the Thai government of doing nothing to prevent Shan rebels from using Thai territory to stage an attack on the Burmese military. The Shan rebels had fired heavy artillery from the Thai Mae Ramat district on Burma's Kok Ko border village. According to the Burmese official, two villagers had died in the attack. Although Thailand denied the allegations, it was clear that it had deployed military along the border with Burma and that it supported the Shan rebels in order to fight the illegal smuggling of narcotics from Burma to Thailand. Bangkok has been claiming for long that the army of one ethnic minority in Burma, which supports the military junta in Rangoon, the Wa, was responsible for the smuggling of narcotics used to produce methamphetamines to Thailand. Thai officials claim that 600 million methamphetamine tablets worth US$1.8 billion are being smuggled to Thailand every year.[3]

In the course of 1999, Thailand increasingly felt the consequences of the military operations of the Burmese military against the ethnic minorities along the Thai border, which were largely designed to suppress independent struggles. In May, 300 Karen rebels fled into Suan Pueng district of Ratchaburi province following a clash between the Karen rebels and Burmese troops. Army intelligence source then predicted more violence as Burma wanted to suppress the minority rebels ahead of the planned ASEAN meeting in Rangoon. An estimated 100 000 individuals of ethnic minorities have fled Burma in the last couple of years and sought refuge in neighbouring Thailand, where they pose a great challenge to the Thai government's ability to provide humanitarian assistance. In September 1999, Burma reinforced security forces at the Thai–Burma border, a development that the Thai Supreme commander downplayed by arguing that the reinforcement did not pose any security threat to Thailand. This perception changed when two months later Burmese pro-democracy activists occupied the Burmese Embassy in Bangkok and took the Burmese ambassador at Bangkok as their hostage. Although Thai officials persuaded the activists to give up the occupation, they later set them free without charging them with a crime.

The Burmese junta immediately claimed that the support of the pro-democracy activists constituted a meddling into the domestic affairs of Burma. It closed all checkpoints along the land and sea border with Thailand and linked the re-opening of the checkpoints to the arrest and prosecution of the dissident students, who had occupied the embassy. Although the checkpoints were later re-opened, the bilateral relationship between Thailand and Burma remained strained and the border conflict intensified. In Thailand, the closing of the borders marked a turn in the public perception of the Thai–Burmese border disputes. It triggered a nationalist reaction within the Thai public. The Thai press openly began to put public pressure on the Thai government to end its policy of 'constructive engagement', which basically proscribes not to interfere into Burma's domestic affairs. Editorials in the *Bangkok Post* argued that:

> The general consensus is that the repressive military regime must be held responsible. Had the generals ended their brutal treatment of Burma's pro-democracy elements and allowed Aung San Suu Kyi and her National League for Democracy to govern the country after they swept the polls in the general election of 1990, the embassy siege almost certainly would never have happened ... The hypocrisy of the Burmese dictatorship over this latest incident just reinforces the doubts of the Thai government and others around the region about the legitimacy of 'constructive engagement', one of the principal platforms of ASEAN, in gradually transforming the Rangoon military leadership into a civilized administration with a human heart.[4]

This call was backed by non-governmental human rights organizations, who quickly after the Burmese embassy had been occupied publicly urged the Thai government, as the chair of ASEAN, to immediately initiate diplomatic offensives to push for positive reforms in Burma.[5] While the Thai military increased its military operations along the border, the press and human rights organisations advocated the conduit through ASEAN to put more pressure on the military junta in Burma.

In February 2001, the longstanding diplomatic feud escalated into an armed confrontation, which led to the death of approximately 50 to 100 Burmese soldiers in heavy shelling as the Royal Thai Army pointed and then retook a military outpost which had been occupied by the Burmese two days earlier and which lay inside Thailand. Prior to the occupation, Burmese forces had requested access to the outpost to launch a military strike against the SSA, a request Bangkok refused. An exchange of artillery followed in which the Thai border town of Mae Sai and, in response, suspected *tatmadaw* positions around Tachilek in Burma were shelled. The resort to military action marked the first escalation of armed conflict and a violation of ASEAN's norm of the non-use of force. On 20 May 2002, the Burmese junta closed all border checkpoints with Thailand and reiterated the charge that the Thai military shelled its territory to assist the SSA.

Meanwhile, in Bangkok, the conflict caused a rift within the administration of Thai Prime Minister Thaksin Shinawatra. Thaksin and Defence Minister Chavalit Yongchaiyudh, who tried to pursue a reconciliatory policy towards Rangoon, faced immense public pressure to pursue a harder policy towards Burma. Especially Surayud Chulanont, the commander of the armed forces, became a major spokesperson for a more astute policy, including military operations.[6] While the Thai public welcomed this stance, Thaksin called on the Thai army not to 'overreact' to the situation.[7] Tensions between the military and the civilian government finally erupted on 3 August 2002 when Prime Minister Thaksin surprisingly announced that he had decided to reshuffle the military, as a result of which Commander-in-Chief of the Armed Forces Surayud Chulanont would be 'promoted' to the post of Supreme Commander. Although the post of supreme Commander is technically a higher post, it is largely seen as ceremonial and therefore regarded a less powerful position.

The reconciliatory approach of the Thaksin administration was widely seen as being motivated by the desire to maintain good business relations with Burma. In September 2001, during the height of the military operations between the two countries, the Thai government discussed possible satellite-link contracts with Burmese Junta leader Khin Nyung in Bangkok, although the Burmese army had overrun the military outpost inside Thailand just a few days earlier. This move contributed to widespread suspicions that the prime minister put business interests over national security, a suspicion that echoed the concerns of reformists in the military. It fits the picture that Defence Minister Chavalit Yongchaiyudh, a conservative former army commander, envisions an active role for the army in building up the economy. The military, according to his plans, could grant contracts to build roads and dams in Burma.

Since Surayud's removal, Prime Minister Thaksin and Defence Minister Chavalit have continued implementing their conciliatory approach towards Burma with the active support of Surayud's successor, General Somdhat Attanand. Somdhat officially announced that the army would take a softer line towards Burma. Since then, the government has not only continued to offer negotiations to the military junta in Burma, but has also undertaken measures, which have aroused domestic opposition. In August 2002, the government deported Burmese pro-democracy activists who had taken refuge from prosecution by Rangoon and who had been arrested in Kanchanaburi on the charge of illegal entry. On 26 August, the *Bangkok Post* reported that Thai Foreign Minister Surakiart Sathirathai was confident that borders would be reopened by Burma.[8] He said that the Burmese government now understood Thailand's policy of non-interference in its neighbour's domestic affairs and that bilateral relations were back to normal.[9] Yet, the envisioned border talks on the opening of the checkpoints by the Burmese military junta have been continually delayed.

In sum, although the border conflict between Thailand and Burma seems to provide *prima facie* evidence that democratization has contributed to an escalation of the conflict; a more careful assessment reveals that the link between democratization and escalation is rather weak. With regards to public opinion, Thailand seems to be an example of how a liberal ideology justifies war (Owen 1994). The Thai press such as the *Bangkok Post* openly argued in terms of 'we – the democracy' and 'them – the autocracy' to justify a tougher stance towards Burma. Yet, first of all, these public demands did not translate into a changed behaviour by foreign policy elites and, second, public demands for a tougher stance remained quite limited in scope. Newspaper editorials did not demand that Thailand resort to war, but rather suggested to take recourse for conflict-resolution through ASEAN channels.

To conclude, there has so far been no indication that Thailand intends to go to war over this matter. Similarly, there is evidence, as epitomized in foreign minister Surin's statement ahead of the AAM meeting, that Thailand's efforts to change 'constructive engagement' into 'flexible engagement' has been one avenue to express Thailand's new identity as a democratic state.[10] Yet, an alternative reading is that this concept is promoted in order to contain the negative impact of Burma's policy towards its minorities in Thailand, like the refugee flows and the smuggling of narcotics. Similarly, there are indications that Thailand increasingly feels the negative effects in security terms. ASEAN had long suspected that the international isolation of Burma through the sanctions regime would bring Burma closer to China and give China the chance to exert greater influence over Southeast Asia. During the Cold War and under the military regime of General U Ne Win, Burma had taken a course of strict neutrality and had neither aligned with Western nor with socialist powers. The military suppression of the democracy movement in the mid-1980s and the democratic elections of 1990, which were won by the opposition under Aung San Suu Kyi but not recognized by the military, brought Burma on the international human rights agenda immediately after the Cold War. When the sanctions regime straightened in the course of the mid-1990s, Burma was left only with China as a major ally in the region. In fact, China and Burma agreed on military co-operation in 1989, an understanding that included several arms transfer deals between 1989 and 1996 that amounted up to US$2 billion. It is believed that in exchange for its military assistance, China wanted access to the Indian Ocean via Burma, which would give China the opportunity to challenge Indian naval superiority and project its power into the Indian Ocean (Rüland 2001). As will become evident in the next section, Thailand's foreign policy with regard to human rights and democracy is far too contradictory as to be linked to its new democratic identity. The following analysis on the Aceh conflict reveals that, in accordance to self-interest, the Thai government has not used the aforementioned ASEAN 'Troika' to promote human rights and democracy in other parts of Southeast Asia. This is now discussed in more detail in the following section.

5. ASEAN and the independence struggle in Aceh

In 1999, ASEAN members established a conflict resolution mechanism. The ASEAN 'Troika' was set up during the Third ASEAN Informal Summit in Manila, 28 November 1999.[11] Thailand, which suggested the establishment, argued that ASEAN needed an instrument that would allow it to address issues of regional peace and stability more effectively. It is widely regarded as a major attempt to address issues that were previously regarded domestic, although the activation of the Troika depends on the agreement of all ten member states and therefore seems to be of little value for conflict resolution (Narine 2002). The Troika was seen by many as the first serious attempt to change the organization's sacrosanct principle of non-intervention, a development that has already become evident in the policy of 'flexible engagement' proposed by Thailand. In the process leading to the establishment of the Troika, the more democratic members, the Philippines and Thailand, played a crucial role, which provides *prima facie* evidence that ASEAN's principle of non-interference is threatened by democratization. Yet, as we will see, concerns for the disintegration of Indonesia and the potentially disrupting effects on other ASEAN members have forced a consensus among all ASEAN members that ASEAN needs to depart from non-intervention. Thus, member states' ultimate decision to establish the Troika is the result of the self-interest of democratic and non-democratic member states alike. For very different reasons, even the autocratic member states in ASEAN supported the setting up of the Troika and a departure of the non-interference principle. The background to this decision was provided by the independence struggle in Aceh, an Indonesian province at the Northern tip of Sumatra, but is equally related to democratization, this time Indonesia's. At the same time, even Thailand and the Philippines have expressed their support for non-intervention and the territorial integrity of Indonesia.

The independence struggle in Indonesia is led by the Free Aceh Movement, which has been actively seeking the separation of Indonesia since the 1980s. Under the military dominated regime of President Suharto (1966–98) these independence struggles were largely contained by military measures. When the Indonesian government under President Habibie announced in January 1999 that East Timor would have the chance to hold a referendum on its independence, and the referendum was finally conducted in August 1999, the independence struggle in Aceh gained a major boost. In November 1999, an estimated 1.5 million people gathered in Lhoksumawe to hold a demonstration demanding an end of human rights violations and a referendum for Aceh. The demand was immediately rejected by the newly elected government of Abdurrahman Wahid. Wahid promised to put an end to widespread human rights violations, but was unable to quell the political violence. After a short period in which he tried to solve the conflict by negotiations, Wahid gave in to pressure by the military and deployed Special Forces to the province. Human rights monitors subsequently reported extra-judicial killings and torture, and an increase in civilian victims from military operations.

When the heads of state were asked to explain why they had decided to set up a Troika that would eventually interfere in the domestic affairs of member states, Philippine President Joseph Estrada explained that it were developments in Indonesia, whose probable disintegration due to separatist conflicts in Aceh and Papua New Guinea would encourage similar separatist rebellions from the Philippines to China.[12] Given this background, it became relatively easy for the more democratic members, the Philippines and Thailand, to convince the other ASEAN member state's governments to sign the agreement setting up the Troika to deal with these problems. Not even Burmese military junta leader Than Shwe nor Malaysian Prime Minister Mahathir Mohammed blocked the undertaking.[13] But what appeared to be a potential dangerous development given that the strict adherence to non-intervention was previously regarded a factor for the long peace of ASEAN, turned out to be a change with only little effect on ASEAN's practice.

The Aceh conflict had the potential of a showcase to test the new Troika and the commitment of the new democracies to promoting peace and democracy in other ASEAN countries. As we will see, however, neither did the ASEAN members initiate the Troika to contain the conflict, nor did the new democracies among ASEAN members pursue a different policy towards the Indonesian government than the autocratic members. The ASEAN members displayed a unified stance on Aceh that centred on the principle of non-interference.

The Aceh conflict has affected neighbouring countries, especially Malaysia. Since the outbreak of the conflict, several thousand Acehnese have fled to Malaysia seeking asylum. During an official visit to Indonesia in March 2000, the Malaysian Prime Minister Mahathir Mohammed expressed his full support for Jakarta's policy with regard to Aceh, commenting that, 'Our stance is that Aceh should be a part of Indonesia. If they want to have more autonomy that is up to them to negotiate, but our stance is that Aceh should remain part of Indonesia.'[14] Moreover, he made clear that the Malaysian government would curb any activities supporting the Acehnese rebels, stating that, 'we will not let anybody use Malaysia as a base for activities which are not good for neighbouring countries such as Indonesia.'[15] Events which were beyond the control of the Thai government forced Bangkok to make explicit its position on the issue of non-interference: Thai police implicated two army officers from the 42nd Army Circle in an attempt to smuggle arms to rebels in Aceh. The investigation revealed that a warehouse on a small Thai island off the Thai province Satun had been used by smugglers to sell arms and ammunition to separatist groups in Aceh (and the Tamils in Sri Lanka). The Commander of the 42nd Army Circle immediately denied that the smuggling of weapons occurred with the knowledge of the army command.

The arrest of the officers became part of the agenda during Indonesia's Supreme Commander, General Widodo's visit to Thailand just two days after the arrest, on 16 May 2000 and during Indonesian President Megawati Sukarnoputri's visit to Thailand in August. When Megawati expressed her concern about the smuggling of weapons to Aceh, Prime Minister Thaksin repeated his position that, 'Thailand does not allow the use of Thai territory by people harbouring ill-intentions towards neighbours.'[16] As these statements reveal, ASEAN members regarded the Aceh conflict primarily as a domestic issue and refrained from intervening verbally or militarily into Indonesia's affairs. None of the ASEAN members have departed from ASEAN's official position of non-interference. Yet, strict adherence to the principle of non-interference can be seen as largely stemming from self-interest. Thailand and the Philippines both face an internal security threat from the Islamic minorities in the South and are therefore interested in preventing any developments, which would ultimately instigate rebellious developments in their own countries. Malaysia is equally keen on containing an Islamic radicalization in its Northern territory, where the Muslim community is especially devout. It is on this background that Bangkok, Manila and Kuala Lumpur might have extended their support to Jakarta in mediating a truce with the Free Aceh Movement and worked on a trilateral agreement to curb terrorism arising from domestic groups.[17]

In sum, similar to the Thai–Burmese border dispute, individual reactions to the Aceh conflict do not suggest that there is major rift between democratic and non-democratic states. Democratic states have refrained from supporting human rights struggles in Aceh for fear of spillover effects to Muslim communities in their own countries with negative consequences for their own stability. Likewise, non-democratic states were as much inclined to depart from the principle of non-interference when they feared the repercussions of the Aceh conflict. When the conflict escalated after 1998, the Troika concept basically showed that democracies and non-democracies were united, at least in principle, in changing the policy of non-interference to a considerable degree in order to minimize the negative consequences of their previous hands-off policy.

6. Conclusion

This chapter has argued that the democratization of a considerable number of ASEAN member states is unlikely to lead to a destabilization of ASEAN as a regional organization, as social constructivist theories and statistical evidence on states in transition might predict. It has been further contended that if these theories held true, we would expect a closer correspondence between a democratic identity and foreign policy, for example through the promotion of human rights and democracy. This would either lead to a consequent challenge of ASEAN principles or, given opportunity and contiguity, to a greater likelihood of war between democracies and autocracies or both. Either way, we would expect a destabilization of Southeast Asia due to democratization.

As has been shown, there is some evidence for attempts by the more democratic states to challenge ASEAN's cardinal principle of non-intervention. Rather than being promoted in a consistent manner by the more democratic countries of Southeast Asia (Indonesia, Thailand, Philippines) as part and parcel of a new democratic identity, they emerge out of common interests in domestic stability, which most of the ASEAN members share. And this stability is greatly challenged by separation movements in Indonesia and other interdependencies such as transnational refugee flows. Moreover, there are also indications that in the Thai–Burmese border conflict a Thai public increasingly perceives the conflict with Burma as an antagonism between a democracy and a dictatorship. Yet, as has been argued here, so far these developments have neither led to a destabilization of Southeast Asia nor to the weakening of the regional organization. These developments demonstrate that regional developments are to a considerable extent unrelated to questions of a common identity among ASEAN members (ASEAN as club of dictatorships) but largely stem from individual states' interests in domestic stability, economic development and regime survival. This becomes also evident in the fact that all ASEAN members could principally agree on the need to change the non-intervention principle and set up a Troika, even if concrete plans here have been discarded for the moment.

Notes

1. For example, Maoz and Abdolali (1989).
2. The analysis explicitly excluded civil war.
3. According to the Thai military, the United Wa State Army operates 50 methamphetamine factories out of which many are in an area just across the border near a new township, Mong Yawn. *Far Eastern Economic Review*, 12.06.2000.

4. *Bangkok Post*, 13.10.2000.
5. The statement was jointly issued by Forum-Asia, the Foreign Affairs Committee of the National Council of the Union of Burma, Friends Without Border Project, Campaign for Popular Democracy, the Coordinating Committee of Human rights Organizations in Thailand, the Students Federation of Thailand, the Thai Action Committee for Democracy in Burma, the Union for Civil Liberty and the Alternative ASEAN Network in Burma.
6. *Bangkok Post*, 26.08.2002.
7. *Far Eastern Economic Review*, 27.06.2002.
8. *Bangkok Post*, 26.08.2000.
9. Ibid.
10. Jürgen Haacke has presented that argument most clearly: 'Indeed, the proposal for flexible engagement is also illustrative of an earnest struggle for the international recognition of Thailand's democratic credentials. Especially since 1992, Thailand is acknowledged to have had an accomplished record in promoting political stability, civil liberties and human rights through a process of democratization that led to the promulgation of a new constitution in 1997' (p. 173).
11. See Chapters 7 and 8 for further detail here.
12. *Bangkok Post*, 30.11.1999.
13. Ibid.
14. *Jakarta Post*, 10.03.2000.
15. Ibid.
16. *Bangkok Post*, 03.10.1999.
17. See Chapter 7 for more on this.

References

Amitav, A. (1995) 'Human Rights and Regional Order: ASEAN and Human Rights Management in Post-Cold War Southeast Asia', in J.T.H. Tang (ed.), *Human Rights and International Relations in the Asia-Pacific Region*, Pinter, London.

Amitav, A. (2001) *Constructing a Security Community in Southeast Asia. ASEAN and the Problem of Regional Order*, Routledge, London.

Bunyanunda, M.M. (2001) 'Burma, ASEAN, and Human Rights: The Decade of Constructive Engagement, 1991–2001', *Stanford Journal of East Asian Affairs*, Vol. 2(Spring), pp. 118–35.

Busse, N. (2000) *Die Entstehung von kollektiven Identitäten: das Beispiel der ASEAN-Staaten*, Nomos Verlags-Gesellschaft, Baden-Baden.

Freedom House (2001) *Freedom in the World Country Ratings, 1972–73 to 2000–01*, Freedom House, London.

Gowa, J. (1999) *Ballots and Bullets. The Elusive Democratic Peace*, Princeton University Press, Princeton.

Haacke, J. (2003) *ASEAN's Diplomatic and Security Culture: Origins, Developments and Prospects*, Routledge, London.

Hegre, H., Ellingsen, T., Gates, S. and Gleditsch, N.P. (2001) 'Toward a Democratic Civil Peace? Democracy, Political Change, and Civil War, 1816–1992', *American Political Science Review*, Vol. 95, pp. 33–48.

Jones, D.M., Bremer, S.A. and Singer, D. (1996) 'Militarised Inter-state Disputes, 1816–1992: Rationale, Coding Rules, and Empirical Patterns', *Conflict Management and Peace Science*, Vol. 15, pp. 163–213.

Kivimäki, T.A. (2001) 'The Long Peace of ASEAN', *Journal of Peace Research*, Vol. 38(1), pp. 5–25.

Mansfield, E.D. and Snyder, J. (1995) 'Democratisation and War', *Foreign Affairs*, Vol. 74(3), pp. 79–97.

Mansfield, E.D. and Snyder, J. (2002) 'Democratic Transitions, Institutional Strength, and War', *International Organization*, Vol. 56(2), pp. 297–337.

Maoz, Z. and Abdolali, N. (1989) 'Regime Types and International Conflict', *Journal of Conflict Resolution*, Vol. 33(1), pp. 3–35.

Narine, S. (2002) *Explaining ASEAN. Regionalism in Southeast Asia*, Lynne Rienner, Boulder.

Nischalke, T. (2002) 'Does ASEAN Measure Up? Post-Cold War Diplomacy and the Idea of Regional Community' *The Pacific Review*, Vol. 15(1), pp. 89–117.

Owen, J.M. (1994) 'How Liberalism Produces Democratic Peace', *International Security*, Vol. 19(2), pp. 87–125.

Peceny, M., Beer, C.C. and Sanchez-Terry, S. (2002) 'Dictatorial Peace?', *American Political Science Review*, Vol. 96(1), pp. 15–26.

Rüland, J. (2001) 'Burma Ten Years after the Uprising: the Regional Dimension', in R. Taylor (ed.) *Burma. Political Economy Under Military Rule*, Hurst & Co, London.

Russett, B.M. (1993) *Grasping the Democratic Peace: Principles for a Post-Cold War World*, Princeton University Press, Princeton.

Russett, B.M. and O'Neal, J.R. (2002) *Triangulating Peace. Democracy, Interdependence and International Organization*, W.W. Norton & Company, New York.

11

Changing China–Taiwan Relations and Asia-Pacific Regionalism: Economic Co-operation and Security Challenge

Rex Li

1. Introduction

Since the election of Chen Shui-bian as Taiwan's President in 2000, there have been significant changes in China–Taiwan relations. Economically, China and Taiwan have moved closer to each other. Politically, however, they are drifting further apart. Given that both Beijing and Taipei have a wide range of economic and trade connections with most countries in the Asia-Pacific, the future of their relations will have a far-reaching impact on the economic and security situation in the region. This chapter will first examine recent developments in Cross-Strait relations, focusing specifically on two plausible future scenarios. It will then consider the likely implications of each scenario on Asia-Pacific co-operation.

2. Economic integration, political union?

Although no real progress has been made in Cross-Strait talks over the past few years, the economic ties between the People's Republic of China (PRC) and the Republic of China, Taiwan (ROC) continue to expand. This has led to the speculation that reunification, while not imminent, is a distinct possibility (Tucker 2002). Indeed, the size of Taiwanese investment on the mainland has increased substantially which amounts to an estimated US$100 billion. The ROC is now the second largest foreign investor in mainland China which has attracted around 50 percent of Taiwan's total outward investment. In the meantime, Cross-Strait trade reached the level of over US$30 billion in 2002, which has helped create a huge trade surplus for Taiwan.[1] The PRC has replaced the United States as the largest export market of Taiwan, while the ROC is China's second largest source of imports. More significantly, over 3 million Taiwanese have visited China, and about 1 million Taiwanese business people and their families have opted to live in Shanghai and other

Chinese cities. There are estimated to be over 40 000 Taiwanese companies operating in mainland China.

The desire of Taiwanese companies to develop closer commercial and trade links with the PRC reflects the island's recent economic difficulties. Like many other countries in East Asia, Taiwan has suffered from the consequences of the 1997/98 East Asian financial crisis and its lingering effects. The situation is exacerbated by the economic downturn in the United States, especially since the events of 11 September 2001. Growing unemployment, declining economic performance and a fluctuating financial market have forced Taiwanese business people to turn to the mainland. To Taiwan's companies, China offers an auspicious manufacturing base and a lucrative market. The relatively cheap labour in the PRC has allowed Taiwanese manufacturers to remain competitive in the world market.

Over the past few years, Taiwanese investors have put pressure on the Chen Shui-bian administration to relax its restrictions on Cross-Strait trade. In January 2001, the government approved the 'three small links' under which direct trade, transportation and postal services between Taiwan's offshore islands and adjacent ports in China were permitted. On 26 August 2001, President Chen Shui-bian accepted the recommendations of a multiparty Economic Development Advisory Council that the government should ease its control over the island's economic ties with the mainland.[2] It was suggested that the US$50 million ceiling on single investments in China should be scrapped and that mainland investment in Taiwan's real estates and stock markets should be allowed. The advisory body also argued for a more flexible mechanism for transferring funds between China and Taiwan and for the establishment of the three links of direct communication, trade and transportation. In response to the demands of the business community, the Chen government has replaced its 'no haste, be patient' policy by one of 'active opening, effective management'. It appears that President Chen has found it difficult to resist closer economic ties with China.

Indeed, it could be argued that continued economic interactions between China and Taiwan could strengthen their economic bilateralism. Their WTO memberships would certainly help remove trade barriers that would in turn promote further economic integration across the Taiwan Strait. To be sure, both Beijing and Taipei would have to reconsider their bilateral economic relations within the context of multilateralism. As a member of the WTO, the PRC is expected to deepen its economic reform and liberalisation and to open up its domestic market to the wider world. This would no doubt offer more business opportunities for other WTO members including Taiwan. As a political entity that does not enjoy diplomatic recognition by the majority of the states around the world, the ROC will now be able to deal with other governments through various legitimate channels. Protected by the principles, rules and regulations of the WTO, Taiwan will become more confident in conducting economic and trade negotiations with China as well as other countries. Mutual respect and reciprocal treatment in commercial activities would accelerate Cross-Strait economic interactions. Many analysts hope that systemic and regularised contacts between China and Taiwan within the institutional framework of the WTO could create a more stable environment conducive to a peaceful resolution of their political dispute. This view is shared by some Taiwanese scholars who argue that the dual WTO accessions of the PRC and ROC would provide a good opportunity to develop economic confidence-building measures across the Taiwan Strait (Lee 2002). Closer economic links between the PRC and ROC, as the liberals would argue, would lead to a reduction of tensions and an improvement of their relations, and in the longer term, a peaceful resolution of the Taiwan issue.

Many observers believe that economic integration across the Taiwan Strait would serve as a disincentive for Beijing to use force against Taiwan. PRC leaders are, it is argued, fully aware that the success of China's economic modernisation rests ultimately with its access to the global market and with inflows of external funding. A war with Taiwan would undoubtedly have an adverse effect on the PRC's trade and economic relations with the United States, Japan and other nations. In any case, China has benefited immensely from the expansion of Cross-Strait economic relations. For example, the majority of electronic products the PRC exports to the West are in fact manufactured by Taiwanese companies in China. It is estimated that between 5 and 10 million jobs in mainland China have been created by the investment of Taiwanese companies (Siew 2002).

The argument that international trade and economic interdependence can reduce the likelihood of war has long been advanced and continues to influence the thinking of many liberal scholars and policy-makers (Cobden 1903, Angell 1935, Rosecrance 1986).[3] As Cable and Ferdinand (1994) point out, 'the nature of current Chinese development has involved building up strong economic linkages with its neighbours through trade and investment flows...which would make military confrontation all the more costly' (p. 259). Chinese leaders, says Yahuda (1997), have recognised that economic interdependence plays a vital part in sustaining China's economic growth, maintaining its social stability and legitimising the rule of the Chinese Communist Party (CCP). Some liberals such as Findlay and Watson (1997) reject the realist assumption that China 'has "adapted" its outward behaviour but has not "learned" a new way of thinking' (p. 107). They further argue that, 'China's interaction with the world economy has created a level of trade interdependency that has transformed both China's international role and the way in which the rest of the world relates to China' (ibid). Similarly, Harris (1997) notes that 'cognitive learning has taken place in the economic field' in China that 'supports liberal rather than realist views of the world, including the possibility of co-operative international behaviour not only among "liberal" societies, but also among liberal and non-liberal (in the Western sense) societies' (p. 151).

Liberals argue that interdependent countries are unlikely to go to war because of the benefits of trade. Yet the European powers did fight with each other during the First World War, even though there had been a high level of trade among them before the war. So, under what circumstances will economic interdependence lead to war or peace? Copeland (1996) seems to have the answer. He contends that liberal scholars, like the realists, predicate their predictions of a state actor's decision to initiate war on 'a snapshot of the level of interdependence at a single point in time' (p. 7). His theory, however, offers a new variable (i.e. the expectations of future trade) that 'incorporates in the theoretical logic an actor's sense of the future trends and possibilities' (ibid). Peace can be maintained, Copeland argues, for as long as 'states expect that trade levels will be high into the foreseeable future', and goes on to say that, 'if highly interdependent states expect that trade will be severely restricted…the most highly dependent states will be the ones most likely to initiate war, for fear of losing the economic wealth that support their long-term security' (ibid).

Using historical evidence, Copeland (1996) analyses Germany's decisions to fight the two World Wars. In both cases, the findings reveal the same pattern of behaviour: German leaders decided to go to war because of negative expectations for future trade and high dependence on other countries. 'For any given expected value of war', Copeland argues, 'we can predict that the lower the expectations of future trade, the lower the expected value of trade, and therefore the more likely it is that war will be chosen' (p. 19). It does not matter whether present trade level is high or low. If expectations for future trade are low, the expected value of trade will be negative as illustrated by Germany's decisions to take the military option prior to the two World Wars. On the other hand, the expected value of trade can be positive, if expectations for future trade are high, even though present trade level is low or zero. For instance, the relationships between the Soviet Union and the United States and Western countries were relatively amicable during 1971–73 and after 1985 because of Soviet leaders' positive expectations for future trade.

If one follows Copeland's (1996) argument, whether China and Taiwan will deal with their political dispute through military means would depend on their leaders' expectations of future trade. If PRC and ROC leaders feel that their current trade with each other and with the outside world would continue to expand, there would be little incentive for them to resort to the use of force to resolve the status of Taiwan. If, however, they are convinced that their trade prospects would deteriorate substantially in the near future, they would be likely to take the military option to avert vulnerability and decline. In other words, the future behaviour of both China and Taiwan would be determined not only by the level of their economic interdependence but also by their expectations of the future trading environment.

Many fear that China may sooner or later choose the military solution to the Taiwan problem. If one accepts Copeland's assumptions, however, the threat of a Chinese invasion of Taiwan does not seem imminent. This is because China's expectations of future trade with its Asian neighbours and Western nations are by and large positive. In a speech to an academic symposium in Beijing, Chen Jian, a senior Chinese official, said that 'the international situation has moved at a speed faster than expected in a direction favourable to China. ... The ongoing reform and opening up policies and the economic development in China ... are based on the judgement that world peace can be maintained and a new world war will not erupt for the near future.'[4] Similarly, Wu Yi, the PRC's former Minister of Foreign Trade and Economic Co-operation, has noted: 'We are immersed in the irreversible general trend toward world-wide economic integration ... economic co-operation with various countries makes it easier than any time in the past to reach a common view, and can be carried out in a wider area and at a higher starting point. This in turn portends that possibility for successful co-operation is much greater in the future' (Wu 1997: 16). Many Chinese leaders, officials and scholars echo this type of optimistic assessment of the future trading environment. Despite the recent financial turmoil in East and Southeast Asia, they believe that the economic dynamism in the Asia-Pacific will continue into the twenty-first century, and that China will benefit from further economic growth and co-operation in the region (Song 2002).

It is clear that both the PRC and ROC have been actively involved in global economic activities and are fully integrated into the Asia-Pacific economy. Since the late 1990s, Taiwanese leaders have adopted various measures to improve the economic situation of the island, including loosening control over Cross-Strait interactions. As noted above, Taiwan's WTO membership could intensify its economic and trade relations with China. From the liberal perspective, therefore, Beijing and Taipei share a common interest in maintaining economic stability and prosperity across the Taiwan Strait and in the Asia-Pacific. This irreversible and irresistible trend of economic integration may ultimately lead to some sort of political union between them.

3. Economic integration, political stalemate

Another scenario in China–Taiwan relations is persistent political hostility despite growing Cross-Strait economic interactions. This is exactly what has been happening in the past few years. Since his electoral victory, President Chen Shui-bian has on several occasions expressed his willingness to hold peace talks with China. But he maintains that Taiwan must be treated as an equal in any Cross-Strait negotiations. So far his offer has been turned down by Chinese leaders who insist that any talks between Beijing and Taipei must be based on the 'one-China principle' (Qian 2002). There is no sign of any change in the PRC's Taiwan policy under Hu Jintao's new leadership. As far as Chinese leaders are concerned, there is no room for compromise on the 'one-China principle'.

The reunification of China and Taiwan is arguably the single most important issue that unites all the leaders in Beijing. The occupation of Taiwan by Japan before 1945 is seen as part of the shame and humiliation that China suffered while it was weak. Despite their ideological or policy differences, all Chinese leaders share the same national goal, that is, to build a rich, powerful and united nation. As long as Taiwan is separate from mainland China, as Li (1999b) observes, PRC leaders would fear that it could be exploited by the United States and Japan to 'constrain' China (pp. 11–12). This nationalistic sentiment seems to have widespread sympathy from many PRC elites and citizens. Control over Taiwan and its surrounding areas would greatly strengthen China's military position. It would also allow it to dominate the adjacent water, which is extremely important to other great powers strategically and economically. If Taiwan were to be peacefully incorporated into the PRC, its human and financial resources could add additional strengths to Chinese economic power. Reclaiming Taiwan is therefore an integral part of China's efforts to fulfil its great power aspirations.

From a realist standpoint, a great power's behaviour is determined not so much by its intentions but by its capabilities. As a state's economy vastly expands, it will use its newfound power to extend its spheres of influence and defend its economic and strategic interests whenever and wherever these interests are challenged. This pattern of great power emergence has recurred many times in history: Britain, France, Germany, Japan, the former Soviet Union and the United States all went through similar paths (Friedberg 1993/94: 16). As Rachman (1995) notes, 'big countries are more likely to be difficult to live with if they have a strong sense of cultural superiority or historical grievances about their treatment by the rest of the world' (p. 132). As an emerging power with a great civilisation and a history of being humiliated by foreign countries, China will therefore be likely to behave in the same way as other rising powers did in the past.[5]

Realists are particularly critical of the liberal assumption that economic interdependence reduces the possibility of military conflict. Taiwan is undoubtedly an important trading partner of China, yet their close economic relations have not prevented the PRC from threatening to attack Taiwan. According to the late Segal (1996), 'China's behaviour ... suggests that China does not feel that the fruits of economic interdependence are at risk when it pursues its irredentist agenda or seeks greater international status, or else that these are short-term prices worth paying for a greater good' (p. 133). Economic interdependence, realists contend, can in fact increase the likelihood of armed confrontation among trading nations as they seek to gain or maintain their access to vital resources and materials that are essential to the pursuit of wealth and power in an anarchic world (Waltz 1979). Any attempt to separate Taiwan from the mainland will be perceived by China as both a threat to its security and an obstacle to the achievement of its great power status. Thus, economic interests could be forfeited, if necessary, for the sake of national unity and territorial integrity. This is why Beijing has never renounced the use of force against Taiwan. Indeed, the rapid development of China's defence modernisation is designed primarily, though not exclusively, for that eventuality (Zhang 1999). If one looks at China's naval modernisation, the focus has been on extending the People's Liberation Army (PLA) Navy's defence perimeter from coastal waters to between 200 and 400 nautical miles. This kind of offshore defence would be useful for dealing with potential conflict in the South China Sea but the main consideration is the Taiwan factor. In recent years, substantial improvement has been made in the PLA Navy's surface combatants, destroyers, frigates and submarine force. Recent acquisitions from Russia include the well-known *Sovremenny*-class destroyers. Taiwan is also a key consideration in the PLA's air force modernisation. Since the early 1990s, and particularly after the 1995–96 Taiwan Strait crisis, greater attention has been paid to the role of the PLA Air Force in a potential Cross-Strait confrontation. The purchase of Russian aircraft such as Su-27 and Su-30 and the development of indigenous fighters (e.g. Jian-10 fighter-bomber) are clear indications of the PLA Air Force's modernisation efforts. Chinese defence planners are fully aware of the importance of air dominance and defence capability against air strikes in a future conflict with Taiwan (Li 2002).

More important, a sustained effort has been made to improve the range and accuracy of China's missile force. According to the estimates of the International Institute for Strategic Studies, the PRC currently has 20 intercontinental ballistic missiles, 130–150 intermediate-range ballistic missiles, and 12 submarine-launched ballistic missiles (International Institute for Strategic Studies 2001: 188). The 335 short-range ballistic missiles that China possesses are clearly targeted at Taiwan. The number will certainly increase in the coming years. Given its apprehensions of the current Democratic Progressive Party (DPP) government's independence orientation and of the greater willingness of the Bush's administration to defend Taiwan's security, China has stepped up its military build-up in the past few years (Lang 2002, Sheng 2002, Teng 2002, Zen 2002).

Apart from military coercion, China continues to exert economic pressure on Taipei hoping that it would accept reunification talks. The Chinese are well aware of the economic difficulties that Taiwan has been experiencing since the 1997/98 East Asian financial crisis (Li *et al.* 2002). Their economic offensives are aimed at securing greater support from the island's business community for a closer relationship with China. As noted earlier, Beijing has succeeded in attracting a huge amount of investment from Taiwan and in forcing the DPP government to ease its trade restrictions on Cross-Strait trade. Closer economic ties and trade interactions across the Taiwan Strait could make Taiwan more dependent on the mainland for its future economic development. Indeed, the PRC leaders have been consciously trying to frustrate Taiwan's aspirations to become a regional economic centre. They deliberately seek to develop Shanghai as a major financial and economic centre and to assist Hong Kong in stabilising its economy and financial market. Moreover, China's rapid economic development and its ability to attract enormous Taiwanese investment have caused considerable anxiety in the ROC over the marginalisation of Taiwan's economy.

Taiwan's business leaders are interested in making profits from their China trade but it does not necessarily mean that they are in support of political integration with the PRC. Most Taiwanese people would prefer to maintain the status-quo indefinitely, fearing that reunification with China could mean the loss of their democratic rights and economic freedom. Taiwan's economic achievements and progress in democratisation have undoubtedly led to the rise of a new Taiwanese nationalism.[6] This tendency is strengthened immensely by the DPP government, which has become much bolder in promoting a Taiwanese identity over the past two years. According to a report in *Far Eastern Economic Review*, the Taipei government has raised the status of the Taiwanese dialect, increased the teaching of Taiwanese history in schools, removed the map of China in a government department's logo, and introduced many other measures that would reduce Taiwan's traditional links with mainland China.[7]

Meanwhile, the Taipei government is encouraged by the support of President George W. Bush who said in public that the United States would do 'whatever it took to help Taiwan defend itself'.[8] Indeed, the Bush administration offered Taiwan a massive arms package in April 2001. The package includes 4 *Kidd*-class destroyers, 8 diesel-electric patrol submarines, 12 P-3 Orion maritime patrol aircraft, submarine- and surface-launched torpedoes and other naval systems. Together they would enhance Taiwan's capability to break potential Chinese blockades, although it would take some time for Taiwan to receive these systems and to absorb the sophisticated US equipment. Despite the need to secure China's support for its 'war against terrorism', as Li (2003) has pointed out, Washington has not abandoned its commitments to Taiwan. If anything, it has developed closer defence ties with the Taiwanese military and allowed senior Taiwanese leaders and officials to visit the United States. A leaked Pentagon report has allegedly suggested that nuclear weapons could be used against China in the event of a conflict across the Taiwan Strait.[9] The parallel trends of economic integration and political stalemate is likely to continue as long as the positions of the political leaders on both sides of the Taiwan Strait remain unchanged.

4. The future of China–Taiwan relations: regional implications

It is impossible to predict precisely how China–Taiwan relations will develop in future. For the moment, economic integration across the Taiwan Strait has failed to reduce political tensions between both sides. The situation will remain volatile for the foreseeable future (Li 2002). If a Cross-Strait conflict does occur it may lead to a US–China military engagement with unpredictable consequences. Should this happen, the entire Asia-Pacific region would be destabilised which could make the already fragile economies of Japan and other East Asian countries more fragile. While a China–Taiwan military confrontation would have serious effects on Asia-Pacific security, other countries in the region are unable to play any part in finding a solution to the problem. This is because of China's insistence on treating the Taiwan issue as a matter of 'internal affairs'. Despite their concern over the long-term implications of growing Chinese power, East Asian countries are keen to engage the PRC politically and hope to benefit from the China market. They have therefore no desire to challenge Beijing's claim over Taiwan.

In East Asia, no regional security organisation is in a position to consider the Taiwan question, let alone helping to resolve it. If the ASEAN Regional Forum is not competent in dealing with the South China Sea disputes, it cannot be expected to be able to tackle the China–Taiwan dispute. The 'track two' meetings like the Council for Security Co-operation in the Asia-Pacific (CSCAP) and others are even less capable of handling such an issue. The best they can do is to provide a forum for representatives of the PRC and ROC to exchange ideas and air their concerns. These meetings may be useful in enhancing mutual understanding but their influence on the future of Cross-Strait relations should not be exaggerated. Clearly, the Taiwan dispute is not amenable to any regional solution.

On the other hand, if greater economic co-operation across the Taiwan Strait does bring about some kind of political integration between both sides, it could lead to the emergence of a 'Greater China' which would have significant economic and security implications for the Asia-Pacific region. On the positive side, this scenario would mean the removal of a major regional flashpoint that could potentially disrupt Asia-Pacific stability. On the other hand, such a scenario would alter the balance of power in the Asia-Pacific fundamentally. If Japan fails to regain its dominant position in East Asian economic affairs, it could be pushed into the position of a second-rate regional power. More significantly, an economically and militarily powerful Greater China could seek to challenge the dominant position of the United States in the Asia-Pacific. Already China sees itself as a rising power, which will eventually become an economic superpower and a global strategic player. Its long-term goal, as Li's (1999a) research indicates, is to challenge US domination in the global system and to replace it by one of multi-polarity. With a greater power projection capability, Beijing would be more confident to take on the Americans, which could force Japan to either develop an independent nuclear capability or expand its defence relations with the United States. This could exacerbate China's fear of Japanese remilitarisation (Li 1999b), thus intensifying Sino-Japanese rivalry in the region.

On security matters, a unified and stronger China would feel less constrained by multilateral pressure, although it would not wish to be excluded from any regional security forums. Indeed, China would want to play a key role in dealing with regional security issues, for example, the North Korean situation. But a Greater China would be less inclined to compromise on issues of 'national sovereignty and territorial integrity'. It would insist on bilateral solutions to territorial disputes such as the South China Sea dispute. Furthermore, as Dent (2001) has argued, a rising China would also seek to play a more prominent part in regional economic affairs. At the ASEAN Plus Three (APT) summit in November 2002 at Phnom Penh, the Chinese Prime Minister Zhu Rongji and ASEAN leaders decided to establish a free trade area (FTA) by 2010 that could become the world's third largest trading bloc.[10] The ASEAN-China FTA proposal may be an indication of Beijing's long-term economic intentions in the region. In the meantime, a 'Greater China' FTA that includes China, Taiwan, Hong Kong and Macao could become a highly competitive sub-regional economic bloc. Nevertheless, this may not necessarily be detrimental to the economic interests of other Asia-Pacific nations, so long as China is prepared to practise 'open regionalism' and observe the rules and norms of international trade regimes (see Chapter 5). One would hope that a Greater China would be driven by economic forces rather than political ambitions.

5. Conclusion

Whether closer economic links between China and Taiwan would lead to a peaceful solution to the dispute over the status of Taiwan would have profound implications for the Asia-Pacific region. There is a clear linkage between the economic and security dimensions of China–Taiwan relations. The fallout from the 1997/98 East Asian financial crisis continues to hamper Taiwan's economic fortunes, compelling Taiwanese business people to pay more attention to the mainland China market. As discussed above, this could have a long-term impact on Cross-Strait relations as well as Asia-Pacific economic and security affairs.

It is also important to point out that both China and Taiwan are actively seeking to utilise economic diplomacy to achieve their security objectives, respectively. Beijing has been much more assertive in trying to bring Taipei to the negotiation table through economic pressure. At the same time, the ROC government continues to exploit Taiwan's economic and trade relations with other countries to raise its international profile. The tension across the Taiwan Strait shows just how difficult it is to apply a multilateral approach to the resolution of bilateral disputes in East Asia. In this sense, the Taiwan problem could be regarded as an obstacle to Asia-Pacific security co-operation and to the development of Asia-Pacific regionalism in general.

Notes

1. During the 1995–2002 period, Taiwan's trade surplus with China ranged between around an annual US$15 billion to US$19 billion. This was roughly equivalent with Taiwan's total trade surplus figures.
2. *China Post*, 28.08.2001.
3. See also Chapter 10 in this volume for discussion on the 'democratic peace' hypothesis.
4. *Beijing Review*, 27.02.1997, p. 10.
5. For comparisons of Wilhelmine Germany and today's China, see Kristof (1993: 71–2).
6. *Asia Weekly*, 12.08.2002.
7. *Far Eastern Economic Review*, 07.02.2002.
8. *New York Times*, 26.04.2001.
9. *BBC News*, 090.3.2002.
10. *Digital Chosun Ilbo*, 05.11.2002.

References

Angell, N. (1935) *The Great Illusion*, Heinemann, London.

Cable, V. and Ferdinand, P. (1994) 'China as an Economic Giant: Threat or Opportunity?', *International Affairs*, Vol. 70(2), pp. 243–61.

Cobden, R. (1903) *The Political Writings of Richard Cobden*, T. Fischer Unwin, London.

Copeland, D.C. (1996) 'Economic Interdependence and War: a Theory of Trade Expectations', *International Security*, Vol. 20(4), pp. 5–41.

Dent, C.M. (2001) 'Being Pulled into China's Orbit? Navigating Taiwan's Foreign Economic Policy', *Issues and Studies*, Vol. 37(5), pp. 1–34.

Findlay, C. and Watson, A. (1997) 'Economic Growth and Trade Dependency in China', in D.S.G. Goodman and G. Segal (eds), *China Rising: Nationalism and Interdependence*, Routledge, London.

Friedberg, A.L. (1993/94) 'Ripe for Rivalry: Prospects for Peace in a Multipolar Asia', *International Security*, Vol. 18(3), pp. 5–33.

Harris, S. (1997) 'China's Role in the WTO and APEC', in D.S.G. Goodman and G. Segal (eds), *China Rising: Nationalism and Interdependence*, Routledge, London.

International Institute for Strategic Studies (2001) *The Military Balance 2001/2002*, Oxford University Press, Oxford.

Kristof, N.D. (1993) 'The Rise of China', *Foreign Affairs*, Vol. 72(5), pp. 59–74.

Lang, N.L. (2002) 'Joint Operations to Command the Sea of Taiwan Defence', *Taiwan Defence Affairs*, Vol. 2(4), pp. 78–109.

Lee, C.L. (2002) 'Developing Economic CBMs as a Foundation of Security over the Taiwan Strait: Opportunities after the WTO Accessions', paper presented at an international workshop '*Preventing Insecurity: Lessons from and for East Asia*', Centre for Defence and International Security Studies, University of Lancaster, 6–7 June, Lancaster.

Li, F., Xiong, X.L. and Wang, P. (2002) 'Taiwan's Economic Situation and Future Development in the Early 21st Century', *Taiwan Research Quarterly*, Vol. 1, pp. 40–9.

Li, R. (1999a) 'Unipolar Aspirations in a Multipolar Reality: China's Perceptions of US Ambitions and Capabilities in the Post-Cold War World', *Pacifica Review*, Vol. 11(2), pp. 115–49.

Li, R. (1999b) 'Partners or Rivals? Chinese Perceptions of Japan's Security Strategy in the Asia-Pacific Region', *Journal of Strategic Studies*, Vol. 22(4), pp. 1–25.

Li, R. (2002) 'War or Peace? Potential Conflict Across the Taiwan Strait', *World Defence Systems*, Royal United Services Institute for Defence Studies, August, pp. 157–60.

Li, R. (2003) 'China, America and Asia-Pacific Security after September 11', in M. Buckley and R. Fawn (eds), *Global Response to Terrorism: September 11, War in Afghanistan and Beyond*, Routledge, London.

Qian, Q.C. (2002) 'Upholding the Guiding Principles of "Peaceful Reunification and One Country Two Systems," Striving to Promote the Development of Cross-Strait Relations', *Cross-Strait Relations*, Vol. 57, pp. 5–6.

Rachman, G. (1995) 'Containing China', *The Washington Quarterly*, Vol. 19(1), pp. 129–39.

Rosecrance, R. (1986) *The Rise of the Trading State: Commerce and Conquest in the Modern World*, Basic Books, New York.

Segal, G. (1996) 'East Asia and the "Containment of China"', *International Security*, Vol. 20(4) pp. 107–35.

Sheng, L.J. (2002) 'Peace over the Taiwan Strait?', *Security Dialogue*, Vol. 33(1), pp. 93–106.

Siew, V.C. (2002) 'Trade and Investment and the Taiwan Straits – Building Bridges', paper presented at an international conference *Exploring Federalism and Integration: The EU, Taiwan, and Korea* organised by the Strategic Alliance for Asian Studies, 26–27 October, Berlin.

Song , Y.H. (2002) 'China's Current International Economic Environment', *Journal of International Studies* [Beijing], Vol. 3, pp. 49–54.

Teng, H.Y. (2002) 'Joint Operations: Views from ROC Army', *Taiwan Defence Affairs*, Vol. 2(4), pp. 110–27.

Tucker, N.B. (2002) 'If Taiwan Chooses Unification, Should the United States Care?', *The Washington Quaterly*, Vol. 25(3), pp. 15–28.

Waltz, K.N. (1979) *Theory of International Politics*, Addison-Wesley, Reading, MA.

Wu, Y. (1997) 'Prospects for China's Foreign Economic and Trade Development', *Beijing Review*, Vol. 40(7–8), p. 16.

Yahuda, M. (1997) 'How Much Has China Learned about Interdependence?', in D.S.G. Goodman and G. Segal (eds), *China Rising: Nationalism and Interdependence*, Routledge, London.

Zhang Z.Q. (1999) 'Defence Modernisation and the Taiwan Issue', *Strategy and Management* [Beijing], Vol. 6, pp. 45–9.

Zen, I.M. (2002) 'Air Force's View on Improving Joint Operations Capability for ROC Armed Forces', *Taiwan Defence Affairs*, Vol. 2(4), pp. 56–76.

Part V
Cyber Perspectives

12
Global Economic Change and Cyber Networks: East Asia's Economic and Security Threats in Perspective
Neil Renwick

1. Introduction

This chapter assesses the linkages between global economic transformation and the evolution of the cybernetic revolution and evaluates the national economic and security implications of these relationships. It does so with specific reference to Northeast Asia and specifically Japan, South Korea, and Taiwan. The last quarter of the twentieth century was remarkable for a fundamental move towards the creation of a genuinely global political economy. Taking Castells' (2000) definition, this global economy is 'an economy whose core components have the institutional, organisational, and technological capacity to work as a unit in real time, or in chosen time, on a planetary scale' (p. 102). As this definition suggests, this transformation was driven in large part by technological innovation in communications and information technology but has concomitant institutional and organizational transformations that characterizes it for Castells as an 'informational' economy.

This innovatory drive spurred the formation of cybernetic networks within and between government agencies, public utilities, military forces, corporations, non-governmental organizations (NGOs), and community associations. The global reach of the new information networks both reflected and contributed to a wider and deeper transition taking place in the character of industrial activity itself. National economies, particularly those of the developed world, and the international economy of which these economies formed a dominant part underwent structural adjustment towards knowledge-driven growth and wealth creation. This is no less the case in East Asia than in North America or Western Europe. This symbiosis of industrial and communications revolutions were the foundations for the emergence of a truly global political economy.

The cybernetic and industrial revolutions placed the acquisition of a comparative advantage in knowledge at the heart of industrial, military, and socio-political development. Yet, these cybernetic nervous systems are vulnerable to attack by hostile agencies from bedroom hackers and popular movements to military and intelligence forces. It seems, then, both opportune and prudent to assess the security implications of large-scale fundamental economic transformation and the cybernetic revolution. The following discussion outlines the conceptual ideas informing this analysis; traces the state-led processes of post-war industrial restructuring leading to increasingly knowledge-based economic development; details the character of contemporary network connectivity in these economies; identifies the vulnerabilities of such connectivity; and assesses the nature and utility of responses to these vulnerabilities.

2. Conceptual framework

This study is informed by a number of interrelated methodological concepts: a globalized political economy, cyber-threats, strategic security, and societal security. These form an integrated analytical framework. The control over knowledge and globalized Internet connected information networks are placed at the heart of the new global political economy. As noted above, the contest to control knowledge in a variety of social spheres is increasingly being played out across the informational arteries. The concept of cyberwar focuses attention upon inter-state competition for the control of 'battlespace knowledge'. Netwar draws us to explore largely although not exclusively non-state contests over societal knowledge *per se*. These can effectively be considered under the rubric of information operations. Unsurprisingly, therefore, these informational contests raise both orthodox geo-strategic security and societal security concerns. For Castells (2000) the 'new' global economy is constructed through the conjunction of three features: informationalism, globalization, and networking. As he explains:

> It is *informational* because the productivity and competitiveness of units or agents in this economy (be it firms, regions, or nations) fundamentally depend upon their capacity to generate, process, and apply efficiently knowledge-based information. It is *global* because the core activities of production, consumption, and circulation, as well as their components (capital, labour, raw materials, management, information, technology, markets) are organised on a global scale, either directly or through a network of linkages between economic agents. It is *networked* because, under the new historical conditions, productivity is generated through and competition is played out in a global network of interaction between business networks (Castells 2000: 77).

Structural change refers to the deeper and enduring changes in an economy's production structure, and these three key forces of change are central to the transformation of the internationalized economy over the past quarter century. This has spurred national economic responses. Structural adjustment deals with the practical resource allocation responses to such change. As one might expect, such responses vary in character with some states leaving it to the market to adjust whilst others have taken a more actively interventionist approach. This latter route is particularly true of the East Asian experience since the mid-1970s, with Japan, Taiwan, South Korea, and Singapore leading the way. It is through the vehicle of industrial policy – the state-led process of shifting national priorities and resource allocation between industrial sectors – that economies such as these have undertaken structural adjustment to global structural change. The aim has been, and remains, a significant shift to knowledge-intensive industrial production increasingly deploying networked systems as they become more readily available.

As suggested above, networks are vulnerable in many different ways: international crime, military-industrial espionage, nationalist or NGO propaganda 'swarming'. But it is cyberwar and netwar that carries the greatest potency. Arquilla and Ronfeldt (1993) make the important distinction between militarily oriented and societally oriented information warfare that they term, respectively, 'cyberwar' and 'netwar'. Cyberwar 'refers to conducting, and preparing to conduct, military operations according to information-related principles ... [and] ... turning the "balance of information and knowledge" in one's favour' (p. 144). Netwar is broader in scope and refers to 'information-related conflict at a grand level between nations or societies. It means trying to disrupt, damage, or modify what a target population knows or thinks about itself and the world around it' (pp. 146–7). Netwar, as conflict conducted via Internet societal communications networks, is a contest over the very essence of societal knowledge itself. As Harknett (1996) has pointed out, netwar is primarily about 'attacks on or defense of *societal connectivity*' (p. 96). It is perhaps appropriate, given the blurring of traditional distinctions, to refer to information operations. Central to these is 'network connectivity'. Connectivity is concerned with the information technology network. Such a network 'seamlessly connects all of its parts, creating shared situational awareness throughout an organisation' (p. 93). In other words, netwar is about attacking or protecting 'the linkages essential to the functioning of modern society' (p. 96). Our discussion will consider the different dimensions of cyberwar, both in reference to the military security sphere, as well as its conceptual and practical implications for our understanding of information operations in the non-military and especially economic realms.

Cyberwar is pertinent to military/geo-strategic security in two ways. First, it has the potential to disable an adversary's cybernetic military command

and control systems. Second, it has the potential to disable or disorient an adversary by striking the societal informational infrastructure. Contextually located within a Revolution in Military Affairs (RMA) during the 1990s, it is anticipated that in future conflict 'the struggle for information will play a central role, taking the place, perhaps, of the struggle for geographical position held in previous conflicts. Information superiority is emerging as a newly recognised, and more intense, area of competition' (Davis 1996: 49). For Freedman (1998) this RMA's 'most striking feature is its lack of a fixed form' (pp. 9–10). Whilst retaining a principal focus upon battlespace competition, strategic analysts such as Freedman (1998) and Dibb (1998) have noted the blurring of military and civilian realms and the further transcendence of traditional geographical limitations. Clearly, the contest for control of a battlespace is in large part waged over Command, Control, Communications, Computers and Information (C^4I). For Dibb (1998), the capacity to disable an adversary's transport, energy supply, and communications systems 'would take conflict between states onto a different plane' (p. 97).

The character of future warfare is thus distinct in five particular features. *First*, it represents a fundamental and irreversible shift of information and knowledge to become the critical arena for competition and conflict between protagonists seeking to dominate in pursuit of their political objectives. *Second*, the character of this arena is different in kind from those of previous arenas. Just as the nineteenth-century industrial revolution rendered the seasonal character of warfare outdated, those spatial and temporal factors of conflict such as land, sea and air that remained pertinent, albeit waning, influences upon the conflicts of the industrial era are rendered irrelevant other than as potential sources of conflicts between rival claimants. Infowar, cyberwar or netwar take place in cyberspace. Cyberspace being 'that place where computers, communications systems, and those devices that operate via radiated energy in the electromagnetic spectrum meet and interact' (Kuehl 1997: 3).

Third, the character of perceived *threat* is radically altered. Threats perceived to originate from cyberspace are global in nature. Threats can come from anywhere and at an instant. It is profoundly difficult to target a sophisticated source given the potential for the complex re-routing of attack messages. Moreover, the agencies of attack are no longer necessarily armies but individual hackers, terrorists, disaffected employees or service personnel and other cyber-insurgents. The threshold of access is minimal. All that is required is a WAP (wireless application protocol) mobile phone, a handheld, Internet connected e-notepad or the purchase of Internet time at the burgeoning number of cybercafés. Certainly, there is some variegated basis for the claim that information warfare carries a range of new societal warfare characteristics. Evidence for this includes: the systemic impact of the so-called 'Melissa', 'Code Red' and 'lovebug' computer viruses; major hacker attacks on US institutions, such as the hacking attack 'solar sunrise' mentored by an Israeli citizen, and the 'moonlight maze' attack allegedly originating in Moscow's Russian Academy of Sciences; and reported cyber-skirmishes between South Koreans and Japanese and between Chinese and Taiwanese.[1] The weaponry of cyberspace is also different in kind. The inventory of first generation cyberwar and netwar includes designer 'viruses', 'worms', 'logic bombs', 'trojan horses', 'trapdoors', 'backdoors', 'spy chips', high energy radio frequencies, and electromagnetic pulses. As Peterson (1997) puts it, 'we are quickly moving toward a time when highly customised, one-off tools can be used against very specific, small, but very important system subcomponents. We are moving from sledgehammer to tweezers' (pp. 60–2). Second generation weapons are focused upon the manipulation of information in the target society or emergent psychotronic weapons intended to incapacitate human information network operators (Peterson 1997, Richardson 1997, Sher 1998). Defensive counter-measures must be comprehensive across the network or subsystem to counter multi-directional potential sources of intrusion. Such measures include designer 'vaccines', 'firewalls', 'location-based authentication' for access, counter-attack search and destroy 'spiking' incoming cyber attacks, or isolating critical systems through the provision of 'air gapped' computers.

Fourth, traditional notions of victory and defeat may be obsolete. Peterson (1997) makes the point that 'the most sophisticated and important information warfare battles may be waged against adversaries who never learn that they have been "defeated"' (p. 61). *Fifth*, critically, the emergence of societies defined by significant degrees of networked connectivity marks a decisive shift to a genuinely comprehensive warfare. This is delineated not merely by routine cyber insurgency but potential catastrophic systemic disablement depending upon the degree of societal interconnectivity. Infowar is societal to an unprecedented degree, blurring existing distinctions between military and civilian, public and private and reinforcing theoretical shifts emphasising societal security and re-definitions of strategy acknowledging a more complex threat environment rendering conventional military means of response more problematic (Freedman 1998).

Important though the implications of cyberwar are for Northeast Asian societies, given the novel societal features of information operations, their significance must also to be understood within the broader and deeper approaches associated with notions of 'societal' security. It is this dimension and particularly those of an economic character that the remainder of the chapter addresses. Buzan's (1991) early work in extending the security paradigm to non-state 'societal' categories was developed beyond its neo-realist boundaries by Wæver (1993). Wæver, rightly, is critical of the analytical framework that merely establishes 'society' as 'just a sector, an arena, where the state might be threatened', and 'creates an excessive concern with state stability and largely removes any common sense idea about "the security of societies" in their own right' (p. 25). For Wæver, 'societal security concerns the ability of a society to persist in its essential character under changing conditions and possible or actual threats. More specifically, it is about the sustainability, within acceptable conditions for evolution, of traditional patterns of language, culture, association, and religious and national identity and custom...Societal security is about situations when societies perceive a threat in identity terms' (ibid). Through their insidious capacity to strike at the basic infrastructural pillars sustaining an advanced industrial society and in their potential power to infiltrate and manipulate societal knowledge and value orientations, cyberwar and especially netwar, pose considerable potential threats to the 'ability of a society to persist in its essential character' (ibid).

3. Industrial policies: towards knowledge-based economies

In 1945, Northeast Asian economies were left shattered by the long years of conflict. Key factors in the renaissance of these economies included: the inflow of foreign technology; high levels and substantial growth in investment; the productive application of investment capital driven by anticipated high levels of return; favourable labour relations influenced by a strong degree of elasticity in the labour supply in the immediate post-war decades; high domestic savings level releasing capital for investment purposes; export promotion; a burst of entrepreneurial energy led by the emergence of a new entrepreneurial class. Post-war shifts in industrial structure resulted from the application of national industrial policies. The significance of these shifts lies in the incremental movement towards increasingly knowledge-based economies. This movement involved an initial 'recovery' stage driven by a series of national import substitution industrialization plans establishing heavy industrial bases to satisfy the demands of rising domestic consumption levels. In the early 1970s, however, as production growth could no longer be sustained by domestic demand and profitability began to be eroded by increased labour costs, the emphasis of industrial restructuring moved to the encouragement of export-oriented growth and the development of lighter manufacturing bases. Additional production and labour costs in the wake of the 1973/74 oil crisis accelerated domestic adjustment towards light–medium, capital intensive manufacturing and, particularly in the case of Japan, a relocation of heavy industrial production offshore. The economic rewards of export-oriented growth would be offset by heightened trade tensions and protectionist reaction. Corporate strategies followed designed to circumvent tariff barriers such as foreign direct investment to establish local production facilities in the US economy, joint venture manufacture with US firms, or to re-route production to the US market via production facilities located in third countries.

These generational shifts to more knowledge-based economies would take on a much sharper focus and more intensive character over the past two decades. In Japan, preparations for this shift began in the mid-1980s. The Industry Structure Committee of MITI (Ministry of International Trade and Industry) identified a need to move towards a 'technology-intensive industrial structure which is pollution-free, resource-conservative, and consumer responsive' (Yamanaka 1983: 1). Adopted by the Government as a 'vision' for a future economy, the objective was to establish a 'knowledge-intensive industrial structure' built upon 'knowledge workers'. This, in itself, only represented an initial step. As the new technologies revolution and the Internet began to take hold, this initial step would evolve into a strategy for the attainment of an information-based economy for the twenty-first century or 'e-Japan strategy' grounded in advanced internet infrastructures, the facilitation of electronic commerce, electronic government, and a stronger body of skilled and innovative human resources in the country. As the official statement puts it, 'The Government of Japan is working toward the realization of knowledge-creative society in which citizens actively use IT and derive maximum benefits from it. To this end, it established the Strategic Headquarters for the Promotion of an Advanced Information and Telecommunications Network Society (IT Strategic Headquarters) last year [2001], and adopted an "e-Japan Priority Policy Programme – 2002" in this year [2002].'[2]

The first significant moves to establishing a South Korean knowledge-based economy grounded in IT emerged during the régime of Roh Tae Woo (1988–92). Roh's promotion of a Korea Backbone Computer Network was designed to provide the necessary technical infrastructure to move to this new stage of structural adjustment. Roh's democratically elected successor, Kim Young-sam, continued the process with a 1995–2010 strategy for the development of a Korea Information Infrastructure, including IT and Internet skills training programmemes. The late 1970s and 1980s in Taiwan were also important years for early initiatives towards creating a new knowledge and IT based economy. First steps were the creation of the Science and Technology Advisory Group (STAG) under the auspices of the Executive Yuan and the stated intention to create a regional communications hub termed the Asia-Pacific Regional Operations Centre. On this intention an Executive Committee to Develop Strategic Industries was set up by Taiwan's Ministry of Economic Affairs (MOEA) in 1982. This would develop into a Development of New Industrial Products (1984), Statute for Upgrading Industries (1990) and Development of Targeting Leading Products programmeme (1991). Given the central importance of industrial research and development (IR&D), Taiwan implemented a Science and Technology Development Plan for the period 1986–95. A critical characteristic of Taiwan's approach has been a deliberate policy to enter into a series of corporate strategic alliances. As Simon (1998) explains, 'many Taiwan firms have become enmeshed in the global sourcing and subtracting of American multinational firms, serving as critical suppliers of key components and final products – often on an OEM (made to buyer's order) basis' (p. 168). The creation of the Hsinchu Science and Industry Park and Industrial Technology Research Institute in the early 1970s and the later park established at Tainan brought state, corporate and research interests together. These various initiatives would be harnessed to making, in President Chen Shui-bian's phrase, Taiwan a 'Green Silicon Island'.

As the introduction to this chapter suggests, a statistical marker indicative of a shift towards a knowledge-based economy (or 'new economy' as South Korean governments have preferred to call it) is the relative weight of the services sector in an economy. As Chamberlin (2001) has pointed out, the shift to knowledge-based economies is rooted in human resources and is therefore grounded in a structural shift to the services sector. Each of the economies under review here, with the exception of China, demonstrate a significant shift to service-centred economies in terms of the proportion of GDP and of employment accounted for by the services sector (Table 12.1). Investment in IR&D in Northeast Asia historically has tended to lag behind other advanced industrial states. However, there are signs that there is greater investment in IR&D in these economies and that the proportion of corporate investment is beginning to rise. However, questions remain over the extent of innovative rather than adaptive commercial research being undertaken. Technology-intensive goods and services trade is indicative of a shift to knowledge-based economic activity. The extent of two-way trade suggests a more innovative economy, that is, high IT exports and imports. South Korea, Japan, and Taiwan all show high levels of high technology exports and imports with precision and electrical equipment steadily increasing as a proportion of the machinery and equipment categories as general machinery and equipment steadily declines.

4. Networked or networking economies in Northeast Asia?

How far are the policy ambitions of these respective industrial policies being realized? In particular, are these economies demonstrating significant levels of network connectivity and e-commerce? By 2003 global Internet usage is estimated to increase seven-fold to 580 million from its 1997 base of 82 million users. Over this period the Asia-Pacific Region is expected to grow from 15.8 million users to 182 million (Table 12.2).

Whilst absolute numbers and percentage share data give some idea of trends, current assessments of Internet penetration rates (i.e. demographically adjusted) show Taiwan with the highest rates, closely followed by South Korea, Hong Kong, Japan and China (Table 12.3).

Beyond these broad statistics regarding Internet usage and penetration rates, evidence whereby we can determine the extent of network connectivity also comes from data on e-commerce such as Internet trading and transactional values. E-commerce in Asia (South and Southeast and Northeast

Table 12.1 Northeast Asia's industrial structures (2001)

	GDP (PPP) (US$)	GDP (per capita) (US$)	Industry sectors (% of GDP)			Industry sectors by employment		
			Agriculture	Industry	Services	Agriculture	Industry	Services
Japan	3.45 tr.	27 200	2.0	36.0	62.0	5.0	30.0	65.0
South Korea	865 bn.	18 000	5.0	44.0	51.0	9.5	21.5	69.0
Taiwan	386 bn.	17 200	2.0	32.0	66.0	8.0	36.0	56.0
China	5.56 tr.	4 300	17.7	49.3	33.0	50.0	23.0	27.0
Hong Kong	180 bn.	25 000	0.1	14.3	85.6	–	15.0	55.0

Source: CIA, 'World Factbook 2002'.

Table 12.2   Global Internet usage (actual and projected 1997–2003)

End of year	1997	1998	1999	2000	2001	2002	2003 (est.)
US	41.2	64.7	85.0	102.0	115.5	128.0	140.0
Canada	2.4	4.3	9.6	13.0	15.8	18.4	21.0
Europe	21.4	32.9	49.5	72.5	122.0	163.0	212.0
Asia-Pacific	15.8	28.8	42.0	61.5	119.8	149.0	182.0
South America	0.6	1.5	2.3	4.2	6.5	9.5	13.0
Other Regions	0.6	1.3	1.6	3.0	5.0	8.0	12.0
Global	82.0	133.5	193.3	286.2	384.6	475.9	580.0

Source: InfoCom Research Inc. (2002).

Table 12.3 Internet users by country (per cent of Asia-Pacific Region, end 2000) and Internet penetration rates in Asia-Pacific region (per cent by country, end 2000)

	Internet users % of Asia-Pacific region end 2000	Internet penetration rates in Asia-Pacific region by country, end 2000 (%)
Japan	35.8	23.4
South Korea	17.0	36.8
China	18.9	1.5
Taiwan	8.3	37.6
Hong Kong	2.0	31.7

Source: InfoCom Research Inc. (2002).

Asia) was estimated to account for 25 per cent of global e-commerce by 2003. According to another estimate, business-to-business (B2B) e-commerce is anticipated to have reached US$125 billion in China, US$77 billion in South Korea, and US$55 billion in Taiwan by 2005. According to the Japanese Government, Japan's business-to-consumer (B2C) e-commerce market based upon the value of transactions amounted to US$1.7 billion in 1999. This is small compared to the US's US$24.2 billion. However, whilst the United States demonstrated a year-on-year growth rate of 195 per cent for 1988–99, the rate for Japan was 334 per cent (Keizai Koho Centre 2001). Moreover, Japan's e-commerce defined in Governmental terms of final consumption of goods and services grew by almost 79 per cent in the year 2000 alone with business-to-consumer e-commerce showing a year-on-year increase of 145 per cent. The Japanese e-commerce utilization ratio appears to lag behind that of the United States by three years (0.25 per cent to 1.37 per cent in 2000) but is expected to close this gap to about two years by 2005 (4.5 per cent compared to 6.99 per cent in 2005) (InfoCom 2002).

5. Northeast Asia's information vulnerability

Critical infrastructure concerns the energy, communications, and financial assets underpinning survival of the state.[3] These sectors have absorbed IT during the 1990s, which has resulted in new vulnerabilities potentially more susceptible to electronic 'attack', that of physical attack by terror bombs for example, of course also still prevailing. In the First and Second World Wars, countries' infrastructures were targeted; in the present and in future, attacking a country's infrastructure occurs in armed conflict if deemed to be a military target under the Laws of Armed Conflict. Attacks on the information network components of critical infrastructure during times of non-conflict are relegated to criminal acts (whether conducted by a terrorist group, criminals, or hackers), whether part of a state-sponsored or commercial activity associated with espionage, or part of intelligence gathering possibly prior to conflict.

What, then, are the number and types of attacks being experienced in the Northeast Asia region? In 1999, Taiwan's Defence Ministry established an Information Warfare (IW) Committee to co-ordinate and monitor a perceived IW threat from China. In testimony to the Legislative Yuan in August 1999, Taiwan Defence officials claimed that China had begun planning for IW in 1985, and had conducted computer virus interdiction tests of broadcasting and military networks in Nanjing and Beijing in 1995. In July and August 1999, a statement by Taiwan's then-president Lee Teng-hui angered the People's Republic of China (PRC) government. This led Chinese hackers to damage more than 72 000 Taiwanese websites. Taiwan's own hackers reacted by posting anti-PRC slogans and 'Hello Kitty' pictures on dozens of official Chinese sites. In March 2000, Taiwan's Defense Ministry's Director of cyber information, Chang Chia-sheng, stated that Taiwan's security authorities had uncovered over 7000 attempts by Chinese hackers to enter Taiwan's security and military systems through the Internet.[4] In September 2000, Taiwan newspapers reported that several Taiwanese electronic newspapers and web newsletters published by IT companies were attacked by a hacker presumed to be based in China. The intruder posted messages wishing the people of Taiwan a happy Mid-Autumn Festival 'on behalf of their compatriots on the Chinese mainland'.[5]

In South Korea, according to data from the Korea Information Security Agency (KISA), there were 147 hacker attacks in 1996. The number then fell to 64 in 1997. However, hacking began to rise sharply again in 1998 to 158, and 572 in 1999. A total of 1858 cases of hacking were detected in South Korea as of November 2000. KISA noted that major corporations appear to be the main target for hacker attacks. Some 92 attacks (40.5 per cent) of all 227 attacks in November 2000, were targeted against corporations. As the *Korea Herald* reported, KISA identified various hacking methods: in 110 cases, hackers broke into target computers by aiming at their system's most vulnerable point; in 103 cases, hackers stole information from computers after secretly installing a virus programme often referred to as a 'trojan horse'; there were six cases in which hackers used the denial of service strategy; four hacking cases used e-mail; two cases saw hackers steel the ID of website operators; and there were two remotely controlled hacking attacks.[6] South Korea's National Police Agency's Cyber Centre estimates that between August 2001 and March 2002 some 4376 South Korean sites were targeted and actual damaged systems estimated at over 40000. Moreover, South Korea is increasingly identified as an access point to attack other countries. In the same reporting period, the NPA claimed that 11222 server systems were attacked by hackers. Of 6287 identifiable originating addresses, 39 per cent were South Korean. This confirms a report by US-based Predictive Systems that 91 per cent of all non-US originating hacker attacks involve the Pacific Rim countries with South Korea accounting for 34 percent; China 29 per cent; Japan 10 per cent; and Taiwan 7 per cent of these attacks.[7]

Japan's Computer Virus and Unauthorised Computer Access Countermeasures Group (VUAC), operating under the auspices of the Information-Technology Promotion Agency Security Centre (IPA/ISEC), monitors and disseminates information and warnings about intrusive computer virus attacks. According to VUAC's October 2002 Report, the number of attacks on Japanese computer systems rose significantly over the past decade or so. The earliest reports totalled 14 cases between April and December 1990. Full year statistics showed 57 cases reported in 1991 and 253 in 1992. Significant increases in reported attacks are shown from 1993 with 897 cases and 1127 in 1994. The levels of reported attacks then dropped to 668 in 1995 and 755 in 1996. However, this was a temporary reversal with the number of reported attacks surging back to 2391 in 1997 and 2035 in 1998. Statistics for the years 1999–2001 are shown in Figure 12.1. Available statistics for January–June 2002 (contained in the Japanese language version of the PIA/ISEC October 2002 Report) show 11569 recorded hostile incursions (IPA/ISEC 2002).

Overwhelmingly, these virus attacks in Japan are undertaken via e-mail with almost 89 per cent of all attacks reported to VUAC in 2001 accounted for by this medium. Of this form of attack, 73.3 per cent originate domestically with overseas originating mail accounting for 15.62 per cent. In January 2000, sixteen Japanese websites were attacked by hackers and defaced. These sites included that of the Science and Technology Ministry and the *Asahi Shimbun* newspaper. The defacement criticized Japan's role in the Nanjing massacre. Japan's National Police Agency identified 51000

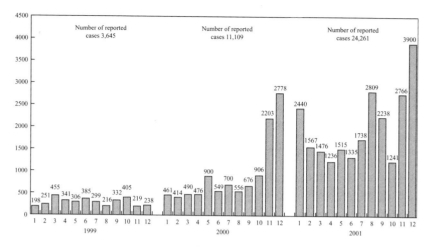

Figure 12.1 Statistics of computer virus damage reports in Japan.
Source: IPA/ISEC (2002).

Table 12.4 Investigation of actual damage by computer viruses in Japan

	1995	1996	1997	1998	1999	2000
Government & municipal offices	84	91	99	82	71	101
Public organisations & universities	212	215	158	154	179	162
Private industries	893	1 094	1 013	1 334	1 279	1 410
Total	1 189	1 400	1 270	1 570	1 529	1 673
No. of damaged bodies	158 (14.2%)	482 (17.9%)	482 (38.6%)	614 (39.8%)	661 (44.1%)	824 (49.3%)

Source: IPA/ISEC (2002).

attempted cyber-incursions into Police computer systems between July and September 2002 amounting to more than 10 attempted attacks daily per monitored computer. Overall, hacking attacks varied from 200 to 2000 a day with a daily average of approximately 560. Apart from Japan itself, attacks originated in the US, China, and South Korea. A little bizarrely perhaps, attacks traced to Italy accounted for more than 20 per cent of all these incursions. The most common hacker incursions (60 per cent) were 'denial of service' attacks produced by the flooding of the system with data causing it to crash. Another 30 per cent of attacks were essentially reconnaissance incursions preliminary to a larger attack.[8] However, as we can see from Table 12.4,

VUAC's annual surveys of actual computer damage caused by such attacks demonstrate that these incursions are increasing in number and are targeted principally at the private industry sector. They also show that the degree of damage being caused is increasing with a five-fold increase in just five years.

6. Responses to perceived threat?

6.1. National policy responses

Given perceived new threats to vulnerable critical infrastructure, processes of institutionalizing its security (e.g. the US Office of Homeland Security) arise, but these processes differ in other countries. Differing country perceptions of the threat will lead to institutions to deal with those threats. Is it that the attacks on computer networks are increasingly from threats that are criminal and thus are dealt with by law enforcement institutions and to what degree are such threats seen to be security that is performed by the military. For example, Taiwan recently placed cyber issues as the main concern in their recently released-Defence Review. As criminals become more sophisticated, to what degree is there increased co-operation between the military and non-military sectors of the state to deal with these threats. One hypothesis might be that conflict may not be changing as quickly as studies in the early 1990s predicted, but that as such threats change and take advantage of new technological vulnerabilities, states reallocate resources accordingly leading to security more by law enforcement than by the military. Increased participation in and strengthening of Interpol reflects this concern.

All three Governments have encountered popular concerns regarding their attempts to implement controls designed to counter hostile information operations. The Japanese, South Korean and Taiwanese Governments have all moved to introduce legislation and establish policing/enforcement agencies against actions that constitute, to use a Taiwanese phrase, 'misuse of devices'. In Taiwan's case, the Government introduced the Computer-Processed Personal Data Protection Law in 1995. Further legislation followed the Council of Europe's Convention on Cybercrime agreed in November 2001. Criticism of Taiwan's attempt at a law-based regulation of the Internet spurred criticism on grounds not only of encroachment upon individual privacy but also that the Taiwanese need not 'dance along with a few European countries'.[9]

The South Korean Government responded to such concerns with privacy guidelines in April 2000 to which Internet Service Providers and e-commerce firms would be required to comply. At the same time, the Personal Information Protection Centre was created to oversee the protection of personal information, and a dispute mediation organization was established in December the same year. South Korea also passed legislation designed to protect the country's major IT infrastructures from hostile information operations. This legislation was aimed at: promoting and disseminating information about such attacks among the corporate sector; establishing effective virus prevention, monitoring, and alert systems; and strengthening established response mechanisms. This signaled a more active international engagement with a more active involvement in bodies such as the Forum of Incident Response and Security Teams (FIRST) established in 1990.

Between August 1999 and June 2001 there were a number of bills enacted by Japan's Legislature (the Diet) that provided for the study of legal issues associated with encryption and authentication, electronic signatures and authorization systems, mandatory confirmation screens for e-commerce transactions, and civil law exemptions. Between May 1987 and 2002, Japan also passed various Acts designed to counter cyber-crime covering the falsification of electromagnetic records, the deliberate damaging of computer equipment to obstruct criminal and other investigations of cyber-crime, unauthorized access to networks, the interception of communications relating to a criminal investigation. In February 2000, the National Police Agency released an Information Security Policy Outline. The sensitivity of these initiatives in Japan relates directly to the ultranationalism and State power of the inter-war years. Legislation was passed in Japan in March 2001 to offer protection for personal information.

6.2. Operational responses

The following outline is drawn from Proctor and Byrnes (2002). There are four key goals in the protection of information assets, namely: (1) *confidentiality* – the protection of knowledge and data; (2) *integrity* – sustaining the purity and uncontaminated nature of the system; (3) *availability* – the maintenance of authorized access; and (4) *non-repudiation* – the identification and tracking of message authenticity. Network security draws strength from a combination of 'enforcement technology' and 'operations technology'. The former embraces: 'access control', restricting entry to the system; 'identification and authentication', involving individual identification via technologies ranging from smart cards to biometric authentification; firewalls; VPN (Virtual Private Network) technologies, harnessing advanced encryption technologies to intra-net systems protection; PKI (Public Key Infrastructure), designed for large open systems such as the Internet that involve millions of users; SSL (Secure Sockets Layer) SSL2 and SSL3, web message encryption/authentification protocol systems; and Single Signon (SSO), involving single password access across common computer systems. 'Operations technology' covers user account management, intrusion detection, vulnerability scanning, and anti-virus strategies and controls. Both aspects are intimately tied to risk assessment, forensic detection, and rapid reaction. The provision of corporate or organizational security programmemes are an inescapable concomitant of enhanced network connectivity.

To try to meet these challenges of critical infrastructure protection and network security, biometric measures are also being promoted by the South Korean Government. In particular, there is encouragement of a more widespread use of digitial signatures backed by a certification system to try to give greater confidence in e-money transactions both domestically and internationally and thereby further encourage e-commerce. Furthermore, Japan's VUAC agency conducts activities to promote computer virus prevention measures. These include the provision of a Help Desk, exhibiting at IT-related shows, the distribution of anti-virus information and CD-ROMs, operating an anti-virus website, disseminating anti-virus articles on magazines and papers, and undertaking information exchange with anti-virus software vendors. In Taiwan, a series of laws have been introduced to regulate and police information networks have been introduced since the mid-1990s. These include the Telecom Law (1996); Communication Protection and Surveillance Law (1999) and the Electronic Signature Law (2001). A Computer Crime Detecting Team has been established within the Department of Police, Ministry of Justice and is responsible for investigating and prevention of computer crimes. Crime reporting in Taiwan is now routed through a dedicated website and a Centre for Preventing Computer Crime has been created by the Department of Prosecution within the Ministry of Legal Affairs. This Centre co-ordinates the various agencies investigating, prosecuting and policing network crime. Finally, planning has been undertaken towards the establishment of a national network security reporting system and a response centre to develop technology and assess network security weaknesses (ITIS 2001).

6.3. Regional responses

The foregoing discussion has emphasized the national responses to perceived threats to information networks in the region. This emphasis reflects the absence of specifically Northeast Asian regional co-operative initiatives. As Chapter 13 discusses, the Association of Southeast Asian Nations (ASEAN) group has a well-developed régime of deliberation with a range of policy, action strategies, and working groups designed to both facilitate the development and the security of regional information networks. Northeast Asia, however, has no process of institutionalized inter-governmental organisation (IGO) co-operation equivalent to that of Southeast Asia. This is not to say that there is a complete lack of dialogue or initiatives taking place. Academic and expert conferences and workshops are undertaken such as the Asia Pacific Regional Internet Conference on Operational Technologies (APRICOT).[10] Practical moves have also emerged in recent years, most notably the Asia Pacific Security Incident Response Co-ordination (APSIRC) initiative developed since 1998 with its task force and national co-ordination centres, and which includes Taiwan, South Korea, Hong Kong, China, and Japan. Other regional functional internet security organizations operate such as the Asia Pacific Network Information Centre (APNIC) that is a regional Internet registry established by the Asia Pacific Networking Group (APNG) in 1993. More widely still, as noted earlier with respect to South Korea, Northeast Asian countries are members of FIRST.

There are four principal reasons why regional inter-state co-operation remains relatively limited in Northeast Asia. First, regional sensitivities grounded in the security apprehensions of geopolitical orthodoxy remain highly salient to governmental and societal perspectives limiting co-operative initiates in this sensitive area of policy. Second, transnational flows of capital, trade and labour within a regionalizing economy notwithstanding, these are also developed national economies in competition with one another. Third, there is no Northeast Asian equivalent of ASEAN wherein multilateral co-operation can be initiated, developed and implemented. Fourth, despite the history of structural adjustment strategies, these governments almost seem to have been taken by surprise by the existence of informational networks. Even more surprising perhaps, given the shadow of geopolitical distrust in Northeast Asia, they have been slow to wake up to the reality of network vulnerability and to develop effective national strategies of response never mind regional co-operation.

Given the momentum and inherent logic of network connectivity, this co-operative vacuum would suggest that Northeast Asia is likely to fall behind the EU and ASEAN states. However, the picture is far from barren. The potential for intra-regional, or wider multilateral *imperative co-operation* between these developed Northeast Asian economies lies with four indirect extra-regional influences. The first of these is the Organisation for Economic Co-operation and Development (OECD), which has been actively developing security guidelines for information systems since 1992 (Japan and South Korea are full OECD members). In 1995, it sponsored the OECD-ASEAN-PECC[11] Vancouver Conference on Global Informational Infrastructure incorporating a Business Forum, a Global Forum on Policy Frameworks for the Digital Economy, and a workshop on a World Summit on the Information Society. The most far reaching initiative is the August 2002, post-9/11 revision of the global security guidelines ('Guidelines for the Security of Information Systems and Networks') designed to create a culture of security among member governments, business enterprises, and other users. Although these are non-binding guidelines, organizational suasion couched in terms of consensus among members offers potential weight for adherence to the nine basic principles regarding security awareness, responsibility, and respect for ethical and democratic values.

The second potential influence for greater Northeast Asian co-operation are the pan-Asia-Pacific organizations to which these Northeast Asian economies claim membership. These include the Asia-Pacific Economic Co-operation (APEC) forum and the Economic and Social Commission for Asia and the Pacific (ESCAP). These organizations are actively engaged in encouraging information networking, e-commerce, and critical infrastructure security régimes. APEC's involvement emerged in May 1995 with the Seoul Declaration for the Asia-Pacific Information Infrastructure committing the members to strengthen technical co-operation, inter-connectedness, and inter-operability. More recently, post-9/11 concerns led to the APEC Shanghai Statement on Counter-Terrorism in October 2001 including action to protect information and communications networks against cyber insurgency (see Chapter 1). Meanwhile, ESCAP has sponsored a conference of its 20 government members, business enterprises, and regional telecommunications organizations to counter hackers, virus infection, and cyber crime.

The third influence is that of ASEAN. With its e-ASEAN strategy and Task Force, ASEAN is well advanced in its promotion of regional Internet exchange provision (ARIX), legal infrastructure, ISP Association (ARISPA), e-readiness guides and evaluations, and certification authentification (see Chapter 12). Although the Northeast Asian States are not members of ASEAN, their growing links through the ASEAN Plus Three (APT) framework offers Japan, China, and South Korea the potential for functional spillover into Northeast Asian practice. The fourth influence is the International Telecommunications Union (ITU) within the UN family of agencies. Of particular importance is the process leading to the World Summit on the Information Society (WSIS) in Geneva in December 2003 and Tunis in 2005. A series of conferences and preparatory deliberations by IGOs, governments, business, and NGOs were timetabled to take place around the world leading up to the WSIS. The Asian Regional Conference for WSIS was held in Tokyo in January 2003 and brought together IGOs such as the ITU, ESCAP, UNCTAD (United Nations Conference on Trade and Development), regional governments, NGOs, and business. The ITUs contribution drew on the organization's 'Input' document to the declaration of principles and plan of action of the WSIS and the 'Guidelines' for the ITU's 'input'. Part III (sections 18, 19, 20) of the 'Guidelines' identified imperatives of co-operation necessary to provide confidence and security in the use of information and communications technology. ESCAP's contribution included the Draft Action Plan on Cybercrime and Information Security for the Asia-Pacific Region adopted at the November 2002 Asia-Pacific Conference on Cybercrime and Information Society held in Seoul.

The point here is that, in the absence of distinct processes of Northeast Asian regional co-operation, the cumulative and mutually reinforcing character of these global and pan-Asia-Pacific IGOs to which Japan, South Korea and China hold membership or 'dialogue' status are creating an international régime of principles, guidelines, legal frameworks, and programmes for action, including provisions for the enhanced security of information networks. This emergent régime embodies 'habits of dialogue' that include the Northeast Asian states and offer commonalities to which policy and practices of regulation and security in Northeast Asia can come to conform.

7. Conclusion

This review of Northeast Asia's connectivity and network vulnerability suggests that there is a steady shift to knowledge-based economies. Moreover, constituent to this shift is an increasingly central and critical role for e-commerce carried on cybernetic lines of communication transmitted through rapidly expanding computer networks, as well as a perceptibly growing level of information operations mounted against such networks. The security of these critical infrastructures is thus increasingly recognized as vital to the economic well-being of these societies. Whilst the importance of making the shift to knowledge-based societies has certainly been recognized for over two decades by the region's public and private sectors, it is also fair to say that these sectors have been relatively slow to recognize the potential threats to their emergent computer network systems and their rapidly growing associated levels of national and international connectivity. There has been, and remains to a declining degree, some intransigence on behalf of some enterprises in these economies to accept the financial on-costs involved in the necessary security protection for their systems. Indeed one leading commentator on these issues in Japan has spoken of an 'iron triangle' (*jokun-chitsujo*) of vested interests apparently threatened by change and resistance to change (Miyawaki 1999).

However, the past few years have seen a change in attitudes in Japan, South Korea, and Taiwan with national policy and legislative responses setting the frameworks for public and corporate responses, and enhanced awareness and operational action within the corporate sector itself to increase its protection. These national responses are encouraging. However, as we have seen, specifically Northeast Asian regional responses have not really developed. It may be that recent changes in national attitudes, combined with the operational realities of transnational networking, will make co-operative efforts imperative with respect to regional policy co-ordination, infrastructural development, and network security. In this respect the evolution of wider multilateral (e.g. UN, OECD), other regional (e.g. APT) and wider trans-regional (e.g. APEC, ESCAP) co-operation may offer broader and stronger institutional contexts for régime-building and habits of dialogue for Northeast Asian states.

Yet, the essential and defining nature of hostile information operations is chimerical making long-term solutions highly elusive. Hence, the truth of the statement that security cannot be absolute but only relative and contingent upon the balance between innovative threats and innovative defence is perhaps more true today than ever before. The capacity for an adequate response in these countries will, though, also be governed by historical and political sensitivities, not least with respect to public concerns over privacy and the degree of state intrusiveness. This is a particular feature of Northeast Asia's recent political culture given the legacy of Japan's mid-twentieth-century history, the shadow of the Park Chung Hee years in South

Korea, and the martial law years in Taiwan. The trick will be to strike a balance between the imperatives of economic development on the one hand and the requirements of democracy on the other.

Notes

1. *BBC News*, 10.10.2000, 'Taiwan on guard for cyberwar'.
2. Government of Japan (2002), *IT Commerce in Japan*, <http://www.stat.go.jp/English/data/it/index.html>.
3. The author is grateful to Dr Olivia Bosch, then of the IISS, for her suggestions and insights related to the issues of critical infrastructure. The opening discussions of this section and of the next section of the chapter draw heavily upon Dr Bosch's written contribution to related collaborative project work undertaken with the author during November 2002.
4. *The Standard*, 07.03.2000, 'Taiwan Says Prepared for Internet Attack'.
5. *Internet News*, 20.12.2000, 'Taiwan Government Website Hacked'.
6. *Korea Herald*, 26.04.2002, 'Hackers exploit Korea to attack global systems'.
7. Ibid.
8. *Asahi Shimbun*, 08.11.2002, 'Police systems under assault by hackers'.
9. *The Taipei Times*, 02.01.2002, 'Beware of legislating the Internet'.
10. CICEC Beijing Conference, 27 August, 2002; GLOCOM CAN Forum and Global Forum (for regional enterprises and netizens for information sharing).
11. PECC stands for Pacific Economic Co-operation Conferences, which commenced in the late 1970s and are closely associated with APEC.

References

Arquilla, J. and Ronfeldt, D. (1993) 'Cyberwar is Coming!', *Comparative Strategy*, Vol. 12, Spring, pp. 141–65.

Buzan's, B. (1991) *People, States and Fear*, Harvester Wheatsheaf, Hemel Hempstead.

Castells, M. (2000) *The Rise of Network Society*, Blackwell, Oxford.

Chamberlin, P. (2001) *Korea 2010: The Challenges of the New Millennium*, CSIS, Washington DC.

Davis, F.S. (1996) 'An Information-Based Revolution in Military Affairs', *Strategic Review*, Vol. 24, Winter, pp. 43–53.

Dibb, P. (1998) 'The Revolution in Military Affairs and Asian Security', *Survival*, IISS, Vol. 39(4), pp. 93–8.

Freedman, L. (1998) *The Revolution in Strategic Affairs*, IISS Adelphi Paper 318, London.

Harknett, R.J. (1996) 'Information Warfare and Deterrence', *Parameters: US Army war College Quarterly*, Vol. XXVI(3), pp. 93–107.

InfoCom Research, Inc. (2002) *Information & Communications in Japan 2002*, InfoCom, Tokyo.

IPA/ISEC (2002) *Computer Virus Incident Reports*, Information-Technology Promotion Agency Security Centre, Tokyo.

Information Technology Information Services (ITIS) (2001), 'National Information Infrastructure Development in R.O.C', http//www.it is.org.tw/forum/content3/01if12b.htm.

Keizai Koho Centre (Japan Institute for Social and Economic Affairs) (2001), *Japan 2002: An International Comparison*, Table 5-22 E-Commerce – B-to-C, p. 51, Tokyo.

Kuehl, D. (1997) 'Defining Information Power', *Strategic Forum*, No. 115, June, pp. 1–4.

Miyawaki, R. (1999) *'The Fight Against Cyberterrorism: A Japanese View'*, CSIS, Washington DC, http://www.csis.org/html/sp990629Miyaaki.html.

Peterson, J.L. (1997) 'Info War: The Next Generation', *Proceedings*, US Naval Institute, Vol. 123(1), pp. 60–1.

Proctor, P.E. and Byrnes, F.C. (2002) *The Secured Enterprise: Protecting Your Information Assets*, Prentice Hall, NJ.

Richardson, D. (1997) 'Hacker Warfare: Threat of the Future?', *Armada International*, No. 4, pp. 64–74.

Sher, H. (1998) 'www.terror', *The Jerusalem Report*, 08.06.1998, pp. 32–41.

Simon, D.F. (1998) 'Charting Taiwan's Technological Future: The Impact of Globalisation and Regionalisation' in Shambaugh, D. (ed.), *Contemporary Taiwan*, Oxford University Press, Oxford.

Wæver, O. (1993) 'Societal Security: The Concept', in O. Wæver, B. Buzan, M. Kelstrup and P. Lemaitre (eds), *Identity, Migration and the New Security Agenda in Europe*, Pinter, London.

Yamanaka, S. (1983) 'Minister for International Trade and Industry: Basic Thinking behind Japanese Industry Policy', *Focus Japan* (May), MITI, Tokyo.

13
Regionalism Online: A Case Study of e-ASEAN

Xiudian Dai

1. Introduction

With the rapid advancement in new information and communications technologies (ICTs)[1] geographical distance is becoming less relevant and boundaries of the nation-state are becoming increasingly permeable. We have inherited from the last century, among other things, the invention of the Internet – a global network of computer networks, which is undoubtedly a major achievement in the emancipation of cross-border human communication. The Internet was accompanied by the establishment of the World Trade Organisation (WTO), which can be said to be a big step forward in multilateral or global trade liberalisation. As against the euphoria of globalisation supported in part by the Internet and the WTO, however, is the proliferation of preferential trade agreements (PTAs), which has led to renewed interest in the economics and politics of regionalism (Freund 2000). One of the most prominent examples of PTAs is the Association of South East Asian Nations (ASEAN). Whilst much has already been said in the current literature about the major regional PTAs (e.g. the EU), the impact of the global communications revolution (arguably the most important globalising factor) on the development of regionalism, and vice versa, is a rather neglected area of study.

As far as ASEAN is concerned, regionalism is evolving along two different directions. On the one hand, ASEAN member states are endeavouring to deepen economic co-operation and regional integration by, for example, the implementation of the ASEAN Free Trade Area (AFTA) to further liberalise intra-ASEAN trade and the development of the ASEAN Investment Area (AIA), which is aimed at promoting and facilitating foreign direct investment (FDI) into the region. On the other hand, ASEAN's vision is not confined to the region's boundaries. Rather, ASEAN is actively seeking new collaborative partnerships through dialogue with countries outside the region. These include, among others, the on-going negotiations on the ASEAN–China Free Trade Area, the ASEAN Plus Three (APT) partnership with

China, Japan and South Korea, and the Enterprise for ASEAN Initiative with the United States. It seems that the ASEAN countries' interest in achieving a greater degree of regional integration among the member states is not separated from their desire for reaching the wider market beyond the boundaries of Southeast Asia. As this chapter examines, the launch of the e-ASEAN initiative appears to be a strategic manoeuvring aimed at further promoting ASEAN regional integration through exploiting the opportunities afforded by new ICTs and effectively preparing the ASEAN countries to collectively cope with the challenges of globalisation in the information age. It thus adds an 'e' ('e' for electronic) dimension to the nature and process of regional integration among the ASEAN countries.

The chapter begins with establishing the context and background against which the e-ASEAN initiative was launched, as well as identifying what objectives this new initiative aims to achieve. Subsequently, the key objectives of the e-ASEAN initiative will be matched with detailed studies of the existing and potential challenges that the ASEAN countries would have to address. One of these challenges is the digital divide (i.e. disparities in ICT development and access between ASEAN countries, as well as between ASEAN as a whole and countries outside the region) that could prevent those lagging countries from effectively participating in cross-border economic co-operation facilitated by new ICTs. The second challenge to the e-ASEAN initiative is posed by the difficulties associated with the governance of online trans-border commercial activities, for example, e-commerce. Finally, as a collective venture between the member states, the e-ASEAN initiative is faced with the dilemma that some countries wish to excel in their own way: their commitment to e-ASEAN is somehow overshadowed by the desire to become *the* regional ICT hub on their own.

2. Towards an e-ASEAN: building on the information age optimism

It is often argued that instantaneous electronic communication is the new driving force behind the much debated phenomenon of globalisation (Giddens 1999), a process that is poised to create a globalised or homogenised world of socio-economic and political sphere through increased transborder flow of not only capital and goods but increasingly digital information and communications facilitated by inter-connected electronic networks (see Chapter 2). It has been argued that new ICTs can significantly advance transnational co-operation and regional integration in both economic and political terms (Bangemann *et al.* 1994, CEC 2000). Over the last decade the EU has, for example, been actively promoting a European Information Society (EIS) Programme aimed primarily at creating a common European information area to complement the on-going single market enterprise (Dai 2000). In the case of the EU, the information society is treated very much as 'a transnational integration agenda' (Venturelli 2002: 80). New ICTs also have important implications for the developing countries. The World Bank believes that ICTs are not only a key input for economic development and growth but also creating opportunities for global integration while retaining the identity of traditional societies and, therefore, developing countries face opportunity costs if they delay greater access to and use of ICTs in a rapidly evolving global environment (World Bank 2002a). Some are deeply concerned with the fact that, 'we live in a brutal and unjust world, where astonishing developments in science and technology are not matched by the ability of governments to marshal forces to overcome social and economic inequities of their countries'.[2]

There are indeed many voices advocating for global solutions to the socio-economic and political challenges raised by the development of ICTs. The G8, among others, published the Okinawa Charter on Global Information Society in 2000 calling for orchestrated actions at the international level to close the digital divide (G8 2000). The European Commission argues that international co-ordination in the governance of globalisation and the information society is needed (CEC 1998). Whilst it is difficult to deny that ICTs 'can give many poor countries the chance to leap frog some long and painful stages in the development process',[3] it also seems convincing that, in an ideal world, 'the evolution of policy for the development of an equitable global information society should be co-ordinated internationally to ensure the sharing of information and resources'.[4]

There is a broad recognition by ASEAN governments of the potential impact of new ICTs on economic development, albeit to various degrees. Singapore has already built a nationwide broadband infrastructure providing high-speed electronic connectivity to many countries, including all ASEAN countries, the United States, Australia, Japan, China, Hong Kong, India and Europe (Infocomm Development Authority of Singapore 2000). At the heart of the Singapore government's vision and strategy for the information age is the desire to 'develop Singapore into a vibrant and dynamic global Infocomm Capital with a thriving and prosperous infocomm-savvy e-Society' (ibid. p. 5). Following the lead of Singapore, the Malaysian government is also determined to harness ICTs for the benefit of economic and social development. A central point of the Malaysian government's information age policy and strategy is to fundamentally transform Malaysia from a primarily agricultural economy now into a developed country by the year 2020. In Vietnam, the government is looking to the Internet to create a new economy paradigm in the country.[5] According to Vinh (2002), the Vietnamese government believes that, 'e-commerce is nowadays becoming an efficient tool to support and facilitate economic development, and surely will make greater contributions to the future' (pp. 1–2). In Cambodia, where electricity is still not universally available, computer education and Internet access are being experimented at the village level to demonstrate the benefit of new ICTs for economic development.[6] The government of Myanmar (Burma), which is generally uneasy about the political and social impact of new ICTs, is in the process of developing a cyber park in the capital city of Rangoon to allow for the provision of Internet access in a controlled manner.[7]

Prompted in part by the predominately optimistic views within and outside the ASEAN region on the potential of new ICTs for speeding up economic development, in addition to facilitating transnational co-operation, the e-ASEAN Framework Agreement was signed at the Fourth ASEAN Informal Summit in November 2000 at Singapore.[8] Modelled on the European Information Society Programme, e-ASEAN is 'to develop a broad-based and comprehensive action plan including physical, legal, logistical, social and economic infrastructure needed to promote an ASEAN e-space, as part of an ASEAN positioning and branding strategy'.[9] The e-ASEAN initiative is an ambitious undertaking to promote social and economic integration among its member countries by exploiting the potentials of new ICTs. It furthermore represents a collective response by a regional bloc (i.e. ASEAN) to the opportunities and challenges posed by the information age. Although the same strategy of ICT diffusion and usage might not be applicable across the board, Madon (1998) comments that, 'groups of countries with the need for similar strategies could perhaps be identified' and that, 'greater country to country co-operation to take advantage of the broad range of lessons should be a primary goal' (p. 12). Given the relatively small size of each ASEAN country's own market, advanced or less advanced, unilateral response alone to the challenges of the global communications revolution might prove very limited. Instead, the e-ASEAN initiative serves as a new platform for the ASEAN countries to develop a collective solution. The aims of e-ASEAN, as stipulated in Article 2 of the e-ASEAN Framework Agreement, are to promote:

- co-operation to develop, strengthen and enhance the competitiveness of the ICT sector in ASEAN;
- co-operation to reduce the digital divide within individual ASEAN member states and amongst ASEAN member states;
- co-operation between the public and private sectors in realising e-ASEAN;
- the liberalisation of trade in ICT products, ICT services and investments to support the e-ASEAN initiative.

The aims stated are to essentially enhance transnational co-operation among member states in the information age. This requires, among other things, further liberalisation of trade between member states in goods, services and investments in the ICT sector. In addition to 'showing how the information revolution can make a difference in the daily lives of the people in the region', the e-ASEAN initiative plans 'to use IT (Information

Technology) and the Internet to speed up economic integration of the group, and help them compete better in the global economy' (Ng and Nurbanum 2002: 39). This point explains one of the rationales behind the e-ASEAN Framework Agreement and was reiterated by a senior ASEAN official responsible for the e-ASEAN initiative in these terms: 'In 1999 the ASEAN leaders saw ICTs as the potential force that could accelerate the economic integration process. Also, there is a need for ASEAN to embrace ICTs in a collective manner in order to exploit the potential of the global network economy and to primarily prepare ourselves for the global network economy.'[10]

Following the signing of the Framework Agreement, the e-ASEAN Task Force was set up with its headquarters in Manila. The Task Force has two members from each member state, representing the government and business community. For instance, Malaysia is represented by the Minister from the Ministry of Energy, Communications and Multimedia and the Chairman of the Multimedia Development Corporation (MDC). The Task Force holds periodical meetings (usually at intervals of three to four months) to discuss about matters related to the e-ASEAN initiative.[11] The e-ASEAN Framework Agreement is implemented primarily through 'Pilot Projects', which are overseen by the e-ASEAN Task Force. Since the signing of the Agreement in November 2000, 40 Pilot Projects have already been launched.[12] These Pilot Projects fall roughly into four major categories: (i) e-Commerce; (ii) e-Society; (iii) Information Infrastructure and (iv) e-Governance (see Table 13.1). Each of these Pilot Projects usually involves partner organisations from two or more ASEAN member states. It is hoped that, through these Pilot Projects, knowledge and experience in using ICTs for social and economic development can be shared between the partners from different parts of ASEAN so that the overall competitiveness and economic integration of the region can be improved.[13]

Among the 40 Pilot Projects, 13 were initiated and co-ordinated by Malaysian organisations. This suggests that the more ICT-savvy countries of ASEAN, such as Malaysia, are playing a leading role in promoting the Pilot Projects. However, proponents of the e-ASEAN initiative argue it is not the case that countries such as Malaysia and Singapore with a more advanced ICT sector wanted to sell more products to the less developed ASEAN countries. Rather, 'Each member country has its own specialities...We are interested in combing the specialities of different member countries through developing Pilot Projects. ASEAN countries need to get their actions together through various Pilot Projects before we can collectively jump onto the global stage of the ICT revolution.'[14]

Although the specific objectives differ from project to project, each project is intended to address a particular aspect of the e-ASEAN development. For example, The Cyber-law Training Workshop Project, co-ordinated by the Institute of International Legal Studies of the University of the Philippines Law Centre (UP-IILS), aims to provide lawyers, legislators, judges and enforcement officials in the ASEAN region with an overview of the issues,

Table 13.1 e-ASEAN Pilot Projects (by November 2002)

e-Commerce	e-Society	Information infrastructure	e-Governance
1) ASEAN eTourism Portal	1) ASEAN Information Network (AINet)	1) ASEAN Regional Internet Exchange (ARIX)	1) Cyber-law Training Workshop for CLMV
2) ASEANWorld.com Regional Master Portal	2) ASEAN SchoolNet		
	3) Accelerating e-Learning in ASEAN School (I-tutoring Online)	2) ASEAN Regional Electronic Payment Gateway Solution	2) ASEAN eVisa Portal
3) EastASEANbiz.net			
4) GM SupplyPower			
5) WeASEAN.com	4) ASEAN Institute of Business Technology	4) ASEAN Service Access Platform	
6) SESAMI.com			
7) Real Estate in Cyberspace	5) e-Entrepreneurship Training Program/ Java Competency Project	5) Cybermatrix	
8) ASEAN e-Farmers Project			
9) e-ASEAN Auction & Trading Portal	6) ASEAN Incubator Network (COMPLETED)		
10) ASEAN Global Halal Exchange	7) ASEAN Training Network		
11) e-Halal Solutions	8) Knowledge Workers Exchange (KWX)		
12) ASEAN e-Money			
13) ASEAN Transact	9) ArtPostAsia		
14) ASEAN TEDI	10) Multilingual Site in Asian Languages		
15) ASEAN Electronic Legal Services	11) ASEANVoice.net		
16) ASEAN Trade			
17) VirtualASEAN			
18) Asia Pacific Information & Communications Magazine			
19) e-Cop.net: 24 × 7 Internet Security Surveillance Services			
20) ASEAN Hosted eLogistics Platform (HeLP)			
21) ASEAN Bio Tropical Agriculture Portal (ASEAN-BT)			
22) ASEAN Central Credit Bureau (ASEAN/CCB)			

Source: Project information is based on the e-ASEAN Task Force website, URL (accessed November 2002): www.e-aseantf.org

problems and possible solutions to e-commerce. In particular, the project is focused on helping the CLMV group (Cambodia, Myanmar, Laos and Vietnam – ASEAN's lesser developed member states) to build a legal infrastructure for e-commerce and to eventually harmonise e-commerce regulation in all of the 10 ASEAN countries. Through establishing an ASEAN Agriculture e-Marketplace, the ASEAN e-Farmer Project aims to allow buyers and suppliers to interact directly without having to go through any intermediaries. The project will provide integrated services to support a complete trade cycle.

3. The digital divide: an ASEAN perspective

The goodwill of ASEAN governments to create an ASEAN e-space through the launch of the e-ASEAN initiative is, though, coupled with an imbalanced picture of ICT development. On the one hand, there exists a digital divide between different member states within ASEAN and, on the other hand, there is a big gap between ASEAN as a whole and more advanced countries in the wider Asia-Pacific region.

3.1. The intra-ASEAN digital divide

A prime challenge in the development of e-ASEAN concerns the very poor provision of telecommunications infrastructure and very low level of ICT access. In many parts of the region, and particularly the CLMV group, teledensity is in the low one-digit percentage band and the Internet penetration rate is negligible (Table 13.2). Proponents argue that addressing the issue of digital divide is not, for example, to simply give farmers a PC (personal computer) or offer them Internet access. Instead, a more appropriate and strategic way would be to help farmers apply ICTs and find cost-effective solutions to their problems, such as accessing wider and bigger markets and bringing down the cost of distribution by bypassing the market chain.[15] The e-ASEAN Pilot Projects, such as the ASEAN e-Farmers Project, seem to be concerned more with improving the region's economic productivity, rather than simply making the local farmers consumers of new gadgets.

In order to assess the different levels/stages of development of the information society in the ASEAN countries, it is worth looking at the progress of e-Government projects. As shown in Table 13.3, the ASEAN-6 countries (Brunei, Indonesia, Malaysia, the Philippines, Singapore and Thailand – ASEAN's more developed member states) have already developed their e-Government portals. These e-Government portals already function very well as government information gateways. In particular, the Singapore and Malaysian e-Government portals have been built with sophistication. Both of these two sites provide a one-stop shop for government information as well as a variety of online services to citizens. The Singapore government site has a designated 'e-Citizen' section, under which different aspects of public

Table 13.2   Access to ICTs in ASEAN and other countries (2000)

Country	Telephone mainlines per 1000 people	Mobile phones per 1000 people	PCs per 1000 people	Internet users (% of population)*	Television sets per 1000 people
ASEAN					
Brunei	245	289	70.1	8.82	640
Cambodia	2	10	1.1	0.05	8
Indonesia	31	17	9.9	0.95	149
Laos	8	2	2.6	0.11	10
Malaysia	199	213	103.1	15.88	168
Myanmar	6	0	1.1	0.01	7
Philippines	40	84	19.3	2.65	144
Singapore	484	684	483.1	30.00	304
Thailand	92	50	24.3	3.79	284
Vietnam	32	10	8.8	0.25	185
Non-ASEAN					
Australia	525	447	464.6	34.38	738
Bangladesh	4	1	1.5	0.08	75
China	112	66	15.9	1.78	293
India	32	4	4.5	0.49	78
Japan	586	526	315.2	37.10	725
Korea, Rep.	464	567	237.9	40.25	364
US	700	398	585.2	33.86	854

Note: * Percentages are calculated by the author based on data of total population and Internet users provided by World Bank (2002b).

Source: Adapted from World Bank (2002b).

services have been categorised into 15 online 'e-Towns'. Combined with a nationwide broadband infrastructure, the Singapore e-Government portal can be said to be second to none in the world.

In comparison, the four CLMV countries had no user-friendly e-Government portal by November 2002. Basic government information for Laos and Myanmar is each provided by a commercial (i.e. .com) website. In the case of Cambodia, the best online access to government information one could get is via the 'embassy.org' site based in the United States. The Vietnamese government has developed a website for its Ministry of Foreign Affairs, which is matched by a site for the Vietnamese Communist Party (with most of the contents non-clickable) instead of sites for other government ministries. On the whole, e-Government portal development show in the ASEAN countries shows a somewhat imbalanced picture. Thus, ASEAN consists of world leaders (e.g. Singapore, followed closely by Malaysia) as well as the world's most lagging countries (e.g. the CLMV) in e-Government development. Undoubtedly, the e-ASEAN initiative would have to deal with

Table 13.3   ASEAN governments online (November 2002)

Country	e-Government portal	URL
ASEAN 6		
Brunei	Government of Brunei	http://www.brunei.gov.bn
Indonesia	Indonesian Government	http://www.indonesia.go.id
Malaysia	Malaysian Civil Service Links	http://mcsl.mampu.gov.my
Philippines	Philippines Portal	http://www.gov.ph
Singapore	Singapore Government Portal	http://www.gov.sg
Thailand	Thai Government	http://www.thaigov.go.th
CLMV		
Cambodia	Cambodian Embassy to the US	http://www.embassy.org/cambodia
Laos	Mekongexpresslaos	http://www.mekongexpress.com/laos/index.htm
Myanmar	Golden Pages of Myanmar	http://www.myanmar.com
Vietnam	Ministry of Foreign Affairs	http://www.mofa.gov.vn/English/Home.htm

Source: Adapted from ASEAN Secretary-General (2000).

this digital divide between different member states with a sense of urgency, if the initiative is to be a success and meaningful. For the time being, the four CLMV countries remain largely unconnected *cul-de-sac* to the e-ASEAN information superhighway.

In terms of overall access to information and communications technologies, as indicated in Table 13.2, Singapore, Malaysia and Brunei are far ahead of the rest of the ASEAN countries. In particular, Singapore has already reached the average access level of advanced countries in mainline telephone (484 lines per 1000 people), mobile phones (684 per 1000 people), personal computers (483.1 per 1000 people), Internet users (30 per cent) and television sets (304 per 1000 people). The respective figures for Cambodia, Laos and Myanmar are almost negligible. Five ASEAN countries (Cambodia, Indonesia, Laos, Myanmar and Vietnam) had an average ownership of less than 10 PCs per 1000 people in the year 2000 corresponding to less than 1 per cent of Internet users among the population in the same year. This makes stark contrast with the fact that both Singapore and Malaysia are endeavouring to become the regional ICT hub for the Asia-Pacific.

In view of the significant economic and technological gaps between different ASEAN countries – in addition to that between ASEAN member states and the outside world – the launch of the e-ASEAN initiative, according to the ASEAN Secretariat, was intended to promote collaboration and mutual help rather than eliminating the digital divide between the rich and the poor. At the same time, though, 'e-ASEAN has to be pursued at full speed, with full regard for the need to help the laggard countries to catch up but not necessarily waiting for them' (ASEAN Secretary-General 2000, website reference). The official view over the varied speed of e-ASEAN development in different member countries can be said to be an official 'certificate' for a two-tier or multi-tier e-society to be developed within ASEAN. This is an unfortunate but also realistic scenario of the future shape of e-ASEAN to come. To be sure, for the vast majority of the population in the less developed countries in ASEAN, it would be a long way before they can enter the 'e-space' or e-ASEAN that is being promoted by their governments: they simply do not have the necessary means to participate in the information age.

3.2. The global digital divide

Despite the fact that Singapore is already up to the level of the advanced industrialised countries in ICT access, it is worrying that most ASEAN countries are lagging far behind. At the international level, five less-developed ASEAN countries (i.e. the CLMV plus Indonesia) are in a comparable situation with India and Bangladesh. As Table 13.2 further shows, industrialised economies like the United States, Japan and Australia and South Korea have a significantly higher level of average access to ICTs than the developing and under-developed countries of the Asia-Pacific region. The existence of the digital divide between ASEAN and the more advanced countries outside ASEAN is in part explained by the relatively lower level of commitment to research and development (R&D). As shown in Table 13.4, again with Singapore being an exception, ASEAN countries on the whole have a much lower level of GERD (Gross Expenditure on R&D) to GDP than some of ASEAN's neighbouring countries (e.g. Australia, New Zealand, Japan, South

Table 13.4 Gross expenditure on R&D (GERD) by selected countries

Country	Year	% GERD to GDP
ASEAN		
Indonesia	1994	0.16
Malaysia	1998	0.39
Philippines	1992	0.22
Singapore	1999	1.94
Thailand	1996	0.12
Non-ASEAN		
Australia	1996–97	1.65
China	1998	0.71
New Zealand	1997–98	1.10
Japan	1995	2.98
Korea, Rep.	1998	2.52
Taiwan	1995	1.81

Source: Adapted from ASEAN Secretary-General (2000).

Korea and Taiwan) outside ASEAN. This contrast suggests that most ASEAN countries are less willing, or financially less able, to promote research and development activities that are the foundation for long-term innovation and advancement in ICTs. The success of Singapore in catching up with the western industrialised countries in the ICT sector in terms of infrastructure, access and online public service provision is coupled with the country's relatively high level of financial resources poured into science and technology.[16]

The fundamental reality of economic development in ASEAN is that a substantial proportion of the region's population are still living in poverty. For instance, in 2000 the percentage of population living below US$1 a day in Indonesia was 7.7 per cent, in Laos 26.3 per cent and in Thailand 2 per cent (World Bank 2002b). That is to say, whilst there are good reasons for the ASEAN countries to catch up with some of their more technology-savvy neighbour countries, it is also imperative that their effort in poverty relief should not be diluted. To be sure, this is a dilemma faced by not just ASEAN but also most developing and under-developed countries in the world. In recognising the economic and digital divide, the official view of the ASEAN Secretariat seems to suggest a practical approach towards science and technology:

> ASEAN countries must similarly embrace technology, its development and use, if it is to remain competitive – not even to catch up with the industrialized world but simply to stay in the running. This is a call not for ASEAN necessarily to undertake basic, pioneering scientific research but to adapt, develop and utilize science and technology to strengthen the region's economies and improve the lives of its people (ASEAN Secretary-General 2000, website reference).

At the global level, the more advanced ASEAN countries can probably do many things on their own and do them well in terms of developing and using ICTs for economic development. The same, though, can not be said about the CLMV and Indonesia for the time being. This is partly the reason why the e-ASEAN Framework Agreement urges that 'the more advanced Member States with ICT training facilities would offer training courses to the less advanced Member States' (Article 8-1). Although the e-ASEAN initiative is not about having one size to fit all, the lagging countries in the region are being offered an opportunity to work together and share their experience with the more advanced countries through the e-ASEAN initiative. As an interviewed senior ASEAN official commented:

> We are not forcing everybody to do the same thing. Rather, e-ASEAN provides a good opportunity for the CLMV countries to learn from Singapore and Malaysia. The opportunity that e-ASEAN brings to the table is to

learn through sharing experience – to share the experience of economic development of Singapore and Malaysia by the CLMV. To have a regional programme on ICTs is not to create problems but to bring an opportunity. Sharing experience will benefit all member countries.[17]

If one accepts Webber's (2001) argument that 'the principal obstacle to closer economic co-operation or integration was the disparity in levels of economic development between the ASEAN states' (p. 348), the existing digital divide between the ICT rich countries and the CLMV will continue to be a major concern for ASEAN leaders. The launch of e-ASEAN, in particular the Pilot Projects, has surely made a promising start to address this issue. It is, however, still too early to say how effective these Pilots Projects will be in helping to bridge the intra-ASEAN digital divide and, ultimately, the global digital divide.

4. Closing the legal gap: harmonisation of cyber-laws in ASEAN

The problem for the new international economic order, which is increasingly characterised by the development and application of new ICTs, is 'how to organise and accommodate this phenomenon in such a way as to maximize the benefits to all thus avoid conflict' (Snow 1991: 57–8). In commenting on the experience of the East Asian region, Venturelli (2002) argues that 'without the institutional and regulatory structures to ensure participation and access to knowledge and information, as well as broader foundations for civil society, the East Asian economies would be unable to develop and exploit information technologies and services in the long run' (p. 82). The same observation may also be applicable to the case of ASEAN. In the absence of any international organisation and global regime that is eligible and capable of governing e-commerce, the e-ASEAN Framework Agreement has kick-started a process of harmonisation of e-commerce regulation at the regional level. The e-ASEAN Framework Agreement stipulates that 'Member States shall adopt electronic commerce regulation and legislative frameworks that create trust and confidence for consumers and facilitate the transformation of businesses towards the development of e-ASEAN' (ASEAN 2000, website reference). More specifically, the e-ASEAN Framework Agreement, if implemented effectively, would lead to three major developments. First, each ASEAN country would need to put in place national e-commerce policies and laws. Second, mutual recognition of national e-commerce laws should be achieved. Third, ASEAN-wide regional e-commerce mechanisms need to be established in order to facilitate secure cross-border transactions, payments and settlements.

Malaysia has introduced a comprehensive set of 'cyber-laws' since the late 1990s. These include the Communications and Multimedia Act (1998), the

Malaysian Communications and Multimedia Commission Act (1998), the Digital Signature Act (1997), the Computer Crimes Act (1997) and the Telemedicine Act (1997). The list of cyber laws makes Malaysia one of the early movers in the world to comprehensively regulate certain key issues of the information age. As far as e-commerce regulation in ASEAN is concerned, there are also other national legislations that include the Electronic Transactions Act (ETA, Singapore), the Electronic Commerce Act (ECA, Philippines), the Electronic Transactions Order (ETO, Brunei) and the Draft Electronic Transactions Bill (ETB, Thailand). In order to effectively promote e-commerce under the e-ASEAN initiative, ASEAN countries would have to close two legal gaps. The first gap exists between those member states that already have introduced legislation to govern e-commerce and those that have not drafted their own e-commerce laws. The second gap is created by the differences between the existing national e-commerce laws. To address these two challenges, an e-ASEAN Reference Framework for Electronic Commerce Legal Infrastructure was published by the ASEAN Secretariat in 2001.

The issue about e-commerce governance is further complicated by the fact that in the virtual world of digital information flow and electronic transactions national borders have lapsed. Cross-border e-commerce has raised serious questions about jurisdiction and taxation. Regarding jurisdiction the ASEAN Secretariat has not come up with answers to questions such as which court may hear and resolve the dispute between the contracting parties from two different countries, which law to use and whether the court judgement obtained in one jurisdiction is enforceable in another jurisdiction (ASEAN Secretariat 2001). Over the issue of taxation, the ASEAN authorities are also confused with the questions of where the source(s) of income should be if the e-commerce transaction occurs in multiple countries, which tax regime to use and which jurisdiction the tax (if collectable in the first place) should be paid to.

Furthermore, the differences in the social and political circumstances between the ASEAN member states may well delay, if not completely prevent, the effective harmonisation of e-commerce governance. Due to the fact that the Internet has not only economic and commercial implications but also far-reaching social political implications, governments in the world have adopted rather different policies and strategies towards this new medium. Hachigian (2002) suggests three different categories of East Asian states in relation to the Internet: (i) countries that severely restrict all public use of the Internet, for example, Myanmar and North Korea; (ii) countries with compromised policies and strategies that moderately restrict Internet access and contents, for example, Vietnam, Singapore and China; (iii) countries that actively promote Internet access and allow for online political pluralism, for example, Malaysia. The socio-political divide of the ASEAN member states with regard to Internet policy might prove to be a fundamental challenge to achieving harmonisation in e-commerce legislation in the region.

5. Intra-ASEAN competition

Intra-regional competition is certainly a factor worth considering with regard to countries as Malaysia, where the core national ICT flagship initiative cannot be excluded from this influence (Harris 1998). Although the e-ASEAN Framework Agreement emphasises the importance of cross-border co-operation in order to make a collective response to the opportunities and challenges brought by new ICTs, this does not necessarily suggest an end to competition between the member states. The more ICT-savvy member countries have their own national agenda for the information age, which often centre on making their own country the regional hub for informational and communications technologies. This has naturally led to the head-on competition between, for instance, the Singapore One Network for Everyone (ONE) initiative and Malaysia's Multimedia Super Corridor (MSC) initiative. It is publicly acknowledged in the Malaysian national media that Malaysia is set to rival Singapore as an Information and Communications Technology event Hub with the launch of the annual Malaysia ICT Week.

During the national ICT Week in September 2002, the Malaysian Ministry of Energy, Communications and Multimedia, the Multimedia Development Corporation and the Malaysian National Information Technology Council (NITC) jointly organised three major events including the Multimedia Super Corridor Expo 2002, the ASEAN Communications and Multimedia Expo and Forum (ACM 2002) and the National e-Commerce Expo 2002. These events coincided with the MSC International Advisory Panel (IAP)[18] annual meeting chaired by the Prime Minister Dr Mahathir Mohamad. It is reported that during the Malaysia ICT Week 418 exhibitors from 28 countries were expected to participate in the events.[19] Thus, Malaysia is undoubtedly making considerable efforts to establishing itself as a regional ICT hub to rival Singapore.

In parallel with the e-ASEAN regional initiative, both Malaysia and Singapore have developed their own national agenda to improve *national* competitiveness (n.b. rather than *regional* competitiveness) through fostering a strong national ICT sector. Back to the early 1980s, the Singapore government launched a 5-year National Computerisation Plan (NCP 1980–85). The NCP was focused on three major aspects including a Civil Service Computerisation Programme (CSCP) to: computerise the major functions of the government, facilitate the development and growth of the national ICT sector and develop a pool of ICT skills. The NCP was succeeded by the National IT Plan (1986–91), which afforded more emphasis on networking technologies to integrate computing and communications in order to provide more efficient public services. In another strategic move, the Singapore government launched the IT2000 Plan in 1992 centred on transforming the city state into an 'Intelligent Island'. This was essentially to make ICTs a ubiquitous factor in every sector of the economy and every walk of social life. One of the most important achievements of the IT2000 Plan is Singapore ONE, which is widely recognised as the first nationwide broadband network in the world. Singapore ONE has already reached all schools and nearly all the households in the country. The most recent development in the Singapore government's information age policymaking is the launch of Infocomm 21 (Information and Communications Technology for the 21st Century) in 1999. The centrepiece of Infocomm 21 is the e-Government Action Plan. Pushed by waves of government strategic planning, Singapore has already become one of the most sophisticated ICT hubs for ASEAN and the wider South East Asia area.[20] To a certain extent, Singapore, as some commentators argue, is already ahead of the game and already has much of what Malaysia is talking about.[21]

The Singapore way to ICT prosperity is closely watched by its ASEAN neighbours, in particular Malaysia, with a view to emulating or catching up. Compared to Singapore, Malaysia is a relatively latecomer in the field of government policymaking for the information age. Through mainly the process of five-year planning, the Malaysian government has embarked upon a strategy for economic development with ICTs being a key factor. The Sixth Malaysia Five-Year Plan (1991–95) clearly identified the need for creating an information-rich society. This was followed by the Seventh Malaysia Five-Year Plan (1996–2000), which provided the necessary policy momentum for the launch of the MSC. The MSC would include the creation of an ICT business and technology centre (Cyberjaya) to attract foreign direct investment and an 'intelligent city' as the new federal government administrative centre (Putrajaya) linked with a new international airport (the Kuala Lumpur International Airport or KLIA) and the Kuala Lumpur City Centre (KLCC) through a high-speed communications network and an efficient transportation network.[22] With a firm conviction that ICTs hold the key to transforming the Malaysian economy into a 'K-Economy' (or Knowledge Economy) and the Malaysian society from a developing country into a developed status, the Prime Minister Dr Mahathir assumes personal control at the top level over key policy initiatives such as the MSC.[23] The *Malaysia K-Economy Masterplan*, the latest strategic policy document for information age economic development, was released in September 2002 by the Ministry of Finance, for which Dr Mahathir holds the ministerial portfolio. It is hoped that, 'in a move to make Malaysia a regional IT hub, the country would provide the latest in IT services to encourage multinational companies to set up their research and development (R&D) operations in the country' (Harris 1998: 13).

Geographically, Malaysia and Singapore border each other immediately and both are relatively small countries in the ASEAN context. With the rise of two regional ICT hubs, there is every reason to anticipate waves of fierce competition between the two countries, in particular with regard to opportunities to host ICT sector related foreign investment. This scenario will likely present a specific challenge to the ethos of e-ASEAN, which is to promote regional economic integration and cross-border co-operation in the information age.

6. Conclusion

Bearing in mind the challenges discussed above, it is still too early to declare e-ASEAN as a triumph of ASEAN regionalism. The information age optimism can not be isolated from the fundamental socio-economic and political realities that ASEAN countries are faced with. It is true that Article 8-3(d) of the e-ASEAN Framework Agreement calls for the member states to work towards establishing an e-society by 'facilitating freer flow of knowledge workers'. However, some member states, particularly ASEAN's relatively wealthier ones, are faced with the political challenge of dealing with the cross-border flow of manual or 'non-knowledge' workers from other, often relatively poor member states. Whilst one of the objectives of the e-ASEAN Framework Agreement is to establish a free trade area for goods, services and investments for the ICT industries,[24] the governments of Malaysia and Singapore are still engaged in a high profile bilateral disagreement at the time of writing over the price of freshwater supply from Malaysia to Singapore. In this case, the trade of water, one of the very basic goods, was not 'flowing' freely between the two countries. The fundamental reality today seems to be that ASEAN is still far from being a regional free trade zone. The ASEAN-6 member states will not fully eliminate all import duties until 2010, whilst the CLMV will do so by 2015.[25] It looks likely that the pace of e-ASEAN development would have to be subject to the progress in intra-ASEAN trade liberalisation in general.

Some warn about the danger of over-reliance upon technological determinism, and moreover argue that 'technology alone will not solve any problems – it must be integrated with the social context and the stakeholders' (Davison *et al.* 2000: 8). The social context of the ICT revolution in ASEAN, as shown in this chapter, is a complicated one and the interests of the e-ASEAN's stakeholders are diversified. The ambitious undertaking of the e-ASEAN initiative promises to enable the ASEAN countries to make effective use of new ICTs for the purpose of enhancing cross-border co-operation and, ultimately, deepening ASEAN integration. However, in order to achieve this objective, ASEAN countries are faced with the reality that the digital divide between different member countries would make it very difficult, if not impossible, for the lagging ones to effectively participate in the e-ASEAN process. The uneven development would seem to lead to the creation of a two-tiered or multi-tiered ASEAN regional e-Society. This would in turn be detrimental to ASEAN's ambition of closing the digital divide between ASEAN and the western industrialised countries through the e-ASEAN initiative.

It is also ASEAN's intention that increased trans-border e-commerce activities and communications would be governed by the same cyber-laws. As agreed by the member states, harmonisation of cyber-laws, ought to be achieved through the e-ASEAN initiative. However, whilst some member states (e.g. Malaysia and Singapore) have already implemented national legislations to address the new issues related to the governance of the cyberspace, other member states (e.g. the CLMV) are slow in drafting cyber-laws. In addition to this disparity, ASEAN countries have very different social contexts and diversified attitudes towards the political implications of ICTs, in particular the Internet. This will make it a great challenge to achieving a common approach to the governance of the cyberspace.

Adding to the list of challenges faced by the e-ASEAN initiative is the competition between the ICT-savvy member states' national agenda for the information age. Both Malaysia and Singapore are endeavouring to become *the* regional ICT hub. Whilst each of the two countries' strategy might well be bold and effective at the national level, unconnected and unco-ordinated national agendas may dilute these countries' commitment to the region's collective undertaking under e-ASEAN. As has been previously noted, the national information age strategy is so dear to the heart of Malaysia's Prime Minister Dr Mahathir that he assumes personal responsibility over key national ICT initiatives, such as the MSC. In comparison, the responsibility of championing the e-ASEAN initiative on behalf of Malaysia has fallen onto the shoulders of the Minister of Energy, Communications and Multimedia. Although the e-ASEAN initiative can not be said to be a panacea for all the real problems that are faced by ASEAN, it nevertheless represents a major step forward by the ASEAN member states in promoting cross-border co-operation and deepening regional integration in the information age.

Notes

The author is grateful to the research grant awarded by the British Academy for undertaking fieldwork in the ASEAN region.

1. ICTs, according to ASEAN (2000), 'Refer to Infrastructure, Hardware and Software Systems, Needed to Capture, Process and Disseminate Information to Generate Information-based Products and Services' (Article 1).
2. Dr Mahathir, M. (1996) 'Rich in Hypocrisy', *Sunday Morning Post*, Hong Kong, 6.10.1996, cited in Harris (1998).
3. Kofi Annan, UN Secretary General, 'Welcome' speech at the UN ICT Task Force Conference, www.unjcttaskforce.org/welcome/principal.asp.
4. Nelson Mandela, former President of South Africa, http://itu.int/TELECOM/wt95/pressdocs/manddist.html. Quoted in Davison et al. (2000), p. 8.
5. *New York Times*, 14.11.2000, 'A Nascent Internet Takes Root in Vietnam'.

6. *New York Times*, 07.08.2000, 'It Takes the Internet to Raise a Cambodian Village'.
7. Interview by the author with senior ASEAN official responsible for ICT and the e-ASEAN initiative, Kuala Lumpur, 06.09.2002. The ASEAN official suggested that the cyber park project in Rangoon is being developed in collaboration with the e-ASEAN Task Force.
8. It is worth noting that the e-ASEAN Framework Agreement is a new development based on previous ASEAN Frameworks and Agreements. On its relationship with other ASEAN Agreements, the e-ASEAN Framework Agreement states that 'The Provisions of the Agreement on the Common Effective Preferential Tariff Scheme for the ASEAN Free Trade Area and its Protocols, the ASEAN Framework Agreement on Services and its Protocols, and the Framework Agreement on the ASEAN Investment Area...Shall Not Be Prejudiced By, and Shall Apply to, This Agreement' (ASEAN 2000, Article 14). Nevertheless, the e-ASEAN initiative is poised to add a new dimension and new momentum to the course of regional integration in ASEAN.
9. ASEAN Secretariat, 'Toward an e-ASEAN', http://www.aseansec.org.
10. Interview by the author with senior ASEAN official responsible for ICT and the e-ASEAN initiative, Kuala Lumpur, 06.09.2002.
11. Information is from interview by the author with a senior executive of the Multimedia Development Corporation, Kuala Lumpur, 4.9.2002. The MDC is the overall administrative organisation for the Multimedia Super Corridor (MSC) on behalf of the Malaysia government.
12. A senior ASEAN official suggested during an interview with the author on 06.09.2002 that 47 Pilot Projects have been launched under the auspices of e-ASEAN Task Force by September 2002. This is slightly different from the number of projects introduced on the e-ASEAN Task Force website (http://www.e-aseantf.org).
13. Interview with senior ASEAN official, op. cit.
14. Interview with senior executive of the MDC, op. cit.
15. Interview with senior ASEAN official, op. cit.
16. Singapore spent 1.94 per cent of its GDP on R&D in 1999, which compared to less than half per cent of GERD by each of the other four original ASEAN member countries in 1990s.
17. Op. cit.
18. Most of the IAP members are senior managers of large multinational companies in the ICT sector and leading academics.
19. *New Straits Times*, 03.09.2002, 'Malaysia's Launching of ICT Week to Rival Singapore'.
20. For more detailed information about the Singapore government's strategic planning on ICT, see http://www.egov.gov.sg.
21. *Asia Magazine*, 24–26.10.1997, cited in Harris (1998).
22. The principal objectives of the MSC Scheme are to develop: (i) an e-Government; (ii) a multipurpose smart card, i.e. the MyKad, which has already been launched; (iii) Smart Schools; (iv) TeleHealth; (v) an R&D cluster in the ICT sector; (vi) a worldwide manufacturing web; (vii) a Borderless Marketing Centre to promote e-commerce. These are also known as the 'Flagship Applications'.
23. He actually chairs the MSC International Advisory Panel, which meets annually.
24. See the Preamble and Article 2(d) of the e-ASEAN Framework Agreement.
25. See Chapter 5 for more detail on the ASEAN Free Trade Area (AFTA) project.

References

ASEAN (2000) 'e-ASEAN Framework Agreement', *Fourth ASEAN Informal Summit*, 22–25 November, Singapore.

ASEAN Secretariat (2001) 'e-ASEAN Reference Framework for Electronic Commerce Legal Infrastructure', November, http://www.aseansec.org.

ASEAN Secretary-General (2000), 'Challenges and Opportunities in Information and Communications Technologies', report (excerpts) to the *33rd ASEAN Ministerial Meeting*, July, http://www.aseansec.org.

Bangemann, M. *et al.* (1994) *Europe and the Global Information Society: Recommendations to the European Council*, 26 May, European Council, Brussels.

Commission of the European Communities (1998) *Globalisation and the Information Society: The Need for Strengthened International Co-ordination*, COM(98) 50 final, Brussels.

Commission of the European Communities (2000) *Proposal for a Regulation of the European Parliament and the Council on the Implementation of the Internet Top Level Domain*, COM(2000) 827 final, 12 December, Brussels.

Dai, X. (2000) *The Digital Revolution and Governance*, Ashgate, Aldershot.

Davison, R., VoGel, D., Harris, R. and Jones, N. (2000) 'Technology Leapfrogging in Developing Countries – An Inevitable Luxury?', *Electronic Journal on Information Systems in Developing Countries*, Vol. 1(5), pp. 1–10.

Freund, C. (2000) 'Different Paths to Free Trade: The Gains from Regionalism', *Quarterly Journal of Economics*, November, pp. 1317–41.

G8 (2000) *Okinawa Charter on Global Information Society*, Okinawa, 22 July, http://www.library.utoronto.ca/g7/summit/2000okinawa/gis.htm.

Giddens, A. (1999) 'Runaway World: Globalisation', *BBC Reith Lectures*, December, London.

Hachigian, N. (2002) 'The Internet and Power in One-Party East Asian States', *The Washington Quarterly*, Vol. 25(3), pp. 41–58.

Harris, R. (1998) *Malaysia's Multimedia Super Corridor*, http://is.lse.ac.uk/ifipwg94/pdfs/MalayMSC.pdf.

Infocomm Development Authority of Singapore (2000) *Infocomm 21: Singapore Where the Digital Future Is*, December, Singapore. http://www.ida.gov.sg.

Madon, S. (1998) *The Internet and Socio-Economic Development: Exploring the Interaction*, London School of Economics, http://is.lse.ac.uk/ifipwg94/pdfs/internet.pdf.

Ng, E. and Nurbanum, M. (2002) 'e-Enabling the ASEAN Nations: Malaysia', *Asia Pacific Information & Communication Technology*, September, pp. 38–44.

Snow, D. (1991) *The Shape of the Future: The Post-Cold War World*, M.E. Sharpe, New York.

Venturelli, S. (2002) 'Inventing e-Regulation in the US, EU and East Asia: Conflicting Social Visions of the Information Society', *Telematics and Informatics*, Vol. 19(2), pp. 69–90.

Vinh, L.D. (2002) 'Opening Speech at the Cyber Training Course Organised by the Ministry of Trade and e-ASEAN Task Force', 12–13 June, Hanoi.

Webber, D. (2001) 'Two Funerals and a Wedding? The Ups and Downs of Regionalism in East Asia and Asia Pacific after the Asian Crisis', *The Pacific Review*, Vol. 14(3), pp. 339–72.

World Bank (2002a) *Information and Communication Technologies: A World Bank Group Strategy*, World Bank, Washington DC.

World Bank (2002b) *Data and Statistics: ICT at a Glance Tables*, http://www.worldbank.org/data/countrydata/ictglance.htm.

Part VI
Conclusion

14
Prime Dimensions of the New Economic and Security Co-operation in the Asia-Pacific: A Conclusion

Christopher M. Dent

1. Introduction

In Chapter 1, we presented three 'prime dimensions' to the new Asia-Pacific economic and security co-operation, namely: the tension between the 'post-shock' forces of *imperative co-operation* and the counter-forces of *complex diversity*; the growing conflation between economic and security issues, or the *economics–security nexus*, in Asia-Pacific international relations; the relationship between the *Asia-Pacific's new economic and security bilateralism and regional-level forms of co-operation, integration and governance*. In this chapter, we bring together the main findings and conclusions of preceding chapters and synthesise them within this 'prime dimension' analytical framework.

2. Imperative co-operation and complex diversity in the Asia-Pacific

To restate, *imperative co-operation* refers to how 'shock' events, such as the 1997/98 East Asian financial crisis and the 11 September 2001 terrorist attacks on the United States, invariably expose critical deficiencies or fault-lines in existing co-operative structures, and furthermore heightens the imperative to better manage the interdependence between shock-affected communities and states. This usually also generates sufficient political will to establish new forms and structures of co-operation. Regarding *complex diversity*, we are concerned with a region's highly diverse complexity of defining features that is evident across various domains – economic, business system, political, socio-cultural, socio-religious and so on. It has already been noted that the Asia-Pacific region, or trans-region, is arguably the most *complex diverse* in the world, and that this presents a ubiquitous set of hurdles in the path of *imperative co-operation*. In this section, we make a synthesised overview of both implicit and explicit references to the revealed tensions between these two sets of opposing forces.

The dual 'shock' impacts of the East Asian financial crisis and the 9/11 terrorist attacks on Asia-Pacific economic and security co-operation were examined throughout this book. In Chapters 2 and 3, Simon Lee and Christopher Hughes in their own ways noted how the financial crisis led to a greater understanding of the region's vulnerability to capricious global market forces. Meanwhile, Christopher Dent argued in Chapter 5 how the crisis led to a firmer resolve to better manage regional economic interdependence in East Asia, as well as brought considerable pressures to bear upon existing regional trade institutions or projects, such as the Asia-Pacific Economic Co-operation (APEC) forum. Yet, new forms of region-wide economic co-operation emerged in the form of the increasingly dense proliferation of bilateral free trade agreement (FTA) projects between Asia-Pacific states and the ASEAN Plus Three (APT) framework that incorporated Southeast and Northeast Asian countries into East Asia's first formalised regional grouping. Jürgen Haacke noted in Chapter 7 how the crisis spurred China into substantially strengthening economic and security relations with Association of Southeast Asian Nations (ASEAN) states. Indeed, the fall-out from severe crisis events such as that experienced in East Asia over 1997/98 can create structural or paradigm shifts in international relations generally, leading *inter alia* to new formulations or international co-operation between affected communities and states.

Closely associated with this are 'creative destruction' processes often exacted by post-shock forces of *imperative co-operation*, whereby incumbent co-operative structures are either displaced by new structures or substantively reconfigured into something new itself. This can be clearly seen in the Asia-Pacific. On the economic front, established regional organisations such as ASEAN and APEC have come under competitive pressure from new frameworks of co-operation such as APT and bilateral FTAs. While Alan Collins in Chapter 8 contends it is premature to assert that ASEAN will eventually become subsumed by the wider APT framework, he comments that the 1997/98 financial crisis has led many Southeast Asian states to believe that their future economic development and prosperity (i.e. economic security) lies in closer economic and financial ties with Northeast Asia. Collins makes the further observation that APT-based co-operation in the economic field has mirrored the ASEAN Regional Forum (ARF) process in the security field in that both indicate an appreciation among the ASEAN members that Southeast Asian security and economic problems cannot be considered separately from the rest of East Asia. We may more specifically posit that ASEAN is finding significance through its externalised links with the major Asia-Pacific powers, as may be seen with new economic and security co-operation agreements or dialogue with China, Japan and the United States. It may be worth considering here to what extent does the engagement with these powers help to overcome *complex diversity* challenges facing ASEAN, that is, at the sub-regional level? For example, the compulsion to overcome internal differences and co-operate on external or extra-group diplomacy could derive from the significant collective gains to be had from such engagement, for example, on market access, general security benefits. Yet as we discuss towards the end of this chapter, the ASEAN group's co-operation with third country powers is often being actualised on a separate bilateralised basis (especially in trade and economic diplomacy) mainly owing to *complex diversity* constraints upon ASEAN-level negotiations proceeding.

As we saw from Chapter 1, the 'post-shock' impacts upon APEC have compelled it to both concentrate on its revealed strengths (e.g. trade and investment facilitation) and try to reposition itself as a regional organisation generally, looking to play a new functional role in Asia-Pacific security affairs after the 9/11 terrorist attacks. Whether or not APEC finds new purpose as essentially an economic-oriented body serving new security objectives (and therein is able to remain distinct and therefore of perceived value to its member states amongst a growing number of regional fora) is a key issue. So is more generally the issue of whether the Asia-Pacific is entering a phase of 'competing regionalism' (i.e. where new co-operative frameworks like APT are pitched against incumbents such as APEC) or one of 'congruent regionalism', whereby compatible and even synergetic links may be established between these same fora. In Chapter 9, Jörn Dosch comments on this in his analysis of the Greater Mekong Sub-region (GMS) development project, noting that from China's perspective the GMS project serves the country's interest of strengthening relations with ASEAN in political, social, economic and security co-operation, and moreover has been used to promote the wider aims of the ASEAN–China FTA project. Congruent regionalism in the Asia-Pacific has been studied in the past, for example, in the concentric circle relationship between ASEAN's Free Trade Area (AFTA) project and APEC's much broader scale 2010/2020 'free trade and investment zone' project (Soesastro 1995). It is still too early to draw firm conclusions on whether competitive regionalism or congruent regionalism will generally prevail, but the relationship between new and 'pre-shock' frameworks of economic and security co-operation is another worthy of critical attention.

The connections between the Asia-Pacific's new *imperative co-operation* and global-multilateral co-operative fora and structures of relations were also discussed by certain chapter authors. On the one hand, regional or region-wide co-operative forms of relations may perform important 'multilateral utility' functions, whereby they help realise the indivisible goals of multilateral institutions (Henning 2002, Katzenstein 2002, Dent 2004). This is generally consistent with the multi-layered and 'open' nature of *new regionalism* and may also work conversely, where these institutions may assist regional-level co-operation by the common participation of a region's states in a wider multilateral context. Neil Renwick in Chapter 12 cites the example here of Northeast Asia's states that – in the general absence of sub-regional co-operative ventures – are at least working indirectly with each other on information and communication technology (ICT) matters within Organisation for Economic Co-operation and Development (OECD) and United Nations based initiatives. In Chapter 11, Rex Li notes that China and Taiwan's recent accession to the WTO could also provide a conducive multilateral framework or environment for enhancing their economic and diplomatic relations: the WTO-induced removal of Cross-Strait trade barriers would further stimulate sub-regional economic integration within 'Greater China' and thereafter possibly a more benign political interaction between Beijing and Taipei.

On the other hand, the relationship between regional co-operation and global-multilateral fora can reveal *complex diversity* problematics within the Asia-Pacific. Simon Lee explores this point in Chapter 2, where he warns against locating East Asian or Asia-Pacific regional co-operation within the prevailing institutional and ideological frameworks of global governance, as currently dominated by the so called 'Washington Consensus' – a compound of neo-liberal values and oriented governance structures championed by the United States. This is partly based on the argument that global neo-liberalism was largely culpable for the unravelling of the 1997/98 East Asian financial crisis in that it was the retreat of the state's governance functions over finance (e.g. surveillance, monitoring and investment co-ordination mechanisms) during the liberalisation process of the 1990s rather than state over-involvement in the economy that was primarily to blame. Lee further proposes that the current problems experienced by the free market US economy are similarly portentous, and that regional economic integration and co-operation based on liberalised markets alone is fundamentally flawed. In this context, East Asia's developmental statist approaches to national economic management may offer viable alternatives, extending the principle to regional economic management with application to improved co-operation and the co-ordination of monetary, fiscal and competitiveness policies. In addition, the current trend of embedding free trade agreements within wider bilateral economic co-operation agreements between Asia-Pacific states (sometimes referred to as 'broadband' FTAs, e.g. the Japan–Singapore Economic Partnership Agreement, Japan–Korea Economic Agenda 21) may offer important opportunities for forging developmental linkages between them.

Indeed, it was East Asian resentment against the United States' ardent and somewhat triumphalist neo-liberal advocacy exhibited within the APEC forum that was a significant factor in the organisation's post-crisis demise (Ravenhill 2000). While the aftermath of the 9/11 attacks created a new *imperative co-operation* impetus for the resumption of more positive developments in East Asia – US economic and security diplomacy, many East Asian states remain wary of the values and ultimate objectives of US foreign policy. For example, in Chapter 7, Jürgen Haacke comments that in certain parts of Southeast and East Asia there is a perception that the United States' new security strategy emphasises a doctrine of pre-emption, and is unambiguous about the need to maintain American primacy in global politics. This was despite the United States making it clear that it now afforded Southeast Asia greater strategic security significance and importance after the 9/11 attacks, with all the security benefits this would supposedly confer the sub-region. Alan Collins, in Chapter 8, also notes that the United States might come to oppose developments in the APT framework that lead to exclusive East Asian regionalism, and thus undermine US interests and influence in the region, not least by APT eclipsing APEC as the Asia-Pacific's most pre-eminent regional economic organisation. East Asian states, like many others around the world, continue to view the exercise of US structural power (i.e. the ability to influence and shape international rules, norms and structures in which others must also operate accordingly) with suspicion. However, they appreciate too the importance of working with the United States on economic and security co-operation: the question is *on whose terms* is this co-operation based? In bilateral relations, as we later discuss, great powers such as the United States are able to bring their considerable relational power (i.e. the leverage that an international actor can directly exert on the behaviour of, or decisions made by another) to bear on weaker powers or states.

Other theoretical and ideological perspectives on the Asia-Pacific's new *imperative co-operation* are presented by other authors. In his exposition on 'co-operative realism', Jürgen Rüland postulated in Chapter 4 that co-operation within Asian regional organisations is basically viewed as a means to increase national power, to balance shifts in the international power equation, and to enhance bargaining power in international organisations with the objective of exerting more influence over international rule-making. Thus, he argues, new economic and security co-operation is still very much driven by realist (or neo-realist) premises, and as such new co-operative ventures may prove ephemeral, being displaced or overshadowed by even newer co-operative initiatives in accordance to short-term cycles of shifting national interests. This may be linked to our previous discussion on 'creative destruction' and 'creative reconfiguration' processes concerning the fast changing pattern of regional co-operation in post-shock periods. What Rüland is essentially arguing here is that the forces of *imperative co-operation* may quickly fade, and that no long-term structural or paradigm shift in the international relations of the Asia-Pacific will therefore transpire. Xiudian Dai in Chapter 13 implicitly suggests that such an outcome may come to pass in ICT co-operation within ASEAN, attributing this to the potentially damaging international competition between Singapore and Malaysia over becoming the dominant regional ICT hub. Anja Jetschke, in Chapter 10, also makes the point that national self-interest still remains the defining feature of intra-ASEAN diplomacy, while Jörn Dosch, in Chapter 9, notes that the GMS project has been largely state-centric determined, with civil society in the sub-region exerting very limited stakeholding influence.

More positive views on the prospects of *imperative co-operation* in the Asia-Pacific are presented elsewhere in the text. In Chapter 5, Christopher Dent notes in relation to the APT framework, for example, that notwithstanding the limited regional ambition demonstrated by the Chiang Mai Initiative (CMI) network of currency swap agreements – the APT's most important achievement to date – it does marks a significant step forward in East Asian financial co-operation, not least because of the almost complete lack of region-wide co-operation in this field before the 1997/98 crisis. In addition, the initiation of discourses within the APT framework on the possible longer-term goals of establishing an East Asian Free Trade Area, common market and even full monetary union, while currently very ambitious, is nevertheless a notable achievement in itself. As further mentioned in Chapter 5, East Asia's leaders are generally under no illusions about how long it will take before this level of co-operation and integration is realisable. Yet, Christopher Dent argues that developments within APT and in various bilateral FTA-based co-operation point to important initial steps down this route being made. Furthermore, Neil Renwick and Xiudian Dai consider, in Chapters 12 and 13 respectively, how new ICT developments may play an important facilitating role in economic and security-related co-operation in the region. The ability of ICTs to forge different forms and modes of inter-connectivity between communities and states across a region is particularly relevant in this respect. However, revealed technological divides between those same communities and states present a different set of challenges. This is not only recognised by Renwick and Dai but also Eric Grove in Chapter 6, where he relates this to maritime security concerns. For example, he suggests that America's technological lead is increasing to a point where there are even question marks over its closest allies retaining full inter-operability with the US Navy.

Various implicit references to *complex diversity* counter-forces that oppose the progress of *imperative co-operation* have already been made thus far, and more explicit instances of the former are now provided. In relation to Southeast Asia's war on terrorism, Jürgen Haacke details the particular dilemma facing the Indonesian government in the two-level game of (at the international level) meeting the demands of fellow ASEAN members and extra-regional powers such as the United States in coming to an international agreement, and (at the domestic level) dealing with Indonesia's own radical Muslim organisations with a view to rooting out suspected terrorists they were allegedly harbouring. As he notes, concerns about the political repercussions of cracking down on such organisations largely explained why Indonesia's leadership did not pursue the war on terror with greater vigour. The particular socio-religious fabric of Indonesian society thus made a regional co-operation agreement on counter-terrorism difficult to achieve; and yet the ASEAN group were nevertheless eventually able to sign a Joint Declaration on Anti-Terrorism with the United States, helped by the *imperative co-operation* stimulus of the 12 October 2002 Bali terrorist bombing in Indonesia itself. However, Jürgen Rüland argues in Chapter 4 that this Declaration glosses over intra-ASEAN policy disagreements over fighting terrorist movements, and, second, it touches upon very sensitive national security issues that most ASEAN members are not prepared to discuss in depth with their neighbours. This latter specific point is fundamentally and closely related to sensitivities over dealing with differential socio-cultural or ethnic group issues in Southeast Asia, whether in matters of internal or external security relations, as, for example, has been demonstrated in relations between Malaysia and Singapore. Similar, deep-rooted *complex diversity* impediments to regional co-operation are acknowledged by Neil Renwick in Chapter 12 in his reasons provided for the general lack of co-operation between Northeast Asian states on ICT issues.

Instances of where the Asia-Pacific's diverse socio-cultural features continue to impede new co-operative endeavours are also strongly evident in the economic domain. In Chapter 5, Christopher Dent discusses how the agriculture issue has particularly hampered bilateral FTA negotiations across the trans-region, be it between Japan and South Korea, or between the United States and Australia. This cannot be simply attributed to asymmetric comparative advantages in the sector but perhaps more importantly due to the 'extra-commercial' nature of agriculture itself (i.e. its social, cultural and political aspects), and hence presents a good example of the complex interlinking between these different domains that were first noted in Chapter 1. Thus, on this issue, a number of *complex diversity* factors are brought into play: agricultural protectionism is thus not just about trade but also safeguarding certain aspects of a country's national identity to those that advocate this line of action. In East Asia, this is further reinforced by a strong neo-mercantilist tradition regarding trade policy, which contrasts with the market liberal tradition of Anglo-Pacific and certain Latin-Pacific states; and here there is a long-standing debate on the localised socio-cultural determinism respectively underpinning these different policy approaches. The development of the first and also earliest initiated cross-region bilateral FTA project – that between South Korea and Chile – is testimony to such *complex diversity*. Here, the two sides were engaged in hard negotiations for four years (1999–2002) over agriculture and various other industrial sectors, especially where evidence of South Korea's neo-mercantilist legacy lingered (Dent 2002). More generally, many chapter authors have commented upon the notable asymmetry in the levels of economic development, as well as in the distribution of relational and structural power within the Asia-Pacific (discussed earlier), and this too provides the basis for further *complex diversity* counter-forces. The former has, for example, been officially cited as a major impediment by a Japanese government report into the feasibility of establishing an East Asian FTA, and presumably other ambitious projects most likely launched through the APT framework.

We can also examine the *complex diversity* issue through the comparative political perspective offered by Anja Jetschke in Chapter 10, where she discusses the actual and potential impact of the democratisation of certain Southeast Asian states on intra-ASEAN diplomacy and co-operation. In this context, she explored the hypothesis that 'mixed state dyads' (i.e. democracies and non-democracies) may bring a greater probability of war because they externalise different norms of conflict management. According to this view, more pronounced political system diversity within a regional set of states not only makes international co-operation between them difficult but also may lead to more adversarial intra-regional relations generally. Conversely, democratised states may be expected to be more active promoters of international co-operation, in accordance to the liberal norms of human behaviour normally associated with them. While Jetschke finds that neither hypothesis really applies to recent events and developments in intra-ASEAN diplomacy, political system diversity across the wider Asia-Pacific region has undoubtedly placed hurdles in the path of economic and security co-operation. For example, civil society opposition in New Zealand to the FTA it negotiated with Singapore caused some delay to a final agreement being reached. While their impact has yet to be fully made, human rights, labour rights and environmentalism – all issues increasingly championed by the civil society movements of Anglo-Pacific states in particular – may come increasingly to the fore in future international co-operation negotiations in the Asia-Pacific as the twenty-first century progresses, pitching liberal democratic states against their non-democratic, authoritarian counterparts.

3. The economics–security nexus

The second 'prime dimension' initially outlined in this book's introductory chapter concerns how *economic and security issues have become increasingly conflated in Asia-Pacific international relations*, particularly since the 1997/98 East Asian financial crisis and the 9/11 terrorist attacks on the United States. Moreover, it was noted that this new 'economics–security nexus' is increasingly evident within various regional fora, for example, ASEAN, APT, APEC. It is helpful at this stage to make the conceptual distinction between the economics–security nexus and economic security. Technical aspects of the former generally include the:

- *Economics of military security (or military security economics)*: that concern allocative, productive, techno-industrial, infrastructural and cost-price aspects of resourcing military security capabilities. Eric Grove in Chapter 6 discussed the US's growing comparative advantages here in relation to other Asia-Pacific states. Other chapter authors have also noted the US's huge post-9/11 fiscal commitment to further strengthening its armed forces.

- *Subordination of economic policies to security policy interests*: in the past this has involved the conferment of foreign aid to security partner countries (e.g. US aid to certain East Asian capitalist economies during the Cold War period) and the use of economic sanctions imposed upon security rivals and competitors. More recently, APEC's post-9/11 'Action Plan on Combating the Financing of Terrorism' and the ARF's 'Workshop on Financial Measures against Terrorism' are illustratively relevant here.
- *Subordination of security policies to economic interests*: at a general level, this could relate to making the Asia-Pacific region safe for the expansion of capitalist activities, with this typically attributed to a hegemonic state's (e.g. the US) duties.

The pursuit of economic security, on the other hand, essentially involves 'safeguarding the structural integrity and prosperity-generating capabilities and interests of a politico-economic entity [e.g. a nation-state] in the context of various externalised risks and threats that confront it in the international economic system' (Dent 2002: 17). It is thus more economistic in its conceptual determination, being concerned with realising specific foreign *economic* policy objectives, for example, resource–supply security, market access security, finance–credit security. The economics–security nexus simply observes broader matters of issue-linkage and technical policy linkage between the two domains. It is often, though, difficult to establish whether a certain policy action was driven by economic and politico-military security objectives when the intention was to realise both. For example, as Christopher Dent argues in Chapter 5, the US's Enterprise for ASEAN Initiative (EAI) launched in November 2002 was no doubt motivated as much by politico-military security objectives (e.g. cementing alliance ties in the fight against international terrorism) as it was by economic security ones. Yet, it is this blurring between these two domains that is key to understanding new co-operative developments in the Asia-Pacific: economic and security issues and policy measures are increasingly converging, as manifest in the foreign policy actions of the region's states. Moreover, as Simon Lee commented in Chapter 2, economic prosperity and security are vital public goods, and in a fast-changing globalising world, new forms and structures of co-operation among states are required for their achievement and maintenance. This especially applies where there have been substantive economic and security 'shocks' to a regional system.

The close connections between economics and security have long been appreciated in the Asia-Pacific. In East Asia this has particularly related to how economic development could correspondingly enhance national security, and, with especial regard to ASEAN, how a regional organisation fostering economic co-operation could also consolidate a regional security alliance of states, as noted by Jürgen Rüland in Chapter 4. In his exposition on 'comprehensive security' in Chapter 8, Alan Collins contended that, conversely, regional (security) resilience in turn supports national resilience by creating stable external relations that consequently enables individual countries to concentrate on economic development. These principles still apply today. For instance, one could argue that integral to the post-9/11 war on terror has been the promotion or consolidating of 'lowest common denominator' links (e.g. trade, investment) between the region's states as a means to demonstrate international unity in the broader cause of counter- terrorism. To a lesser extent, the 1997/98 East Asian financial crisis spurred new forays in security co-operation in the region, if not only to deal with the prospect of adverse spillovers emanating from badly crisis-affected states experiencing significant economic, social and political turmoil, e.g. Indonesia. The extent to which such post-crisis security co-operation was consciously intended to help restore semblances of economic confidence to the region (i.e. the subordination of security measures to economic objectives) is questionable. In Chapter 11, Rex Li notes that it was for reasons of national security that Taiwanese governments had proved reluctant to liberalise Cross-Strait commerce with China, even though this would have conferred considerable economic advantages to Taiwan's economy and firms. While, then, the general distinction between 'high' and 'low' politics in the region's economic and security affairs has broken down to a considerable degree – especially in terms of issue-linkage – it still remains instructive when analysing the 'policy subordination' relationship.

However, it is increasingly the case that new economic and security co-operation arrangements across East Asia and the Asia-Pacific have gone hand-in-hand. As Jürgen Haacke comments in Chapter 7, several ASEAN countries supported the war on terror as a means to promote their economic and security relationship with the United States. They were thus generally receptive to Washington's EAI proposal at the same time the ASEAN–US Joint Declaration on anti-terrorism was signatured. Furthermore, Christopher Dent argued in Chapter 5 that the US's new bilateral FTA policy formed part of Washington's broader strategy of international coalition-building against the spectre of terrorism, with these trade agreements viewed as cementing alliance ties amongst 'democratic' or at least like-minded partner states. Other chapter authors also note the coinciding in November 2002 of the ASEAN–China FTA agreement with the ASEAN–China joint declaration on non-traditional security issues, including terrorism. Just as in the US case, China's reasons for this dual-track approach lie in promoting broad co-operative ties with a region deemed to have new strategic and security significance in a post-9/11 world. In addition, Singapore and India announced in February 2003 their plans to develop a bilateral FTA project and an anti-terrorism pact simultaneously, which in the words of India's

Deputy Prime Minister Lal Krishna Advani were seen as 'key to furthering economic and security cooperation between India and Southeast Asia' (*Radio Singapore International*, 04.02.2003).

Developments in the new economics–security nexus may also be viewed from both macro and micro perspectives. Further instances of macro-level developments include the 'creative reconfiguration' of APEC noted earlier, in which the United States is particularly interested in now using APEC as a dual-purpose (i.e. economics *and* security) vehicle for regional co-operation. A similar confluence of economic and security agenda issues is apparent within the APT framework. As Jürgen Haacke explains in Chapter 7, the 12 October 2002 Bali bomb attacks served to focus APT leaders' minds more sharply on dealing with terrorism and new security threats generally. Alan Collins observed in Chapter 8 that at their 2002 summit in Phnom Penh, these leaders decided to formally extend APT's remit of co-operation beyond its original economic realm to include issues of security more readily associated with the ARF.

At the micro-level, Jörn Dosch draws upon Deutsch's (1957) transactionist hypothesis – which posits that an increasing volume of economic, political and cultural transactions across national borders will result in the emergence of regional security communities if the process is accompanied by the growth of integrative institutions among the participating nations – in examining the economics–security nexus in the GMS development project. In this context, the transnational economic co-operative activities promoted under this project should in theory lead to improved security relations between the riparian states of the GMS. Dosch notes that this is an important issue given the Mekong's history of both traditional security (e.g. border disputes) and new security (e.g. migration, environmental degradation) problematics. This economic development project is more specifically viewed by Thailand and Vietnam as a means to build fruitful relations in the aftermath of the Cold War. As he further notes, many Mekong riparian states are ardently promoting the GMS project in order to exercise some influence over China's plans to build more than a dozen power plants in the river zone, which poses the potentially serious 'environmental security' problem of intense water resource competition between the upper and the lower Mekong states.

Eric Grove, in Chapter 6, offers additional micro-level perspectives by stressing the continued need to promote maritime security in the Asia-Pacific as a means to safeguard its seaborne trade. For a trans-region denoted by an oceanic referent, this remains vital to the economic development and commercial interests of its constituent states. Indeed, he rightly points out that its land-based trade links are nowhere near as important as its seaborne counterparts. Meanwhile, in Chapter 12, Neil Renwick discussed the connections between economics and security in the 'cyber-war' context, whereby the protagonists may target information nerve-centres in either the military security domain (e.g. command control posts) or the economic domain (e.g. financial market operations). Furthermore, 'cyber-security' co-operation has become increasingly pertinent in the post-9/11 era, with new initiatives such as APEC's 'Cybersecurity Strategy' intended to debilitate terrorist communication capabilities while maintaining the free flow of information that permit markets to operate effectively. Rex Li's study of Cross-Strait relations in Chapter 11 considers the extent to which intensifying interaction and co-operation between Taiwan and China's firms can establish a foundation on which politico-diplomatic relations between the two sides may be positively developed, thus addressing one of Asia-Pacific's most difficult security predicaments. He considers the argument that the future behaviour of both China and Taiwan would be determined not only by the level of their economic interdependence but also by their expectations of the future trading environment. If this was considered extremely positive in both bilateral and regional senses, then a benign development in politico-security relations may be anticipated. In sum, then, the more prominent economic–security nexus evident in 'post-shock' Asia-Pacific co-operation may be viewed at multiple levels and across various domains of activity.

4. The new bilateralism and regionalism in the Asia-Pacific

4.1. Introductory comments

This section considers the book's third 'prime dimension', this being the relationship between the *Asia-Pacific's new economic and security bilateralism and regional-level forms of co-operation, integration and governance*. To restate key points made in the introductory chapter, the recent intensification of economic and security bilateralism in the Asia-Pacific may constitute a new paradigm of strategic diplomacy in the region, especially where incumbent regional frameworks have clearly faltered, for example, APEC. In this sense, the Asia-Pacific's new bilateralism forms a key constituent element of its post-shock *imperative co-operation*. How, though, will the relationship between the new bilateralism and regionalism in the Asia-Pacific develop in the immediate and longer-term future? Two main perspectives may be offered in this respect, namely 'region-divergent' bilateralism and 'region-convergent' bilateralism.

Region-divergent bilateralism essentially relates to how dense bilateralism within a region works against the development of regionalism. As a defining feature of a region's international relations or international political economy, dense bilateralism may reflect and also itself create or perpetuate norms of adversarial and competing strategic-alliance behaviour, hence diminishing the prospects of regional community-building processes and endeavours. *Region-convergent bilateralism* in contrast posits that dense bilateralism can make a positive contribution to these same processes and endeavours, for example through its construction of a bilateralised 'lattice' base of international relations from which regionalised links may evolve and develop. Taking these two main perspectives together, we can see that the same bilateralist form or development may be construed in different ways. For example, the Japan–ASEAN Closer Economic Partnership (JACEP) agreement, largely acknowledged to be a strategic response to the ASEAN–China FTA pact, is viewed by some as an exemplar of 'region-divergent' bilateralism while to others as illustrative of 'region-convergent' bilateralism. In addition, there is a third scenario to consider regarding the bilateralism-regionalism relationship, this being the neutral perspective of 'region-static' bilateralism where intensifying bilateralism within a particular region makes no impact upon either existing regional organisations and frameworks, or the development of new regionalist forms of co-operation and integration. However, evidence presented throughout this book does not generally support this argument or prediction. In the debate that follows, we shall therefore concentrate on the relevance of 'region-divergent' and 'region-convergent' bilateralism to understanding new developments in Asia-Pacific economic and security co-operation.

4.2. 'Region-divergent' bilateralism

The 'region-divergent' bilateralism perspective relates to various arguments presented by a number of chapter authors. These arguments may be broadly categorised into four main points of contention. The first relates to how deepening bilateralism within a region can create increasingly convoluted patterns of reactive counter-balancing manoeuvres amongst the region's constituent states, leading to potentially hazardous inter-state rivalry. Such a scenario is obviously not conducive to regional community-building. This argument is most clearly championed by Jürgen Rüland in Chapter 4, who cites the aforementioned case of Japan's act of 'reactive state' diplomacy as revealed by its response to China's FTA project with ASEAN, which reportedly caught Tokyo somewhat unawares. Thus from this perspective, the JACEP project may be viewed as essentially a function of intensifying Sino-Japanese rivalry, and moreover escalating hegemonic competition with respect to the East Asia region. Setting this in the wider context of the recent proliferation of bilateral FTAs in the region, Rüland questions that these help facilitate regionalism owing to the distrust sowed by the inevitable rivalries of successive balancing moves. In Chapter 8, Alan Collins also argues that the competitive bilateralism of Japan and China – where each is trying to establish 'outflanking' bilateral ties with other states in the region – ultimately damages the prospects for East Asian and Asia-Pacific regionalism. Furthermore, Jürgen Haacke in Chapter 7 contends that China's recent manoeuvres on economic and security bilateralism was to some extent intended to challenge American influence in the region, particularly in the security domain and (geographically) with regard to Southeast Asia. He also argued that the Philippines' recent interest in developing closer bilateral military co-operation with the United States should be understood in the context of Manila's continuing security-related suspicions of China. In addition, Rex Li noted, in Chapter 11, how China's push for a FTA with the ASEAN group was no doubt partly motivated by how this could potentially further marginalise Taiwan's geo-economic position in the region. In sum, intensified bilateralism can propagate significant levels of inter-state suspicion and competition, thus creating a poor international relations environment for regionalism to develop within.

The second main point of contention concerns how the bilateral links of sub-regional powers (or of member states therein) with 'great powers' may undermine the former's regional group cohesion. Jürgen Haacke makes such a case in relation to ASEAN and the United States on security co-operation. As he notes, the ASEAN group have experienced considerable difficulties in realising *imperative co-operation* objectives with regard to the post-9/11 security agenda. Haacke follows this by specifically stating that ASEAN's new bilateral security co-operation with the United States, which involves both more and deeper intelligence co-operation and direct military-to-military ties, may yet render existing regional institutions in the ASEAN region less relevant. In addition, the bilateral agreements of individual member states from a sub-regional group with great powers may also undermine group cohesion. Both Alan Collins and Christopher Dent note in their respective chapters the diplomatic tensions between Malaysia and Singapore over the latter's various bilateral FTA projects (e.g. with the United States and Japan), which Malaysia's leadership believes were compromising the integrity of ASEAN's own AFTA regional project by potentially conferring Singapore's FTA partners with 'back-door' non-tariff access to ASEAN's new free trade zone. Even though Singapore countered this charge by stating that rigorous 'rules of origin' applied to its imports would negate any such trade deflection, this was a clear incident of where an activist bilateral approach was deemed to undermine regional cohesion.

Closely related to this is the third main point of contention that unchecked bilateralism serves to further exaggerate or reinforce power asymmetries within a region, which in turn may work against the development of regionalism. Jürgen Rüland argues in general relation to this point that bilateralism eventually works in favour of *realpolitik* as it allows stronger and more resourceful partners to broker better deals, which in turn are not cushioned by the checks and balances otherwise provided by regional organisations. Thus, according to this argument, stronger powers within a region may have greater incentive to exercise 'hub-spoke' bilateralism than promoting or leading regional co-operation or integration projects. In Chapter 2, Simon Lee relates this to the United States' new bilateral FTA diplomacy in the Asia-Pacific, arguing how this leaves weaker states susceptible to compromises demanded by Washington in the economic policy domain.

Indeed, Christopher Dent notes in Chapter 5 that the United States insisted in its bilateral FTA negotiations with both Singapore and Chile on the removal of their respective sets of capital control measures, only normally drawn upon in times of financial crisis. This links directly back to preceding discussions in this chapter on the first 'prime dimension'. On the one hand, this debate connects with the issue of on whose terms is the new *imperative co-operation* in the Asia-Pacific based, and thus matters of asymmetric relational power pertaining to economic and security co-operation. Furthermore, intensified bilateralism may further expose *complex diversity* differences within a region, as revealed in the United States' aggressive neoliberal advocacy noted earlier, which posed a challenge to a particular aspect of Singapore's developmental statism. In its own FTA negotiations, Japan is generally insistent that agricultural trade liberalisation is omitted from the agenda. It is such opportunities created by bilateralism for coercive relational power that may thus undermine the chances for regionalist endeavours to emerge and develop, especially as they invariably depend on the very same strong 'assertive' powers to lead them.

The fourth and final point of contention concerns how intensified bilateralism may come to takeover or in some way 'capture' key aspects of existing regional organisations and fora themselves. For example, Jürgen Rüland notes that Asia-Pacific leaders increasingly use the summits of regional (e.g. ASEAN) and trans-regional fora (e.g. APEC) for bilateral talks at the sidelines of the official programme, and that reducing regional and trans-regional fora to such functions sets the wrong signal in that they serve to rationalise bilateralism instead of regional-multilateralism. Christopher Dent also offers some comment here in particular relation to APEC, whereby he argues that many Asia-Pacific states have come to view the trans-regional organisation's summits – at least in terms of trade diplomacy – as primarily facilitative of their new and existing bilateral FTA projects with other APEC members. He further contends that the new FTA bilateralism has seriously challenged the guiding principles and *modus operandi* of APEC by the clear switch in 'reciprocity choice' in trade liberalisation: that is from the 'diffuse' reciprocity on which APEC's open regionalism is supposedly based to the 'specific' reciprocity of bilateral FTAs. For these and other reasons, bilateralism may invert the fundamental principles on which regional co-operation is based.

4.3. 'Region-convergent' bilateralism

As we have previously indicated, the 'region-convergent' bilateralism perspective represents a more positive view on the relationship between bilateralism and regionalism. Many of the arguments presented above under the rubric of 'region-divergent' bilateralism are based on neo-realist premises of inter-state competition and rivalry and a generally anarchical international system. In contrast, the points of contention made under

256296256296256296

'region-convergent' bilateralism are generally based on institutionalist premises of co-operative interdependence, from which we expect more benign developments in international relations as states and communities increasingly see the comparative benefits of co-operative over rival competitive behaviour in an increasingly interdependent world system, where a deepening and broadening of common interests between them are progressively more exposed. Furthermore, this co-operative interdependence extends to different frameworks and levels of international relations themselves, and hence in this context a purposeful congruence and compatibility may exist between bilateralism and regionalism. 'Region-convergent' bilateralism connects with discourses on the so-called *new regionalism*, may itself be generally contrasted with its more narrow 'old', Euro-centric counterpart by its particular emphasis on: multiple and co-existent levels and forms of regional co-operation and integration (e.g. state-driven, market-driven; sub-regional, trans-regional); a less technocratically determined and more socially constructed or ideational view to understanding regional community-building; the connections between regionalism and extra-regional processes and structures at the global and multilateral levels. It is contended here that the contributions bilateralised links can make to regionalist developments thus form a sub-set of *new regionalism* analysis. Three main points of contention are presented here with respect to 'region-convergent' bilateralism.

The first point concerns how intensifying bilateralism can provide a progressively developed 'latticed' foundation on which wider regional-level relations and agreements later emerge. Christopher Dent especially champions this view in Chapter 5 in his study of the Asia-Pacific's new economic bilateralism. The general line he takes is that a gradual evolutionary process of bilateral-to-plurilateral rationalisation may eventually lead to regional-level agreements and forms of co-operation arising. Dent argues that bilateral-to-regional evolution should be particularly expected where a dense and overlapping spread of bilateral agreements is evident. For example, if three states have separate bilateral FTA links with each other, significant commercial and policy-technical benefits are to be realised by rationalising these into one unified trilateral FTA arrangement. Moreover, the benefits of 'rationalised bilateralism' become greater as the number of bilaterally linked states increases. Given, though, the challenge of harmonising customs procedures and addressing various *complex diversity* factors between multiple Asia-Pacific economies, a generally slow evolutionary process should be anticipated. As Christopher Dent notes, however, this process has already begun. In October 2002, Singapore, New Zealand and Chile launched their 'Pacific-3' trilateral FTA project that primarily arose out of previously initiated bilateral FTA projects. A month later, at the 2002 APT summit, Chinese Premier Zhu Rongji announced his country's proposal for a Northeast Asian trilateral FTA between China, Japan and South Korea. While this particular action may be interpreted as a strategic counter-balancing move by Beijing (i.e. in reaction to the development of Japan – South Korea FTA project), the end product – if realised – would be one of notably significant sub-regional integration between East Asia's three largest economies. Other scenarios in bilateral-to-plurilateral-to-regional FTA evolution are suggested by Dent in Figure 5.7.

Jürgen Haacke in Chapter 7 also makes reference to a trilateral security agreement signed between Malaysia, the Philippines and Indonesia in May 2002, which covered a variety of transnational issues. Cambodia and Thailand became signatories to the agreement later that year, with other ASEAN member states perhaps likely to follow suit soon. He also suggests that despite his aforementioned argument articulated under 'region-divergent' bilateralism concerning ASEAN–US security relations, that there is in principle no intrinsic incompatibility between ASEAN member states enhancing their respective bilateral security co-operation with the United States and effectively functioning as a sub-regional diplomatic community and security regime. This is not least because regional consent to the parallel pursuit of defence ties with external powers is explicitly covered by ASEAN's 1976 Treaty of Amity and Co-operation. Haacke further notes that from the simultaneous promotion of bilateral security contacts between the United States and ASEAN member states and a multilateral approach to regional security (i.e. US–ASEAN, or ARF) was perceived by some as the most effective strategy, whereby efforts within each track of diplomacy could have positive spillovers into the other.

This latter issue provides a link to the second point of contention, which concerns how bilateralism and regionalism may be involved in serving similar ends, and even working in concert with the other. Recent developments in the APT framework perhaps best demonstrate this. As Christopher Dent argues in Chapter 5, bilateral FTA projects between East Asian states are increasingly viewed as coinciding with integrational developments within the APT framework itself. On the one hand, these projects have undoubtedly stimulated and even catalysed discourses within the APT group at various levels (e.g. amongst political leaders, in academic circles) on broader regional trade integration, for example, in the possible future creation of an East Asian Free Trade Agreement (EAFTA). In addition, the same bilateral FTA projects are being developed at the sidelines of APT meetings, with the effect of further augmenting the regional cohesion and co-operative behaviour this new framework is attempting to propagate between East Asia's states. This is effectively the converse argument to that articulated in the previous section that bilateralism can takeover or 'capture' regional co-operation processes. One could argue that a similar encroachment of FTA diplomacy in APEC meetings affords it comparable 'networking the region' benefits in that it broadly assists APEC's attempts at Asia-Pacific regional community-building (Dent 2003b). However, in APT's case the conflation of

FTA bilateralism with the regional framework has helped add a 'trade' dimension to its regional agenda rather than dislocate the main regional agenda, as generally applies to APEC with regard to its centrepiece trade liberalisation project. Yet, we must not forget that APT leaders have only thus far discussed the possibility of an EAFTA.

Christopher Dent further argues that bilateralism may be the practically deployed means by which regional or region-wide co-operation is realised. This particularly related to how the APT's network of bilateral currency swap agreements under its CMI constituted the sub-structure on which regional financial co-operation and governance was essentially based. He noted too how a similar 'bilateralism within regionalism' principle was at work in the country-to-subregion trade agreements sought by China, Japan and the United States with the ASEAN group. In the JACEP and EAI especially, these agreements were to be gradually implemented on a bilateral basis, for example, Japan–Thailand, US–Thailand. While as mentioned previously under 'region-divergent' bilateralism this leaves individual ASEAN member states susceptible to abuses of relational power from these much stronger trade partners than had ASEAN-level deals were being negotiated, this bilateral methodology was generally accepted by both sides as being the most practical way to proceed.

This directly leads on to our third point of contention regarding 'region-convergent' bilateralism, namely that bilateralism can offer viable circumventing routes around *complex diversity* factors in the development of regionalist endeavours. For example, ASEAN-level negotiations with extra-regional trade partners are deemed largely unworkable in implicit acknowledgement of the ASEAN group's *complex diversity*. A similar interpretation may also be made of why Japan did not specifically re-promote its Asian Monetary Fund (AMF) idea within the APT framework, preferring instead to advocate a network of bilateral currency swap agreements rather than a regional-level arrangement. As Christopher Dent claimed in Chapter 5 in relation to trade, 'one-on-one' (i.e. bilateral) agreements help negate the *complex diversity* predicament in that resolving problems at the domestic political level (e.g. over agriculture) becomes easier if just a couple of countries are involved in the 'two-level game' dynamic rather than a multiple, asymmetric set of trade partners. This, he admits, may appear a somewhat messy and diplomatic resource-intensive method of proceeding but yet at the same time the most effective way of advancing regional or region-wide co-operation in such a *complex diverse* region as the Asia-Pacific.

5. Concluding summary

This final chapter has synthesised the main findings of preceding chapters within the 'prime dimension' analytical framework first presented in Chapter 1, which has been more substantively developed here also. It has been proposed that there are three 'prime dimensions' to the Asia-Pacific's new economic and security co-operation, this being: (i) the tensions between 'post-shock' forces of *imperative co-operation* and *complex diversity* counter-forces; (ii) the changing *economic–security nexus* in the international relations of the region; (iii) the relationship between the *new bilateralism and regionalism* in the Asia-Pacific. To conclude, we will briefly summarise the main salient points of each.

Regarding the first 'prime dimension', various sources and manifestations of *imperative co-operation* were identified and discussed in relation to the numerous *complex diversity* constraints that impede the progress of economic and security co-operation in the Asia-Pacific generally. Various debates and arguments were presented here. Particular 'creative destruction' and 'creative reconfiguration' processes were studied in relation to both incumbent and new forms of region-wide and regional co-operation. How the forces of *imperative co-operation* may also be connected to issues of 'competing regionalism' and 'congruent regionalism' was briefly considered as well, as was the links between the Asia-Pacific's new *imperative co-operation* and global-multilateralism. In addition, this chapter discussed a number of relational and structural power issues, especially in relation to questions concerning on whose terms is the 'post-shock' *imperative co-operation* based? Important theoretical and ideological perspectives on these debates offered by chapter authors were incorporated here, such as Jürgen Rüland's 'co-operative realism' which suggested that the forces of *imperative co-operation* might quickly fade. Finally, various instances of *complex diversity* constraints were case-studied, in which a number of inter-related economic, political, socio-cultural and socio-religious factors were cited.

With respect to the new 'economics–security nexus' in the Asia-Pacific, the distinction between this concept and that of 'economic security' was initially made. It was noted that the former is broadly concerned with matters of issue-linkage and technical policy linkage between the economic and security domains. Moreover, it was generally argued that appreciating the increasingly blurred demarcation between these domains in the economics–security nexus was key to understanding new co-operative developments in the Asia-Pacific. Various chapter authors presented evidence of this, especially in relation to recent foreign policy actions of Asia-Pacific states wherein economic and security issues and policy measures can be seen to increasingly converge. This is particularly so for certain states, such as the United States in the aftermath of the September 11 terrorist attacks in which its new invigorated bilateral and regional trade diplomacy is partly designed and motivated to cement inter-state alliance ties in the broad offensive against terrorism. The 'policy subordination' relationship between economics and security was discussed in relation to this. Developments in the new economics–security nexus were also viewed from both macro and micro perspectives. Examples of the former included the 'creative reconfiguration' of

APEC whereby this 'economic' regional organisation has been recently been used to serve overt security objectives. Instances of the latter included Jörn Dosch's study on the extent to which transnational economic co-operative activities promoted within the GMS development project were improving security relations between its participating states.

Concerning the third 'prime dimension', we discussed how the relationship between the new bilateralism and regionalism in the Asia-Pacific might develop in the immediate and longer-term future. Two broad and opposing perspectives were offered here, that of 'region-divergent' bilateralism and 'region-convergent' bilateralism. Four main points of contention were presented in this chapter regarding 'region-divergent' bilateralism. The first related to how deepening bilateralism within a region can create increasingly convoluted patterns of reactive counter-balancing manoeuvres amongst the region's constituent states, leading to potentially hazardous inter-state rivalry. The second concerned how the bilateral links of sub-regional powers (or of member states therein) with 'great powers' may undermine the former's regional group cohesion. The third point of contention posited that unchecked bilateralism serves to further exaggerate or reinforce power asymmetries within a region, which in turn may work against the development of regionalism. The fourth related to how intensified bilateralism may come to takeover or in some way 'capture' key aspects of existing regional organisations and fora themselves. Three main opposing points of contention were then presented under the rubric of 'region-convergent' bilateralism, which offered a more positive view of the bilateralism-regionalism relationship as well as a niche analysis on *new regionalism* development. The first of these argued that intensifying bilateralism can provide a progressively developed 'latticed' foundation on which wider regional-level relations and agreements later emerge. The second point considered how bilateralism and regionalism may be involved in serving similar ends, and even working in concert with the other, while the third suggested that bilateralism can offer viable circumventing routes around *complex diversity* factors in the development of regionalist endeavours. The arguments presented across both perspectives were invariably based on the converse premises of the other, and hence the perspective you would most readily prescribe depends on your particular views or understandings of the nature of the international system itself. This same principle can, of course, be applied to the broad issues and debates presented in this book. One argument that can perhaps be commonly supported is that it is currently both a fascinating and critical time to be studying economic and security co-operation in the Asia-Pacific.

References

Dent, C.M. (2002) *The Foreign Economic Policies of Singapore, South Korea and Taiwan*, Edward Elgar, Cheltenham.

Dent, C.M. (2004) 'The Asia-Europe Meeting (ASEM) and Inter-Regionalism: Towards a Theory of Multilateral Utility', *Asian Survey*, Vol. 44(1).

Dent, C.M. (2003) 'Networking the Region? The Emergence and Impact of Asia-Pacific Bilateral Free Trade Agreement Projects', *The Pacific Review*, Vol. 16(1), pp. 1–28.

Deutsch, K.W. (1957) *Political Community and the North Atlantic Are: International Organization in the light of Historical Experience*, Princeton University Press, Princeton.

Henning, C.R. (2002) *East Asian Financial Co-operation*, Institute for International Economics, Washington DC.

Katzenstein, P. (2002) 'Regionalism and Asia', in S. Breslin, C. Hughes, N. Phillips and B. Rosamond (eds), *New Regionalisms in the Global Political Economy*, Routledge, London.

Ravenhill, J. (2000) 'APEC Adrift: Implications for Economic Regionalism in Asia and the Pacific', *The Pacific Review*, Vol. 13(2), pp. 319–33.

Soesastro, H. (1995) 'ASEAN and APEC: Do Concentric Circles Work?', *The Pacific Review*, Vol. 8(3), pp. 475–93.

Index